Financial Economics

Financial Economics

By

G. Yoganandham

Associate Professor and Head,
Department of Economics,
Thiruvalluvar University, Vellore, Tamil Nadu

New Century Publications
New Delhi, India

NEW CENTURY PUBLICATIONS
74, Ansari Road, Ground Floor,
Daryaganj,
New Delhi – 110 002 (India)

Tel.: 011-4101 7798; 4358 7398; 98117 88655
E-mail: info@newcenturypublications.com
www.newcenturypublications.com

Editorial office:
4800 / 24, Bharat Ram Road,
Ansari Road, Daryaganj,
New Delhi – 110 002

First Published: **2021**

ISBN: **978-81-7708-527-3**

Published by New Century Publications and printed at Milan Enterprises, New Delhi

Designs: Patch Creative Unit, New Delhi

PRINTED IN INDIA

About the Book

Financial economics is a branch of economics that analyzes the distribution and use of resources in markets in which decisions are made under uncertainty. Financial decisions must often take into account future events, whether those are related to individual stocks, portfolios or the market as a whole.

The subject is concerned with the allocation and deployment of economic resources, both spatially and across time, in an uncertain environment. It, therefore, centres on decision-making under uncertainty in the context of financial markets. It is built on the foundations of microeconomics and decision theory.

Financial economics is important in making investment decisions, identifying risks, and valuing securities and assets. It relies heavily on microeconomics and basic accounting concepts. In addition, it requires familiarity with basic statistics and probability since these are the standard tools used to measure and evaluate risk.

Financial economics employs economic theory to evaluate how time, risk, opportunity costs and information can create incentives or disincentives for a particular decision. Financial economics often involves the creation of sophisticated models to test variables affecting a particular decision. Often, these models assume that individuals or institutions making decisions act rationally, though this is not necessarily the case. Irrational behaviour of parties has to be taken into account in financial economics as a potential risk factor.

This book provides a comprehensive description of the theory and functioning of financial economics (or economics of finance).

It is spread over 28 chapters which have been organized into 5 theme parts.

Part I (chapters 1 and 2) is titled Basics of Financial Economics. It gives a bird's eye view of financial system, financial economics, financial institutions, financial markets and financial instruments.

Part II (chapters 3 to 10) is titled Investment Theory and Portfolio Analysis. It deals with discussion on theory of the rate of interest, reasons for interest rate differentials, term structure of interest rates and yield curves, portfolio of assets, mean-variance portfolio analysis, Markowitz model, capital asset pricing model (CAPM), capital market line (CML) and security market line (SML).

Part III (chapters 11 to 17) is titled Derivatives, Forwards, Futures and Options. It covers emergence and popularity of financial derivatives, forward contracts, future contracts, options, Black-Scholes-Merton option pricing model, binomial option pricing model, and principles of arbitrage.

Part IV (chapters 18 to 22) is titled Corporate Finance. It focuses on the patterns of corporate financing, capital structure and the cost of capital, corporate debt, dividend policy models, and Modigliani-Miller theorem.

Part V (chapters 23 to 28) is titled Indian Financial System. It delves into financial institutions, financial markets, financial instruments, financial inclusion, financial regulators, and legislative and institutional measures to strengthen financial sector in India.

About the Author

Dr. G. Yoganandham is currently Associate Professor and Head, Department of Economics, Thiruvalluvar University, Vellore, Tamil Nadu. He received his M.A. (Economics) degree from Loyola College, Chennai and M.Phil. and Ph.D. degrees from Department of Economics, University of Madras, Chennai. He was awarded Doctoral Research Fellowship by the Ministry of Social Justice and Empowerment, Government of India, New Delhi. The Indian Council of Social Science Research (ICSSR), New Delhi awarded him General Research Fellowship to pursue his post-doctoral research studies. He has actively participated and presented papers at various regional, national, and international conferences, seminars, and workshops. In 2019, he won the Eminent Social Scientist Award, for his outstanding contribution in applied economic research, from Global Peace University, USA.

He has published a number of books including *Causes and Consequences of Demonetization in India: A Critical Assessment*, Asian Management Economics and Commerce Association Publications, 2017. He has 24 years of teaching and research experience in the field of applied economics. Till date, 8 Ph.D. degrees and 32 M.Phil. degrees have been awarded under his guidance and supervision.

Contents

About the Book..*v*
About the Author...*vi*
Preface..*xiii-xiv*
Explanation of Select Terms Related to Financial Economics........................*xv-xxii*
Abbreviations/Acronyms..*xxiii-xxiv*

Part I: Basics of Financial Economics

1. Financial System and Financial Economics   1-9
1.1 Meaning and Importance of Financial System
1.2 Functions of Financial System
1.3 Role of the State in Financial Development
1.4 Determinants of Access to Financial Services
1.5 Financial Neutrality versus Financial Activism
1.6 Financial Volatility versus Financial Stability
1.7 Regulation and Supervision of Financial System
1.8 Meaning and Significance of Financial Economics
1.9 Aspects of Financial Economics

2. Financial Institutions, Financial Markets and Financial Instruments   10-14
2.1 Financial Institutions
2.2 Financial Markets
2.3 Financial Instruments

Part II: Investment Theory and Portfolio Analysis

3. Theory of the Rate of Interest   15-21
3.1 Significance of Interest Rate
3.2 Types of Rate of Interest
3.3 Loanable Fund Theory of the Rate of Interest
3.4 Liquidity Preference Theory of the Rate of Interest

4. Reasons for Interest Rate Differentials   22-26
4.1 How Are Interest Rates Determined?
4.2 What is an Interest Rate Differential?
4.3 Causes of Differences in Interest Rates
4.4 Types of Credit (Loans)

5. Term Structure of Interest Rates and Yield Curves   27-32

5.1 What is Term Structure of Interest Rates?
5.2 Shapes and Uses of Yield Curve
5.3 Three Theories to Explain Yield Curve
5.4 Fixed Income Securities

6. Portfolio of Assets   33-38

6.1 Portfolio Defined
6.2 Portfolio Manager
6.3 Portfolio Management
6.4 Diversification of Portfolio
6.5 Efficient Portfolio and Risk Categories
6.6 Problems with Diversification

7. Mean-Variance Portfolio Analysis   39-43

7.1 Importance of Portfolio Theory
7.2 What is Mean-Variance Analysis?
7.3 Investment Strategy
7.4 Main Components of Mean-Variance Analysis
7.5 Assumptions of Mean-Variance Analysis
7.6 Calculation of Expected Return and Variance
7.7 Criticism

8. Markowitz Model   44-47

8.1 Assumptions
8.2 Markowitz Efficient Set
8.3 Markowitz Efficient Frontier
8.4 Limitations of the Markowitz Model

9. Capital Asset Pricing Model (CAPM)   48-53

9.1 Risk and Return
9.2 Systematic Risks versus Unsystematic Risks
9.3 Risk-Return Trade-off
9.4 CAMP Formula
9.5 Assumptions of CAMP
9.6 Limitations of CAPM
9.7 Consumption Capital Asset Pricing Model (CCAPM)
9.8 Inter-temporal Capital Asset Pricing Model (ICAMP)

10. Capital Market Line (CML) and Security Market Line (SML)   54-60

10.1 Capital Market Line (CML)
10.2 Security Market Line (SML)

Part III: Derivatives, Forwards, Futures and Options

11. Financial Derivatives: Emergence and Popularity   **61-71**
11.1 Emergence of Complex Financial Products
11.2 Meaning of Derivatives
11.3 Reasons for the Popularity of Derivatives
11.4 Variants (or Types) of Derivative Contracts
11.5 Participants in the Derivatives Market
11.6 Economic Role of Derivatives
11.7 History of Derivatives
11.8 International Experience of Derivatives

12. Forward Contracts (or Forwards)   **72-76**
12.1 What is a Forward Contact?
12.2 Salient Features of Forward Contracts
12.3 Example of a Forward Contract
12.4 Advantages of Forwards
12.5 Problems of Forward Contracts
12.6 Risks with Forward Contracts
12.7 Forward Markets Commission (FMC) of India

13. Future Contracts (or Futures)   **77-84**
13.1 What is a Future Contract?
13.2 History of Futures
13.3 How Do Future Contracts Work?
13.4 Hedgers and Speculators
13.5 Role of Clearing House
13.6 Currency Futures
13.7 Distinction between Forwards and Futures
13.8 Introduction of Futures in India

14. Options   **85-93**
14.1 What is an Option?
14.2 Options in Historical Perspective
14.3 Call Options
14.4 Put Options
14.5 Example of an Option
14.6 Advantages of Option Trading
14.7 Forms of Option Trading
14.8 Valuation Models
14.9 Options Risk Metrics: The Greeks

15. Black-Scholes-Merton Option Pricing Model   **94-97**

15.1 What is Black-Scholes Model?
15.2 Basics of the Black-Scholes Model
15.3 Assumptions of Black-Scholes Model
15.4 Black-Scholes Formula
15.5 Limitations of the Black-Scholes Model

16. Binomial Option Pricing Model   **98-102**

16.1 What is Binomial Option Pricing Model (BOPM)?
16.2 Basics of the BOPM
16.3 Assumptions of BOPM
16.4 Calculating Price with the Binomial Model
16.5 Option Valuation
16.6 Advantages and Disadvantages of BOPM

17. Principles of Arbitrage   **103-110**

17.1 What is Arbitrage?
17.2 Conditions for Arbitrage
17.3 Risks Involved in Arbitrage
17.4 Types of Arbitrage
17.5 Arbitrage Pricing Theory (APT)

Part IV: Corporate Finance

18. Patterns of Corporate Financing   **111-117**

18.1 Meaning of Corporate Financing
18.2 Sources of Capital
18.3 Capital Investments

19. Capital Structure and the Cost of Capital   **118-124**

19.1 Capital Structure Defined
19.2 Cost of Capital

20. Corporate Debt   **125-132**

20.1 What is Debt?
20.2 Need for Corporate Debt
20.3 Corporate Bonds
20.4 Emergence of Private Placement Market
20.5 Other Types of Corporate Debt
20.6 Significance of the Corporate Debt Market
20.7 Lessons from East Asian Crisis

21. Dividend Policy Models   133-138
21.1 Dividend Policy Explained
21.2 Types of Dividend Policy
21.3 Dividend Irrelevance Theories
21.4 Dividend Relevance Theories

22. Modigliani-Miller Theorem (M&M Theorem)   139-142
22.1 Historical Background
22.2 M&M Theorem in Brief
22.3 M&M Theorem in Perfectly Efficient Markets
22.4 M&M Theorem in the Real World

Part V: Indian Financial System

23. Financial Institutions   143-153
23.1 Classification of Financial Institutions in India
23.2 Financial Institutions in India at a Glance
23.3 Regulation and Supervision of Financial Institutions in India

24. Financial Markets   154-163
24.1 Importance of Financial Markets
24.2 Regulation and Supervision of Financial Markets in India
24.3 Money Market
24.4 Government Securities Market
24.5 Capital Market
24.6 Foreign Exchange Market

25. Financial Instruments   164-171
25.1 Direct Financial Instruments
25.2 Derivative Financial Instruments

26. Financial Inclusion   172-184
26.1 Origins of the Current Approach to Financial Inclusion
26.2 Financial Exclusion and Financial Inclusion Defined
26.3 Advantages of Financial Inclusion
26.4 Measures Taken by Reserve Bank of India (RBI) for
     Financial Inclusion
26.5 Financial Inclusion Measures by NABARD
26.6 Committee on Financial Inclusion
26.7 Committee on Comprehensive Financial Services for Small
     Businesses and Low-income Households (CCFS), 2014
26.8 Pradhan Mantri Jan-Dhan Yojana (PMJDY), 2014

27. Financial Regulators   **185-196**

27.1 Ministry of Finance, Government of India
27.2 Reserve Bank of India (RBI)
27.3 Ministry of Corporate Affairs
27.4 Securities and Exchange Board of India (SEBI)
27.5 Insurance Regulatory and Development Authority (IRDA)
27.6 Pension Fund Regulatory and Development Authority (PFRDA)
27.7 Monitoring Framework for Financial Conglomerates (FCs)

28. Legislative and Institutional Measures to Strengthen Financial Sector   **197-206**

28.1 Prevention of Money Laundering Act (PMLA), 2002
28.2 Credit Information Companies (Regulation) Act, 2005
28.3 Government Securities Act, 2006
28.4 Payment and Settlement Systems Act, 2007
28.5 Black Money (Undisclosed Foreign Income and Assets) and
     Imposition of Tax Act, 2015
28.6 Benami Transactions (Prohibition) Amendment Act, 2016
28.7 High Level Committee on Financial Sector Reforms, 2008
28.8 Committee on Financial Sector Assessment (CFSA), 2009
28.9 Financial Sector Legislative Reforms Commission (FSLRC), 2013
28.10 Indian Financial Code (IFC)
28.11 Financial Stability and Development Council (FSDC)
28.12 Financial Action Task Force (FATF)
28.13 Financial Stability Board (FSB)

Suggested Readings   **207-210**
Index   **211-216**

Preface

Financial system of an economy is a multi-faceted term. It refers to the whole gamut of legal and institutional arrangements, financial intermediaries, markets and instruments with both domestic and external dimensions.

A well-functioning financial system is a pre-requisite for the pursuit of economic growth with stability. The core function of a financial system is to facilitate smooth and efficient allocation of resources from savers to the ultimate users. The financial infrastructure contributes to the effective functioning of institutions and markets and thereby to stability. Hence, it serves as the foundation for adequate access to financial services and sustained financial development.

Financial markets create an open and regulated system for companies to acquire large amounts of capital. This is done through the stock and bond markets. Markets also allow these businesses to offset risk. They do this with commodities, foreign exchange future contracts, and other derivatives. Since the markets are public, they provide an open and transparent way to set prices on everything traded.

They reflect all available knowledge about everything traded. This reduces the cost of obtaining information because it is already incorporated into the price. The sheer size of the financial markets provides liquidity. In other words, sellers can unload assets whenever they need to raise cash. The size also reduces the cost of doing business. Companies don't have to go far to find a buyer or someone willing to sell.

The maturity and sophistication of financial system depends upon the prevalence of a variety of financial instruments to suit the varied investment requirements of heterogeneous investors so as to enable it to mobilize savings from as wide section of the investing public as possible.

The emergence of the market for derivative products, most notably forwards, futures and options, can be traced back to the willingness of risk-averse economic agents to guard themselves against uncertainties arising out of fluctuations in asset prices. By their very nature, the financial markets are marked by a very high degree of volatility. Through the use of derivative products, it is possible to partially or fully transfer price risks by locking-in asset prices. As instruments of risk management, derivatives generally do not influence the fluctuations in the underlying asset prices. However, by locking-in asset prices, derivative products minimize the impact of fluctuations in asset prices on the profitability and cash flow situation of risk-averse investors.

Financial economics is a branch of economics that analyzes the distribution and use of resources in markets in which decisions are made under uncertainty. Financial decisions must often take into account future events, whether those are related to individual stocks, portfolios or the market as a whole.

The subject is concerned with the allocation and deployment of economic resources, both spatially and across time, in an uncertain environment. It, therefore, centres on decision-making under uncertainty in the context of the financial markets. It is built on the foundations of microeconomics and decision theory.

Financial economics is important in making investment decisions, identifying risks, and valuing securities and assets. It relies heavily on microeconomics and basic accounting concepts. In addition, it requires familiarity with basic statistics and probability since these are the standard tools used to measure and evaluate risk.

Financial economics employs economic theory to evaluate how time, risk, opportunity costs can create incentives or disincentives for a particular decision. Financial economics often involves the creation of sophisticated models to test the variables affecting a particular decision. Often, these models assume that individuals or institutions making decisions act rationally, though this is not necessarily the case. Irrational behaviour of parties has to be taken into account in financial economics as a potential risk factor.

While traditional economics focuses on exchanges in which money is one, but only one, of the items traded, financial economics concentrates on exchanges in which money of one type or another is likely to appear on both sides of a trade.

The ultimate benefit of financial economics is providing investors with the instruments to make sound and informed decisions in relation to their investment options. They are presented with the risks and risk factors involved in their investments, the fair value of the asset they wish to acquire, and the regulations in the financial markets where they are involved, as well as the various financial institutions.

Risk is inherent in almost all financial activities. Anyone who keeps monitoring the stock market will notice that the stocks being traded can change trends anytime. The returns from stock investing are sometimes high, as the risk is also high, and it is the most effective way to lure investors to buy and trade the stocks. Ideally, if an investor holds two risky assets, their individual performances should compensate for the other.

Many advertisements for financial products based on the stock market remind potential buyers that the value of investments may fall as well as rise. So although stocks yield a return which is high on average, this is largely to compensate for risk.

Financial institutions are always looking for ways of insuring (or *hedging*) this risk. It is sometimes possible to hold two highly risky assets but for the overall risk to be low. If share A only performs badly when share B performs well (and vice versa) then the two shares perform a perfect hedge.

An important part of finance is working out the total risk of a portfolio of risky assets, since the total risk may be less than the risk of the individual components.

The present work is an attempt to explain various aspects of financial economics in simple and lucid. It would connect teachers and students of the subject to the basic concepts, components and processes of financial economics.

Vellore
August 2021

G. Yoganandham

Explanation of Select Terms Related to Financial Economics

Annuity: It is a fixed sum of money paid to an annuitant yearly, usually for the remaining part of his life. It is a form of pension which provides a regular annual income. An annuity may be purchased by making a lump sum cash payment.

Arbitrage Pricing Theory (APT): APT is a model of pricing that is based on the concept that an asset can have its returns predicted. To do so, the relationship between the asset and its common risk factors must be analyzed. APT was first created by Stephen Ross in 1976 to examine the influence of macroeconomic factors. It allows for the returns of a portfolio and the returns of specific asset to be predicted by examining the various variables that are independent within the relationship. It is based on the idea that in a well-functioning securities market, there should be no arbitrage opportunities available. That makes it possible to predict the outcome of that security over time.

Arbitrage: Arbitrage means the simultaneous buying and selling of securities, currency or commodities in different markets in order to take advantage of differing prices for the same asset. Arbitrage is basically the act of buying a security in one market and simultaneously selling it in another market at a higher price, profiting from the temporary difference in prices. This is considered risk-free profit for the investor/trader.

Arbitrageurs: They are in business to take advantage of a discrepancy between prices in two different markets. If, for example, they see the futures price of an asset getting out of line with the cash price, they will take offsetting positions in the two markets to lock-in a profit. Arbitragers are traders and market-makers who deal in buying and selling derivatives contracts hoping to profit from price-differentials between different markets. A market maker is one who provides two-way quotes for a given product and thereby runs a position in that product.

Binomial Option Pricing Model (BOPM): BOPM is an options valuation method which uses an iterative procedure, allowing for the specification of nodes, or points in time, during the time span between the valuation date and the option's expiration date. In finance, BOPM) provides a generalizable numerical method for the valuation of options. Essentially, the model uses a *discrete-time* (lattice based) model of the varying price over time of the underlying financial instrument, addressing cases where the closed-form Black-Scholes formula is wanting. The binomial model was first proposed by William Sharpe in the 1978.

Binomial Tree: A binomial tree is a graphical representation of possible intrinsic values that an option may take at different nodes or time periods.

Black-Scholes Model: Black-Scholes model, also known as the Black-Scholes-Merton (BSM) model, is a mathematical model for pricing an options contract. In particular, the model estimates the variation over time of financial instruments. It assumes these instruments (such as stocks or futures) will have a lognormal distribution of prices. Using this assumption and factoring in other important variables, the equation derives the price of a call option.

Bond: A bond is a promise to pay a stated sum of money as interest each year and to repay the face value of bond at some future redemption date. Some bonds, called *perpetuities*, pay a fixed sum of interest each year forever but never repay the principal, i.e. they have no redemption date.

Call Option: A call option is an option to buy a stock at a specific price on or before a certain date. In this way, call options are like security deposits.

Capital Asset Pricing Model (CAMP): It provides a formula that calculates the expected return on a security based on its level of risk. The formula for CAMP is the risk free rate plus beta times the difference of the return on the market and the risk free rate. There are five principal risk measures, and each measure provides a unique way to assess the risk present in investments that are under consideration. The five measures include the alpha, beta, R-squared, standard deviation, and Sharpe ratio.

Capital Market Line (CML): CML represents portfolios that optimally combine risk and return. It is a theoretical concept that represents all the portfolios that optimally combine the risk-free rate of return and the market portfolio of risky assets. Under CAPM, all investors will choose a position on CML by borrowing or lending at the risk-free rate, since this maximizes return for a given level of risk.

Capital Market: Capital market is a market for long-term funds. Capital market channelises household savings to the corporate sector and allocates funds to firms. In this process, it allows both firms and households to share risks associated with business. Moreover, capital market enables the valuation of firms on an almost continuous basis and plays an important role in the governance of the corporate sector.

Capital Structure Substitution Theory: This theory is based on the hypothesis that company management may manipulate capital structure such that earnings per share (EPS) are maximized. The model is not normative. It does not state that management should maximize EPS. It simply hypothesizes they do so.

Capital Structure: In corporate finance, capital structure is the way a corporation finances its assets through some combination of equity, debt, or hybrid securities. It refers to the make up of capitalisation of a firm. It is the mix of different sources of long-term funds such as equity shares, preference shares, long-term debt, retained profits etc. To put it differently, capital structure is the *composition* or *structure* of the liabilities of a firm.

Commercial Paper: Commercial paper refers to a short-term unsecured promissory note issued in public market through private placement. It is a low-cost funding source for working capital, seasonal cash flow demand and bridge financing.

Consumption Capital Asset Pricing Model (CCAPM): CCAPM is an extension of CAPM that uses a consumption beta instead of a market beta to explain expected return premiums over the risk-free rate. The beta component of both the CCAPM and CAPM formulas represents risk that cannot be diversified away. The consumption beta is based on the volatility of a given stock or portfolio.

Corporate Financing: It deals with sourcing capital in the form of debt or equity. A company may borrow from commercial banks and other financial intermediaries or may issue debt securities in the capital markets through investment banks. A company may also choose to sell stocks to equity investors, especially when need large amounts of capital for business expansions.

Derivatives: Derivative instruments comprise financial products which have grown up around securities, currency and commodity trading and whose price is a function of some other underlying security, currency rate or other commodity. The term is usually used to include swaps, futures, options, forwards and a wide range of financially engineered instruments which are hybrids of other financial products.

Financial Economics: Financial economics is a branch of economics that analyzes the distribution and use of resources in markets in which decisions are made under uncertainty. Financial decisions must often take into account future events, whether those are related to individual stocks, portfolios or the market as a whole.

Financial Intermediaries: Financial intermediaries are an integral part of a modern industrial economy. They are institutions, such as commercial banks, which act as middlemen between the lenders and the borrowers. Financial intermediaries are beneficial both to lenders and borrowers. Lenders stand to gain because they can invest their funds at low risk and greater liquidity with financial institutions. The main advantage to borrowers is availability of adequate credit at reasonable rate of interest.

Financial Market: It is a market in which financial assets of various kinds like shares, debentures and bills are dealt with. A financial market consists of: (a) money market which deals in short-term credit and (b) capital market which provides medium-term and long-term credit.

Financial System: It refers to the whole gamut of institutional arrangements which help to mobilise financial surpluses of an economy and transfer them to areas of financial deficit. Financial system of a country rests on three pillars: (a) financial institutions or financial intermediaries, (b) financial markets and (c) financial assets. Financial system is the linchpin of a modern industrial economy.

Forward Contracts (or Forwards): A forward contract is a customised contract between two entities, where settlement takes place on a specific date in the future at today's pre-agreed price. A forward contract is an agreement to buy or sell an asset on a specified date for specified price.

Forward Markets Commission (FMC) of India: FMC was merged with SEBI in September 2015. FMC was the chief regulator of forwards and futures markets in India. Headquartered in Mumbai, it was overseen by the Ministry of Consumer Affairs, Food and Public Distribution, Government of India. Established in 1953 under the provisions of the Forward Contracts (Regulation) Act, 1952, it consisted of 2 to 4 members, all appointed by the Government of India. The Commission allowed commodity trading in 22 exchanges in India.

Future Contracts (or Futures): Future contracts are special types of forward contracts in the sense that the former are standardised exchange-traded contracts. Future contract markets are designed to solve the problems that exist in forward markets. A future contract is an agreement between two parties to buy or sell an asset at a certain time in future, at a certain price. However, unlike forward contracts, future contracts are standardized and stock exchange-traded.

Hedgers: Hedgers face risk associated with the price of an asset. They use future or option markets to reduce or eliminate this risk. In other words, hedgers are those who wish to protect their existing exposures and essentially are safety-driven.

Hedging: It is a method to guard against fluctuations in the prices of commodities (particularly raw materials) scheduled for future delivery by dealing in futures market. *Buying hedge* and *selling hedge* are the two basic types of hedge operations.

Inter-temporal Capital Asset Pricing Model (ICAMP): ICAPM is a consumption-based capital asset pricing model (CCAPM) that assumes that investors hedge risky positions. ICAPM is an extension of CAPM and was introduced by Nobel laureate Robert Merton in 1973.

Liquidity of an Asset: Liquidity of an asset means how easily it can be converted into cash and at what loss of its capital value. If an asset cannot be converted into cash easily (i.e. at short notice) or at minimum loss of its value, it is less liquid.

Liquidity Preference Theory of the Rate of Interest: According to British economist John Maynard Keynes (1883-1946), rate of interest is a reward for parting with liquidity for a specified period of time. Rate of interest, he believed, is a purely monetary phenomenon determined by the demand for and supply of money (liquidity). The supply of money is given by the government, and it is an exogenous (or autonomous) factor and accepted as it is. However, the demand for money (or preference for liquidity) varies and hence plays active role in the determination of the rate of interest.

Loanable Fund Theory of the Rate of Interest: Loanable fund theory is attributed to Swedish economist Knut Wicksell (1851-1926) and the British economist Dennis Robertson (1890-1963). According to this theory, the rate of interest is determined by the demand for and the supply of loanable funds in an economy. The demand for loans originates from three types of borrowers, viz. producers, consumers and government. Supply of loans comes from the current savings of households as well as business firms.

Markowitz Model: Markowitz model is a portfolio optimization model. It assists in the selection of the most efficient portfolio by analyzing various possible portfolios of the given securities. By choosing securities that do not *move* exactly together, the Markowitz model shows investors how to reduce their risk. Markowitz model is also called mean-variance model due to the fact that it is based on expected returns (mean) and the standard deviation (variance) of the various portfolios. It is foundational to modern portfolio theory.

Mean-Variance Analysis: Mean-variance analysis is a technique that investors use to make decisions about financial instruments to invest in, based on the amount of risk that they are willing to accept (risk tolerance). Ideally, investors expect to earn higher returns when they invest in riskier assets. When measuring the level of risk, investors consider the potential variance (which is the volatility of returns produced by an asset) against the expected returns of that asset. Mean-variance analysis essentially looks at the average variance in the expected return from an investment.

Modigliani-Miller Theorem: It states that the market value of a company is correctly calculated as the present value of its future earnings and its underlying assets, and is independent of its capital structure. At its most basic level, the theorem argues that, with certain assumptions in place, it is irrelevant whether a company finances its growth by borrowing, by issuing stock shares, or by reinvesting its profits.

Money Market: It is a market for short-term funds with a maturity of up to one year and includes financial instruments that are close substitutes for money. The main instruments comprising the money market are call money/notice money, certificates of deposit, commercial bills, commercial paper and inter-corporate funds.

Money Market: Money market is the most important segment of the financial system as it provides the fulcrum for equilibrating short-term demand for and supply of funds, thereby facilitating the conduct of monetary policy. It is a market for short-term funds with a maturity of up to one year and includes financial instruments that are close substitutes for money.

Options: Options are fundamentally different from forward and future contracts. An option gives the holder of the option the right to do something. The holder does not have to necessarily exercise this right. In contrast, in a forward or future contract, the two parties commit themselves to doing something.

Pecking Order Theory: Pecking order theory tries to capture the costs of asymmetric information. It states that companies prioritize their sources of financing (from internal financing to equity) according to the law of least effort, or of least resistance, preferring to raise equity as a financing means *of last resort*. Hence, internal financing is used first and when that is depleted, debt is issued; and when it is no longer sensible to issue any more debt, equity is issued. This theory maintains that businesses adhere to a hierarchy of financing sources and prefer internal financing when available, and debt is preferred over equity if external financing is required.

Portfolio: A portfolio can be defined as different investment instruments namely stocks, shares, mutual funds, bonds, cash etc., all combined together depending specifically on the investor's income, budget, risk appetite and the holding period. It is formed in such a way that it stabilizes the risk of non-performance of different pools of investment.

Portfolio Manager: A portfolio manager is a professional responsible for making investment decisions and carrying out investment activities on behalf of interested individuals or institutions. Portfolio managers are primarily responsible for creating and managing investment allocations for private clients. A portfolio manager determines a client's appropriate level of risk based on the client's time horizon, risk preferences, return expectations and market conditions.

Portfolio Management: Portfolio Management is the art and science of making decisions about investment mix and policy, matching investments to objectives, asset allocation for individuals and institutions, and balancing risk against performance. Portfolio management includes a range of professional services to manage an individual's and company's securities, such as stocks and bonds, and other assets, such as real estate.

Put Option: A put option is an option to sell a stock at a specific price on or before a certain date. In this way, put options are like insurance policies.

Residuals Theory of Dividends: One of the assumptions of this theory is that external financing to re-invest is either not available, or that it is too costly to invest in any profitable opportunity. If a firm has good investment opportunity available then it will invest the retained earnings and reduce the dividends or give no dividends at all. If no such opportunity exists, the firm will pay out dividends.

Security Market Line (SML): SML is the representation of the capital asset pricing model (CAMP). It displays the expected rate of return of an individual security as a function of systematic, non-diversifiable risk. The risk of an individual risky security reflects the volatility of the return from security rather than the return of the market portfolio. The risk in these individual risky securities reflects the systematic risk.

Speculative Bubbles and Crashes: A speculative bubble exists in the event of large, sustained overpricing of some class of assets. One factor that frequently contributes to a bubble is the presence of buyers who purchase an asset based solely on the expectation that they can later resell it at a higher price, rather than calculating the income it will generate in the future. If there is a bubble, there is also a risk of a *crash* in asset prices. Market participants will go on buying only as long as they expect others to buy, and when many decide to sell the price will fall. However, it is difficult to predict whether an asset's price actually equals its fundamental value, so it is hard to detect bubbles reliably.

Speculators: They bet on future movements in the price of an asset. Future and option contracts can give them an extra leverage; that is, they can increase both the potential gains and potential losses in a speculative venture. Speculators are willing risk takers who are expectation-driven.

Stock Market: A stock (or share) market deals mainly in corporate securities like shares and debentures. It is an important component of the capital market of the financial system.

Syndicated Loan: A syndicated loan is a loan advanced by a syndicate, a group of banks (joined sometimes by pension funds, insurance companies etc.) to a single company. One bank acts as a lead (also called originator) and it manages the whole process. Even a secondary market has recently developed in the syndicated loans market in which syndicated loans are securitized and sold to investors.

Systematic Risk: These are market risks, i.e. general perils of investing which cannot be diversified away. These systematic factors include macroeconomic factors such as inflation, interest rates, economic growth, exchange rates, recessions etc.

Trade-off Theory: Trade-off theory of capital structure allows bankruptcy cost to exist as an offset to the benefit of using debt as tax shield. It states that there is an advantage to financing with debt, namely the tax benefits of debt and that there is a cost of financing with debt the bankruptcy costs and the financial distress costs of debt. This theory also refers to the idea that a company chooses how much equity finance and how much debt finance to use by considering both costs and benefits. Empirically, this theory may explain differences in debt-to-equity ratios between industries, but it doesn't explain differences within the same industry.

Unsystematic Risk: Also known as *specific risk*, this risk relates to individual stocks. In more technical terms, it represents the component of a stock's return that is not correlated with general market moves.

Venture Capital: It is a term used for investment made in those lines where risk element is very high, especially in new lines of production, new markets or new processes.

Virtual Currency: According to the European Central Bank, virtual currency is a digital representation of value, not issued by a central bank, credit institution or e-money institution, which, in some circumstances, can be used as an alternative to money. Virtual currency is a type of unregulated, digital money, which is issued and usually controlled by its developers, and used and accepted among the members of a specific virtual community.

Weighted Average Cost of Capital (WACC): WACC is a calculation of a firm's cost of capital in which each category of capital is proportionately weighted. A firm's cost of capital is typically calculated using the weighted average cost of capital formula that considers the cost of both debt and equity capital. Each category of the firm's capital is weighted proportionately to arrive at a blended rate, and the formula considers every type of debt and equity on the company's balance sheet, including common and preferred stock, bonds and other forms of debt.

Yield Curve: Yield curve depicts the interest rates of similar quality bonds at different maturities. Generally, yields increase in line with maturity, giving rise to an upward-sloping, or normal, yield curve. The yield curve is primarily used to illustrate the term structure of interest rates for standard government-issued securities. This is important as it is a measure of the debt market's feeling about risk.

Zero-tax Company: Income tax laws usually provide for a host of deductions and incentives to promote socio-economic objectives of state policy. It is likely that a profit-making company may arrange its affairs in such a way that the cumulative effect of all deductions is to reduce its income declared in the tax return to zero. To deal with such situations, some countries have introduced minimum alternative tax.

Abbreviations/Acronyms

ADB	Asian Development Bank
APT	Arbitrage Pricing Theory
BCs	Business Correspondents
BOPM	Binomial Option Pricing Model
BSE	Bombay Stock Exchange
CAL	Capital Allocation Line
CAMP	Capital Asset Pricing Model
CBOE	Chicago Board Options Exchange
CBOT	Chicago Board of Trade
CCAPM	Consumption Capital Asset Pricing Model
CD	Certificate of deposit
CDOs	Collateralised Debt Obligations
CDSs	Credit-Default Swaps
CGD	Centre for Global Development
CME	Chicago Mercantile Exchange
CML	Capital Market Line
CP	Commercial Paper
CSS	Capital Structure Substitution
DFIs	Development Finance Institutions
DPs	Depository Participants
EMI	Equated Monthly Instalment
EPS	Earnings Per Share
FIF	Financial Inclusion Fund
FIIs	Foreign Institutional Investors
FITF	Financial Inclusion Technology Fund
FMC	Forward Markets Commission
FSDC	Financial Stability and Development Council
GCC	General Credit Card
GNMA	Ginnie Mae
HFCs	Housing Finance Companies
ICAMP	Inter-temporal Capital Asset Pricing Model
IMF	International Monetary Fund
IPO	Initial Public Offer
IRDA	Insurance Regulatory and Development Authority
IT	Information Technology
KYC	Know Your Customer
LEAPS	Long-term Equity Anticipation Securities
LIBOR	London Inter-bank Offer Rate
M&M Theorem	Modigliani-Miller Theorem
MFIs	Micro Finance Institutions

Financial Economics

NBFCs	Non-banking Financial Companies
Nifty	National Stock Exchange Fifty
NPV	Net Present Value
NSCC	National Securities Clearing Corporation
NSE	National Stock Exchange
OECD	Organisation for Economic Cooperation and Development
OTC	Over-the-Counter
RBI	Reserve Bank of India
RFA	Revolving Fund Assistance
RRBs	Regional Rural Banks
SCRA	Securities Contracts (Regulation) Act
SEBI	Securities and Exchange Board of India
SENSEX	Sensitive Index
SHGs	Self-help Goups
SHPIs	Self-help Promoting Institutions
SIMEX	Singapore International Monetary Exchange
SML	Security Market Line
TVM)	Time Value of Money
UCBs	Urban Co-operative Banks
WACC	Weighted Average Cost of Capital
YTM	Yield-to-Maturity

Part I
Basics of Financial Economics

1

Financial System and Financial Economics

Finance is the life blood of a modern economy. A financial system helps to mobilize the financial surpluses of an economy and transfer them to areas of financial deficit. It is the linchpin of any development strategy. The financial system promotes savings by providing a wide variety of financial assets to the general public. Savings collected from the household sector are pooled together and allocated to various sectors of the economy for raising production levels. If the allocation of credit is judicious and socially equitable, it can help achieve the twin objectives of growth and social justice.

1.1 Meaning and Importance of Financial System

Financial system of an economy is a multi-faceted term. It refers to the whole gamut of legal and institutional arrangements, financial intermediaries, markets and instruments with both domestic and external dimensions.

A well-functioning financial system is a pre-requisite for the pursuit of economic growth with stability. The core function of a financial system is to facilitate smooth and efficient allocation of resources from savers to the ultimate users. The financial infrastructure contributes to the effective functioning of institutions and markets and thereby to stability. Hence, it serves as the foundation for adequate access to financial services and sustained financial development.

In the context of relatively under-developed capital market and with little internal resources, firms or economic entities depend largely on financial intermediaries for their fund requirements. In terms of sources of credit, they could be broadly categorised as institutional and non-institutional. For example, the major institutional sources of credit in India are commercial banks, development finance institutions (DFIs) and non-banking financial companies (NBFCs) including housing finance companies (HFCs). The non-institutional or unorganised sources of credit include moneylenders, indigenous bankers and sellers for trade credit. However, information about unorganised sector is limited and not readily available.

The relationship between finance and development has been a crucial subject of public policy for long. As early as in the 19th century, a number of economists stressed the importance of financial development for the growth of an economy. The banking system was recognised to have important ramifications for the level and growth rate of national income via the identification and funding of productive investments. This, in turn, was expected to induce a more efficient allocation of capital and foster growth. A contrary view also prevailed at the same time suggesting that economic growth would create demand for financial services. This meant that financial development would follow growth more or less automatically. In other words, financial development could be considered as a by-product of economic development.

1.2 Functions of Financial System

Following are some of the functions performed by a financial system:

1. It facilitates trading and hedging of risks. Risk mitigation reduces uncertainty and enables resources to flow towards most profitable projects. Such a situation raises the efficiency of investments and the rate of growth.
2. By acting as an efficient conduit for allocating resources, the financial system enables improvement in technical progress. Technological innovations take place when entrepreneurs exploit the best chances of successfully imitating technologies in their production processes and introducing new products.
3. To the extent that financial development leads to the creation of financial infrastructure and enables better and more efficient provision of goods and services, costs of transactions would be lower, with positive spill over on economic growth.

The role and importance of the financial sector in the process of economic growth has evolved over time along with the changing paradigms. Till the late 1960s, the role of financial intermediaries in general, and banks in particular, in the process of economic growth of a country was largely ignored.

1.3 Role of the State in Financial Development

An important aspect of the process of financial development has been the role of the government. In many developing economies the governments traditionally played a significant role in fostering financial development. In the context of developing countries, this role is all the more important because financial systems in these countries are characterized by nascent accounting frameworks and inadequate legal mechanisms.

Several developing countries, therefore, undertook programmes for reforming their financial systems. In the initial stages of the development process, the financial sector in developing countries was characterised by directed credit allocation, interest rate restrictions and lending criteria based on social needs etc. These policies retarded the nature of financial intermediation in developing countries and the recognition of the same paved the way for financial sector reforms. Since the late 1970s and the 1980s, financial sector reforms encompassing deregulation of interest rates, revamping of directed credit and measures to promote competition in the financial services became an integral part of the overall structural adjustment programmes in many developing economies.

The interface between financial system and economic development revolves around on a wide range of issues, the following being more prominent.

1. Extant of state ownership of financial entities vis-à-vis private sector ownership.
2. Corporate governance in banks and other segments of the financial system.
3. Transparency of policies and practices of monetary and financial agencies.
4. Prudential requirements of market participants.
5. Maintenance of best practices in accounting and auditing.
6. Comprehensive and efficient regulation and supervision of the financial system.

7.   Collection, processing and dissemination of information in order to meet market needs.
     The commonality among these concerns has given rise to a wide recognition and acceptance of having a set of international standards and best practices that every country should strive to foster and implement.

1.4 Determinants of Access to Financial Services

In the literature on finance, a number of factors have been mentioned which affect the access to financial services. Some important factors among these are as under:

1.   **Level of Income:** Financial status of people is always important in gaining access to financial services. Extremely poor people find it difficult to access financial services even when the services are tailored for them.
2.   **Type of Occupation:** Many banks have not developed the capacity to evaluate loan applications of small borrowers and unorganised enterprises and hence tend to deny loan requests by them.
3.   **Legal Identity:** Lack of legal identities like identity cards, birth certificates or written records often exclude ethnic minorities, economic and political refugees and migrant workers from accessing financial services.
4.   **Attractiveness of the Product:** Benefits of financial products offered and how their availability is marketed are crucial in accessing financial services.
5.   **Terms and Conditions:** Terms and conditions attached to products such as minimum balance requirements and conditions relating to the use of accounts often dissuade people from using such products/services. Generally, transaction is free as long as the account has sufficient funds to cover the cost of transactions made. However, there is a range of other charges that have a disproportionate effect on people with low income.
6.   **Socio-cultural Barriers:** Lack of financial literacy (basic accounting skills) and cultural and religious barriers to banking often constrain demand for financial services. Access to credit is often limited for women who do not have, or cannot hold title to assets such as land and property or must seek male guarantees to borrow.
7.   **Living Conditions:** Factors like density of population, rural and remote areas, mobility of the population (i.e. highly mobile people with no fixed or formal address), insurgency in a location etc. also affect access to financial services.
8.   **Age Factor:** Financial service providers usually target the middle of the economically active population, often overlooking older or younger customers.

1.5 Financial Neutrality versus Financial Activism

The views on neutrality of financial intermediaries to economic growth, however, came under attack during the late 1960s. It was pointed out that there exists a strong positive correlation between financial development and economic growth of a country. Financial experts started emphasising the negative impact of *financial repression*, under which the government determined the quantum, allocation and price of credit, on the growth process. They argued that credit is not just another input and instead, credit is the engine of growth.

The world of finance has changed markedly over the last 30 years or so. The change has been brought about by a number of events and circumstances. The growing dissatisfaction with the working of the fixed exchange rate system during the 1960s led many countries, especially of the industrialised world, to adopt a floating exchange rate system by the early 1970s. There was also a growing realisation that for achieving sustained growth with stability, it would be necessary to have freer trade, liberalised external capital movements, and a relatively flexible use of domestic monetary policy. With trade being subject to multilateral negotiations, industrialised countries and some of the emerging market economies took steps to liberalise capital movements across countries since about the middle of the 1970s. Simultaneously, efforts were made to remove distortions in the domestic financial sector through elimination or containment of reserve requirements and interest rate regulations. These initiatives coincided with the rapid technological improvements in electronic payments and communication systems. The interaction among these factors helped the process of internationalisation of financial markets.

Under the impact of economic liberalisation, the industrialised countries, as a group, improved their relative economic position in the world economy, and posted high growth rates in the 1980s and thereafter. This experience has confirmed the release of growth impulses following financial liberalisation.

Developing countries, on their part, have been adopting, since the early 1980s, market-oriented strategies of financial development, partly supported by international financial institutions, and partly to avail of the large pool of resources available in international financial markets. They either dismantled or sharply contained *financial repression* and undertook financial reforms with a view to enhancing allocative efficiency and competitiveness. Financial development required the deepening and widening of the existing financial markets as well as the introduction of new products and instruments to cater to the needs of savers and investors.

Financial development depends on market-based regulatory framework and incentives (disincentives) that promote market discipline. If market discipline is not well-understood or not complied with, there would arise possibilities of inefficiencies and/or volatilities in asset prices and capital movements. Financial stability, therefore, is a pre-requisite for sustained financial development which in turn would impact growth rate positively.

1.6 Financial Volatility versus Financial Stability

The process of deregulation and globalisation of financial markets gained momentum in the 1990s, and expanded the choices for investors, and helped to improve the prospects of reducing the costs of financial transactions and improving operational and allocative efficiency of the financial system. A number of developing countries, especially in Asia, that moved early on to the path of economic liberalisation had experienced large capital inflows through the 1980s and the first half of the 1990s. Large capital inflows, however, carry the risk of financial sector vulnerability, where the use of such flows is not administered by application of appropriate mix of macroeconomic measures. The currency and financial crises in Mexico and Thailand, followed by Korea and Indonesia, provide many insights about the problems that would arise when exchange rates are inflexible, and banking and financial systems are weak.

The experience of the crisis-affected countries highlights the need for setting in place regulatory and supervisory frameworks to ensure the safety and stability of financial systems. Their experience also underscores the premise that financial development is only a necessary condition for sustainable growth, and by no means a sufficient condition. In view of the costs of financial crises falling on the sovereign governments, financial stability has come to occupy a centre-stage in formulating public policy for economic development.

1.7 Regulation and Supervision of Financial System

An efficient and robust regulatory structure is an essential pre-requisite for the stability of the financial system. The implications of increased cross-sectoral and cross-border conglomeration of financial companies highlight the need for increased focus on co-ordination and information sharing among regulators. The emergence of the holding company structure and its legal implications has given rise to concerns about their regulation and supervision. The recent international financial turbulence has shown that there is no single fail-proof method of financial regulation and that an ideal system would have elements of both principles-based and rules-based regulation.

The recent global financial crisis has highlighted the importance of liquidity management for institutions. In this context, it is imperative to have an adequate liquidity infrastructure in place. In the Indian context, active liquidity management has been an integral part of the Reserve Bank of India's monetary operations and it is being achieved through various instruments. However, the use of monetary policy requires to be further honed in order to deal with the impact of external capital flows.

1.8 Meaning and Significance of Financial Economics

Financial economics is a branch of economics that analyzes the distribution and use of resources in markets in which decisions are made under uncertainty. Financial decisions must often take into account future events, whether those are related to individual stocks, portfolios or the market as a whole.

It is a branch of economics characterized by a concentration on monetary activities, in which money of one type or another is likely to appear on both sides of a trade. Its concern is thus the interrelation of financial variables, such as prices, interest rates and shares, as opposed to those concerning the real economy. It has two main areas of focus: asset pricing and corporate finance; the first being the perspective of providers of capital, i.e. investors, and the second of users of capital.

According to Edmund Cannon, financial economics concentrates on decision making when two considerations are particularly important: first, some of the outcomes are risky; second, both the decisions and the outcomes may occur at different times. The subject is usually applied to investment decisions, particularly in financial markets such as the stock market, but it also has close links to the parts of microeconomics connected with insurance and saving.

The subject is concerned with the allocation and deployment of economic resources, both spatially and across time, in an uncertain environment. It, therefore, centres on decision-making under uncertainty in the context of the financial markets. It is built on the foundations of microeconomics and decision theory.

Financial economics is important in making investment decisions, identifying risks, and valuing securities and assets. It relies heavily on microeconomics and basic accounting concepts. In addition, it requires familiarity with basic statistics and probability since these are the standard tools used to measure and evaluate risk.

Financial economics employs economic theory to evaluate how time, risk, opportunity costs and information can create incentives or disincentives for a particular decision. Financial economics often involves the creation of sophisticated models to test the variables affecting a particular decision. Often, these models assume that individuals or institutions making decisions act rationally, though this is not necessarily the case. Irrational behaviour of parties has to be taken into account in financial economics as a potential risk factor.

While traditional economics focuses on exchanges in which money is one, but only one, of the items traded, financial economics concentrates on exchanges in which money of one type or another is likely to appear on both sides of a trade.

The ultimate benefit of financial economics is providing investors with the instruments to make sound and informed decisions in relation to their investment options. They are presented with the risks and risk factors involved in their investments, the fair value of the asset they wish to acquire, and the regulations in the financial markets where they are involved, as well as the various financial institutions.

Financial econometrics is the branch of financial economics that uses econometric techniques to study relationship among financial variables.

1.9 Aspects of Financial Economics
There are two basic aspects of financial economics, namely discounting and risk management diversification.

1.9.1 Discounting: Every investor is aware that the value of his money today would not be the same in after say 10 years. In other words, money today will not provide the same purchasing power after 10 years. It is an important fact that needs to be recognized by investors when making decisions. They should discount the 10 years difference because of inflation and risk. The discounting aspect is very important because associated problems such as under-funded pension schemes are already present.

1.9.2 Risk Management and Diversification: Risk is inherent in almost all financial activities. Anyone who keeps monitoring the stock market will notice that the stocks being traded can change trends anytime. The returns from stock investing are sometimes high, as the risk is also high, and it is the most effective way to lure investors to buy and trade the stocks. Ideally, if an investor holds two risky assets, their individual performances should compensate for the other.

Many advertisements for financial products based on the stock market remind potential buyers that the value of investments may fall as well as rise. So although stocks yield a return which is high on average, this is largely to compensate for risk.

Financial institutions are always looking for ways of insuring (or *hedging*) this risk. It is sometimes possible to hold two highly risky assets but for the overall risk to be low. If share A only performs badly when share B performs well (and vice versa) then the two shares perform a perfect hedge.

An important part of finance is working out the total risk of a portfolio of risky assets, since the total risk may be less than the risk of the individual components.

2

Financial Institutions, Financial Markets and Financial Instruments

2.1 Financial Institutions

Financial institutions are at the heart of an economic system. A modern economy, characterised by acute specialisation and exchange, is unthinkable without financial intermediaries.

The banking system forms the core of the financial institutions in an economy. The role of commercial banks is particularly important in underdeveloped countries. Through mobilisation of resources and their better allocation, commercial banks play an important role in the development process of underdeveloped countries. By offering attractive saving schemes and ensuring safety of deposits, commercial banks encourage willingness to save among the people. By reaching out to people in rural areas, they help convert idle savings into effective ones. Commercial banks improve the allocation of resources by lending money to priority sectors of the economy. These banks provide a meeting ground for the savers and the investors. Savers may not invest either because of inadequate savings and/or lack of risk-taking spirit.

The banking industry all over the world has undergone transformation since the early 1980s under the impact of deregulation, advances in information technology and globalisation. These forces have increased competitive pressures which have: (a) unleashed the strong forces of restructuring and consolidation with the number of banks declining all over the world, and (b) prompted banks to seek new sources of revenue beyond traditional products. These, in turn, have led to the blurring of distinctions among providers of various financial services and emergence of financial conglomerates. Although these developments have made institutions more efficient by lowering transaction costs, they have also challenged the traditional regulatory arrangements based on institutions. Also, heightened competitive pressures, by squeezing profit margins of institutions, could lead them to pursue riskier strategies, raising the possibility of failure. Financial instability can also impinge on a country's ability to pursue a prudent macroeconomic policy. The safety and soundness of financial institutions, therefore, have come to occupy a centre-stage in the policy making.

Under the forces of liberalisation and globalisation, many banking institutions have expanded beyond their home countries and traditional lines of business leading to emergence of large international banks. Many product innovations and new ways of doing business have also emerged that have led to widespread use of securitisation, derivatives and other financial products linking traditional banking functions to the operations of capital markets, whereas these developments have led to some degree of efficiency in financial intermediation, new issues have emerged over the past year that merit attention. Most, if not all of these large banks have become financial conglomerates operating in all the different segments of the financial sector. This movement has been enabled both by technological developments leading to faster transmission of financial transactions and financial innovations, and by falling national barriers allowing cross border capital flows.

A bank can generate revenue in a variety of different ways including interest, transaction fees and financial advice. The main method is via charging interest on the capital it lends out to customers. The bank profits from the difference between the level of interest it pays for deposits and other sources of funds, and the level of interest it charges in its lending activities. This difference is referred to as the spread between the cost of funds and the loan interest rate. Historically, profitability from lending activities has been cyclical and dependent on the needs and strengths of loan customers and the stage of the economic cycle. Fees and financial advice constitute a more stable revenue stream and banks have therefore placed more emphasis on these revenue lines to smooth their financial performance.

A commercial bank generally performs the following functions.

1. It accepts deposits which are of various types like current, savings, recurring and fixed deposits.
2. It grants credit in various forms such as loans and advances, discounting of bills and investment in open market securities.
3. It collects cheques, drafts, bills and other instruments for its depositors.
4. It provides remittance facilities through drafts and telegraphic transfers.
5. It renders investment services such as underwriter and banker for new issues of securities to the public.
6. It provides such agency services as purchase and sale of foreign exchange, acceptance of tax payments, electricity bills etc.
7. It provides facilities like travellers' cheques, gift cheques and safe deposit vaults to its customers.

2.2 Financial Markets

Financial market is a mechanism which allows people to buy and sell financial securities and other fungible items of value. Fungible means interchangeable or exchangeable items (like goods, services, currencies) as contrasted with non-fungible items such as human beings. Thus, financial market can mean capital market (trading in shares and bonds etc.), commodity market (trading in gold and silver etc.), foreign exchange market (trading in different currencies) and other such markets.

A well-functioning financial market enables efficient use of market-based instruments of monetary policy by improving interest rate signals in the economy. Apart from enhancing the efficiency of monetary policy, deep and well-functioning financial markets promote mobilisation of domestic savings and improve the allocative efficiency of financial intermediation, and foster the necessary conditions to emerge as an international or a regional financial centre. Strong domestic financial markets also act as a buffer against external disturbances and help in absorbing shocks to the domestic banking system during crises. Further, they provide incentives for development of hedging instruments, and lower macroeconomic volatility and financial instability. Efficient financial markets also have several indirect benefits such as rapid accumulation of physical and human capital, more stable investment financing, and faster technological progress.

Developed and well-integrated financial markets are critical for sustaining high growth, for the effective conduct of monetary policy, for developing a diversified financial system, financial integration and ensuring financial stability. The question therefore is not whether developed financial markets are needed, but how to go about in developing them fully. Financial markets presently deal with complex and sophisticated products. Introduction of such products would require clear regulatory frameworks, appropriate institutions and development of human resource skills. The speed for further changes in the financial markets would thus depend on how quickly are we able to meet these requirements.

The need for developed financial markets also arises in the context of increasing integration of domestic financial markets with international financial markets. The concept of globalisation is no longer restricted to its traditional sense—variety of cross-border transactions in goods and services—but also extends to international capital flows, driven by rapid and widespread diffusion of technology. In fact, most of the literature in recent years on globalisation has centred around financial integration due to the emergence of worldwide financial markets and the possibility of better access to external financing for a variety of domestic entities.

Financial market development is a complex and time-consuming process. There are no short cuts for developing well-functioning markets with depth and liquidity. Some of the preconditions for financial market reform are the following.

1. Macroeconomic stability.
2. Sound and efficient financial institutions and structure.
3. Prudential regulation and supervision.
4. Strong creditor rights.
5. Contract enforcement.

2.2.1 Types of Financial Markets
The financial markets can broadly be divided into money and capital market.

A. Money Market: Money market is a market for debt securities that pay off in the short term usually less than one year, for example the market for 90-days treasury bills. This market encompasses the trading and issuance of short term non equity debt instruments including treasury bills, commercial papers, bankers acceptance, certificates of deposits etc.

B. Capital Market: Capital market is a market for long-term debt and equity shares. In this market, the capital funds comprising of both equity and debt are issued and traded. This also includes private placement sources of debt and equity as well as organized markets like stock exchanges. Capital market can be further divided into primary and secondary markets.

In the primary market securities are offered to public for subscription for the purpose of raising capital or fund. Secondary market is an equity trading venue in which already existing/pre-issued securities are traded among investors.

Secondary market refers to a market where securities are traded after being initially offered to the public in the primary market and/or listed on the stock exchange. Majority of the trading is done in the secondary market. Secondary market comprises of equity markets and the debt markets.

For the general investor, the secondary market provides an efficient platform for trading of his securities. For the management of the company, secondary equity markets serve as a monitoring and control conduit by facilitating value-enhancing control activities, enabling implementation of incentive-based management contracts, and aggregating information (via price discovery) that guides management decisions.

2.2.2 Primary Market and Secondary Market: Capital market can be classified into two segments, viz. primary market and secondary market.

A. Primary Market: It deals with issuance of new securities. It has the following features:

1. The process of selling new issues to investors is called underwriting.
2. New stock issue is called *initial public offer* (IPO). When an unlisted company makes either a fresh issue of securities or an offer for sale of its existing securities or both for the first time to the public, it is called IPO.
3. In a primary issue, the securities are issued by the company directly to investors.
4. The company receives money from the investors and issues new security certificates to them.
5. Primary issues are used by companies for the purpose of setting up new business or expanding/modernizing the existing business.
6. Borrowers in the new issue market may be raising capital for converting private capital into public capital. This is known as *going public.*

B. Secondary Market: It deals with the sale and purchase of previously issued securities and financial instruments such as shares, bonds, options and futures. It has the following features:

All the securities are first created in the primary market and then they enter the secondary market.

Securities are sold by and transferred from one investor to another.

Secondary equity market serves as a monitoring and control conduit for the decision-makers of a company.

In the stock exchange, all the shares belong to the secondary market.

The main financial products/instruments traded in the secondary market are shares and bonds. Shares are risky investments and offer higher returns with higher risks. Bonds are low-risk investments and offer low returns with low risk.

2.3 Financial Instruments

The maturity and sophistication of financial system depends upon the prevalence of a variety of financial instruments to suit the varied investment requirements of heterogeneous investors so as to enable it to mobilize savings from as wide section of the investing public as possible.

Capital market instruments fall into two broad groups:

1. Direct instruments.
2. Derivates instruments.

2.3.1 Direct Instruments: These include the following:

1. Ordinary (or equity) shares.
2. Preference shares.
3. Debentures.
4. Bonds

While the ordinary and preference shares represent ownership instruments, debentures and bonds are creditorship securities.

For details, see chapter 18 of this book.

2.3.2 Financial Derivatives: In recent years, complex financial products such as asset-backed securities, derivatives, credit-default swaps (CDSs) and collateralised debt obligations (CDOs) have proliferated in developed countries. These products have become highly popular with banks and financial institutions as they allow them to hedge their risks and manage their regulatory and economic capital more efficiently.

Derivative in mathematics means a variable derived from another variable. The term *derivative* indicates that it has no independent value, i.e. its value is entirely *derived* from the value of the underlying asset. The underlying asset can be security, commodity, bullion, currency, live stock or anything else. In other words, derivative means a forward, future, option or any other hybrid contract of pre-determined fixed duration, linked for the purpose of contract fulfilment to the value of a specified real or financial asset of an index of securities. Similarly, in the financial sense, a derivative is a financial product, which has been derived from a market for another product. Without the underlying product, derivatives do not have any independent existence in the market.

In other words, derivatives are financial instruments/contracts whose value depends upon the value of an underlying. Since their value is essentially derived out of an underlying, they are financial abstractions whose value is derived mathematically from the changes in the value of the underlying.

For details, see chapter 11 of this book.

Part II
Investment Theory and Portfolio Analysis

3

Theory of the Rate of Interest

Interest is defined as a payment made or received for the use of money. It is calculated as a percentage of the principal amount, payable annually. Rate of interest is important because it affects saving and investment decisions of the people in an economy.

3.1 Significance of Interest Rate

The efficacy of monetary policy depends on the magnitude and the speed with which policy rate changes are transmitted to the ultimate objectives of monetary policy, viz., inflation and growth. With the deepening of financial systems and growing sophistication of financial markets, most monetary authorities use interest rate as the key instrument to achieve the ultimate objectives of monetary policy. Adjustments in the policy interest rate, for instance, directly impact short-term money market rates which then transmit the monetary policy impulses across financial markets and maturity spectrum, including banks' deposit and lending rates. These, in turn, influence consumption, saving and investment decisions of firms and households, which ultimately influence aggregate demand, and hence, output and inflation. The interest rate channel of transmission is the leading channel of transmission in several countries, including many emerging market economies.

3.2 Types of Rate of Interest

3.2.1 Gross and Net Rate of Interest: Gross interest means the rate of interest actually charged in the loan market. However, the lender has to spend some money to maintain accounts and collect payment of interest. If the lender is to be compensated for all these administrative expenses, the gross rate will be somewhat above the net rate which is actually available to him. Thus,

Net interest = Gross interest - Administrative costs.

3.2.2 Real and Money Rate of Interest: Money rate of interest is calculated simply in terms of money paid. Real rate of interest pertains to the ratio of the purchasing power of money returned to the purchasing power of money borrowed. This distinction is important in the context of inflationary pressures in the economy. Real rate of interest is the difference between the money rate of interest and the rate of inflation. For example, if the money rate of interest is 15 percent and the inflation rate is 10 percent, the real rate of interest is 5 percent. If inflation rate is 18 percent, the real rate is -3 percent.

Among the various explanations provided by economists for the determination of the rate of interest, the following two are important:
1. Loanable fund theory.
2. Liquidity preference theory.

They are explained below.

3.3 Loanable Fund Theory of the Rate of Interest

Loanable fund theory is attributed to Swedish economist Knut Wicksell (1851-1926) and the British economist Dennis Robertson (1890-1963). According to this theory, the rate of interest is determined by the demand for and the supply of loanable funds in an economy. It is based on the assumption of perfect competition. The demand for loans originates from three types of borrowers, viz. producers, consumers and government. Producers borrow in order to make investment in industrial and commercial activities. Consumers borrow primarily for financing the purchase of durable consumer goods. Government borrows to finance public works (roads, bridges etc.) in peace-time and to meet emergencies like a war.

Adding up the demand for loans by producers, consumers and the government, a combined demand curve for loans is obtained. Like any other demand curve, it slopes downward, signifying that lower the rate of interest, greater the demand for loans and vice versa.

Supply of loans comes from the current savings of households as well as business firms. These savings are channelled through commercial banks, insurance companies and other financial institutions. They are made available to various types of borrowers. Adding up the personal and business savings, a combined supply curve is obtained which, like any other supply curve, slopes upwards, denoting that lower the rate of interest, the lower the supply of loans and vice versa.

By bringing together the demand and supply curves of loanable funds, one can see the determination of the rate of interest at the point where the two curves intersect. In Figure 3.1, this point of intersection (or equilibrium) is represented by E.

Loanable fund theory is a very simplistic explanation of an otherwise complex phenomenon. In real world, rate of interest is influenced by a host of subjective and objective factors.

3.4 Liquidity Preference Theory of the Rate of Interest

According to British economist John Maynard Keynes (1883-1946), rate of interest is a reward for parting with liquidity for a specified period of time. Rate of interest, he believed, is a purely monetary phenomenon determined by the demand for and supply of money (liquidity).

The supply of money is given by the government, and it is an exogenous (or autonomous) factor and accepted as it is. However, the demand for money (or preference for liquidity) varies and hence plays active role in the determination of the rate of interest.

3.4.1 Motives for Holding Cash: Why do people demand money (i.e. liquidity) when they know that holding of cash does not earn them any interest income? If wealth can be held in the form of interest-earning bonds why hold it in the form of cash? Keynes explained public preference for liquidity in terms of the following three motives.

A. Transactions Motive: People prefer to hold some money for meeting current transactions of daily life.

Figure 3.1: Equilibrium Interest Rate (Loanable Fund Theory)

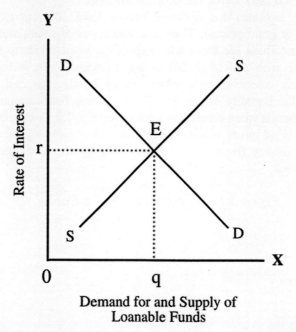

Demand for and Supply of
Loanable Funds

B. Precautionary Motive: People hold liquidity to provide for contingencies requiring sudden expenditure, e.g. accident, illness etc.

According to Keynes, the demand for liquidity for transaction and precautionary motives (labelled L_1) is positively related to the level of income. It is generally a fixed proportion of an individual's income. Thus, $L_1 = kY$.

C. Speculative Motive: People may hold surplus cash over and above what is required to satisfy transaction and precautionary motives. Keynes called this extra demand for liquidity (labelled L_2) as speculative demand for money for speculative motive. It arises due to fluctuations of interest rates and uncertainty about them. Thus, it is a function of the rate of interest, $L_2 = f(r)$.

Let us assume that the normal expected rate of interest is 10 percent and the bonds also carry 10 percent rate of interest. If the actual market rate of interest falls below the normal rate, the bond prices will lie above their normal price because there is inverse relationship between bond prices and interest rates. In such a situation people in general will expect rate of interest to rise (i.e. bond prices to fall) in the near future. Bond holders would like to sell their bonds now at their high price and hold cash with a view to repurchase bonds when their prices fall to normal (i.e. rate of interest rises to normal). In this process they expect to make capital gains. Thus, individuals prefer to hold cash rather than bonds when the rate of interest is low relative to their expectations. The reverse holds when actual rate of interest lies above the normal rate (i.e. bond prices are below their normal price). Thus, Keynesian theory postulates a negative relationship between interest rate and the speculative demand for cash.

Keynesian theory assumes that different people have different expectations about future interest rates (or bond prices). There are two types of speculators in the market, the bulls and the bears. Bulls are those who expect the bond prices to rise in the future while bears are those who anticipate fall in bond prices. Thus, bulls invest all their surplus cash in bonds whereas bears move out of bonds into cash. Therefore, the speculative demand for liquidity arises from bears. These bears accumulate their cash reserves to purchase bonds when either bond prices have fallen as expected or when they start anticipating that bond prices will rise in future.

The demand for money (liquidity) is represented by the downward-sloping curve labelled LP in Figure 3.2.

Figure 3.2: Liquidity Preference Curve

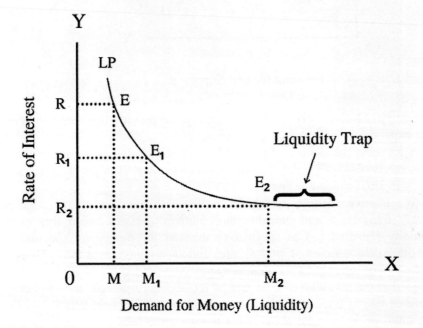

Since money supply is determined by monetary authorities, it can be considered as fixed at a particular time.

The demand curve for liquidity describes an inverse relation between interest rate and the demand for money. The quantity of money demanded declines as interest rate rises because the opportunity cost (interest foregone) of holding money is high. The LP curve comes closer and closer to the vertical axis.

Conversely, at lower interest rates, larger money balances will be held because the cost of holding money (interest foregone) is low. Keynes suggested the possibility of *liquidity trap* which refers to a situation when the demand for liquidity for speculative purpose is very high because the rate of interest is very low. Everybody wants to hold as much cash as possible in expectation of future rise in the rate of interest. Expansion of money supply by the government cannot lower the rate of interest below a certain point. The extra money released by the government is held by the public, i.e. it gets trapped in public hands. The rate of interest R_2 in Figure 3.2 is the minimum below which it cannot fall.

A major criticism of the Keynesian theory of demand for liquidity is that it does not explain how people form their expectations about future normal rate of interest. In order to explain the rate of interest it assumes the existence of a normal rate about which the actual rate gravitates. Thus, the theory assumes what it intends to explain.

4

Reasons for Interest Rate Differentials

Borrowers pay interest because they must pay a price for gaining the ability to spend now, instead of having to wait years to save up enough money. For example, a person or family may take out a mortgage for a house for which they cannot presently pay in full, but the loan allows them to become homeowners now instead of far into the future.

Businesses also borrow for future profit. They may borrow now to buy equipment so they can begin earning those revenues today. Banks borrow to increase their activities, whether lending or investing and pay interest to clients for this service.

Interest can thus be considered a cost for one entity and income for another. It can represent the lost opportunity or opportunity cost of keeping money as cash in almirah as opposed to lending it.

As interest rates are a significant factor of the income one can earn by lending money, it is important that one understand how prevailing interest rates change. Interest rates change primarily by the forces of supply and demand, which are also affected by inflation and monetary policy.

4.1 How Are Interest Rates Determined?

Interest rate levels are a factor of the supply and demand of credit. An increase in the demand for money or credit will raise interest rates, while a decrease in the demand for credit will decrease them. Conversely, an increase in the supply of credit will reduce interest rates while a decrease in the supply of credit will increase them.

An increase in the amount of money made available to borrowers increases the supply of credit. For example, when you open a bank account, you are lending money to the bank. Depending on the kind of account you open, the bank can use that money for its business and investment activities. In other words, the bank can lend out that money to other customers. The more banks can lend, the more credit is available to the economy. And as the supply of credit increases, the price of borrowing (interest) decreases.

Credit available to the economy decreases as lenders decide to defer the repayment of their loans. For instance, when you choose to postpone paying this month's credit card bill until next month or even later, you are not only increasing the amount of interest you will have to pay but also decreasing the amount of credit available in the market. This, in turn, will increase the interest rates in the economy.

Supply and demand are the primary forces behind interest rate levels. The interest rate for each different type of loan, however, depends on the credit risk, time, and tax considerations.

For details, see chapter 3 of this book.

4.2 What is an Interest Rate Differential?

An interest rate is the cost of borrowing money. Or, on the other side of the coin, it is the compensation for the service and risk of lending money. In both cases it keeps the economy moving by encouraging people to borrow, to lend, and to spend. But prevailing interest rates are always changing, and different types of loans offer different interest rates. A lender or a borrower must understand the reasons for these changes and differences.

In the real world varying interest rates prevail at the same time in a country. Thus, individual borrowers pay a higher rate of interest than corporate bonds just like corporate bonds carry a higher interest rate than government bonds.

Interest rate differentials pertain mainly to gross interest (or market rate of interest) though there can be differences in pure rate of interest. Pure rate of interest is defined as the rate received on riskless loan.

In general, an interest rate differential weighs the contrast in interest rates between two similar interest-bearing assets. Interest rate differentials simply measure the difference in interest rates between two securities. If one bond yields 5 percent and another 3 percent, the differential would be 2 percentage points. Such diffetentials are most often used in fixed income trading, forex trading, and lending calculations.

4.3 Causes of Differences in Interest Rates

The important causes of differences in interest rates are the following:

4.3.1 Risk of Default: Rate of interest varies directly with the risk attached to the loan. Thus, lower is the risk, the lower the interest rate and vice versa. Governments can obtain loans at lower rates than private firms. In fact, investment in government bonds is risk-free (gilt-edged investment) and therefore the interest earned is almost pure rate of interest. The higher rate of interest earned from non-government agencies is a premium for risk-taking.

4.3.2 Duration of the Loan: Rate of interest differs with the term (duration) of a loan because duration is related to uncertainty. Thus, the shorter is the term of a loan, the lower the interest rate and vice-versa. Lenders expect a higher rate of interest on long-term loans because the risk element is greater. Also, the face value of a long-term loan, compared to that of a short-term loan, is more vulnerable to the effects of inflation.

Return on risk is a part of gross interest in addition to pure interest. Moreover, a short-term loan is more liquid type of investment and therefore the lender would be willing to charge a lower rate of interest.

Other things being the same, rates of interest also differ according to term to maturity (time-length) of debt. The resulting structure is called the term structure of interest rates and the curve showing the relation between yield and term to maturity is called the *yield curve*.

See yield curve in chapter 5 of this book.

4.3.3 Liquidity of the Security: Liquidity of an asset refers to the degree of ease and certainty with which it can be converted into cash at short notice without any loss.

Creditors generally prefer more liquid to less liquid assets. This means, that, other things being the same, a lender would be willing to charge a lower rate of interest on more liquid debt than on a less liquid debt.

Risk refers to the likelihood of the loan being repaid. A greater chance that the loan will not be repaid, leads to higher interest rate levels. If, however, the loan is *secured*, meaning there is some sort of collateral that the lender will acquire in case the loan is not paid back (such as a car or a house), the rate of interest will probably be lower. This is because the risk factor is accounted for by the collateral.

Interest rate varies with the nature of securities offered by the borrowers. Loans against the security of gold or government bonds carry less interest since these securities can easily be converted into cash by the lenders. But loans are also sanctioned by giving securities of immovable properties, like land and house. Rate of interest against those securities will tend to be high since these are not easily converted into cash.

4.3.4 Financial Standing of the Borrower: Rate of interest may vary due to the lender's idea about the financial strength or creditworthiness of the borrower. A borrower with known integrity and reputation can get loans at low rates. The reverse will be the case if the credibility of the borrower is doubtful. Usually, whenever government takes loans from its own citizens, it pays low interest rate as no one casts any doubt on the ability of the government to pay back money in due time.

4.3.5 Market Imperfections: Market imperfections seem to be another reason for the variation in interest rates. There is variety of institutions that carry on money-lending business. For instance, banks, insurance companies, house building bank specialize in different kinds of loans charging different interest rates.

Interest rate may differ due to monopolistic/oligopolistic advantages enjoyed by the lenders. A lending institution in a small town may have no competitors and the loan-seekers there will have to pay higher rate of interest than prevalent in a big city. Moneylenders and pawnbrokers in Indian villages provide good examples of such monopolistic advantage. Because they know each other well and live in the same community, they understand each other's financial circumstances and can offer very flexible, convenient and fast services. These services can also be costly and the choice of financial products limited and very short-term.

Historically, moneylenders have played a significant role in meeting the credit needs of the rural producers. With stringent laws against money lending and the phenomenal growth of the formal credit delivery system, the role of moneylenders has decreased, but they are still in business under several disguises.

Moneylenders usually charge higher rates from poorer borrowers. While moneylenders are often demonized and accused of usury, their services are convenient and fast, and they can be very flexible when borrowers run into problems. Moneylenders are popular because, unlike government agencies, they give credit for every purpose. They are easily approachable by the credit seekers and there are not many formalities in transacting a loan. However, the malpractices adopted by the moneylenders to exploit the needy farmers cannot be overlooked. These malpractices pertain to charging of high rate of interest and adopting unfair means in the maintenance of accounts.

4.3.6 Rate of Inflation: The moneylender takes a risk that the borrower may not pay back the loan. Thus, interest provides a certain compensation for bearing risk. Coupled with the risk of default is the risk of inflation. When one lends money now, the prices of goods and services may go up by the time one is paid back. Therefore, the original purchasing power of money decreases. Thus, interest protects against future rises in inflation.

The higher the inflation rate, the more interest rates are likely to rise. This occurs because lenders will demand higher interest rates as compensation for the decrease in purchasing power of the money they are paid in the future.

4.3.7 Cost of Servicing Loans: Giving a loan often entails a certain cost of keeping records, making collections and sometimes resorting to legal measures to recover the money. These costs differ from borrower to borrower. It is administratively economical for a bank to lend large sum of money to an industrial company than to lend small sums to a large number of individuals. In general, the bigger is the loan with fewer instalments, the lower the cost per rupee of servicing the loan.

4.3.8 Government Policy: The government has a say in how interest rates are affected. In India, Reserve Bank of India (RBI) often makes announcements about how monetary policy will affect interest rates. RBI announces various types of interest rates periodically.

4.4 Types of Credit (Loans)

Based on repayment and interest options, there can be various types of credit.

4.4.1 Revolving Line of Credit: Bank decides on the limit up to which a borrower can withdraw from this facility. Flexibility of withdrawal and repayment is provided to the borrower. Interest is charged on the balances either on a monthly basis or on daily basis depending on the agreement. Examples of this type of credit include credit cards and overdraft loans.

4.4.2 Flat Rate Loans: Interest on the loan is charged on the original principal amount disbursed and not on the outstanding loan balance as, for example in the case of personal loans.

4.4.3 Floating Rate Loans: Loan is disbursed at the beginning. The tenure and monthly payments are also fixed. But interest rate is not fixed. If the interest rate undergoes change either monthly payment is revised or tenure is revised. Home loans are good example of this type of loan.

4.4.4 Equated Monthly Instalment (EMI): The entire loan is disbursed at the beginning to the borrower. The monthly repayment amount and the number of payments are fixed in the beginning. The repayment mostly starts one month after disbursal of loan, and sometimes first instalment is taken at the time of disbursal. Car loans and home loans are cases in point.

4.4.5 Loan without Collateral: Some loans like personal loans and credit card loans are given without any collateral or guarantee. Loans which are given without any guarantee attract higher rate of interest.

4.4.6 Loan with Collateral: Loans with lesser interest rate can be availed by giving gold or some other collateral. If the loan is not repaid on time, the lender can auction the collateral and recover the borrowed amount.

4.4.7 Mandatory Interest but Flexible Principal Repayment: The entire loan is disbursed at the beginning. The borrower has to compulsorily pay only interest periodically. The principal repayment can be done by the borrower any time. Examples include loan against LIC policy, gold or securities.

5

Term Structure of Interest Rates and Yield Curves

5.1 What is Term Structure of Interest Rates?

Term structure of interest rates, commonly known as the yield curve, depicts the interest rates of similar quality bonds at different maturities.

Essentially, term structure of interest rates is the relationship between interest rates or bond yields and different terms or maturities. When graphed, the term structure of interest rates is known as a yield curve, and it plays a crucial role in identifying the current state of an economy. The term structure of interest rates reflects expectations of market participants about future changes in interest rates and their assessment of monetary policy conditions.

Generally, yields increase in line with maturity, giving rise to an upward-sloping, or normal, yield curve. The yield curve is primarily used to illustrate the term structure of interest rates for standard government-issued securities. This is important as it is a measure of the debt market's feeling about risk.

Although some financial instruments are issued by the same borrowers and have the same characteristics except for maturities, they have often different interest rates.

5.2 Shapes and Uses of Yield Curve

Yield curve has three primary shapes.

1. **Upward-sloping Curve:** It means long-term yields are higher than short-term yields. This is considered to be the *normal* slope of the yield curve and signals that the economy is in an expansionary mode.
2. **Downward-sloping Curve:** It indicates that short-term yields are higher than long-term yields. Labelled as an *inverted* yield curve, it signifies that the economy is in, or about to enter, a recessive period.
3. **Flat Curve:** It shows very little variation between short- and long-term yields. It signals that the market is unsure about the future direction of the economy.

The term structure of interest rates reflects expectations of market participants about future changes in interest rates and their assessment of monetary policy conditions.

The yield curve is considered the benchmark for the credit market, as it reports the yields of risk-free fixed income investments across a range of maturities. In the credit market, banks and lenders use this benchmark as a gauge for determining lending and savings rates.

Ordinarily, yield curve is upward-sloping. One basic explanation for this phenomenon is that investors demand higher interest rates for longer-term investments as compensation for investing their money in longer-duration investments. Occasionally, long-term yields may fall below short-term yields, creating an inverted yield curve that is generally regarded as a harbinger of recession.

The term structure of interest rates and the direction of the yield curve can be used to judge the overall credit market environment. A flattening of the yield curve means longer-term rates are falling in comparison to short-term rates, which could have implications for a recession. When short-term rates begin to exceed long-term rates, the yield curve is inverted, and a recession is likely occurring or approaching.

When longer-term rates fall below shorter-term rates, the outlook for credit over the long term is weak. This is often consistent with a weak or recessionary economy, which is defined by two consecutive periods of negative growth in the gross domestic product (GDP).

Yield curve is a plot of the interest rates (yield to maturity) for particular types of bonds with different terms of maturity, but the same risk, liquidity, and tax treatments. Yield curves are classified in terms of their shapes and are used to explain the condition in financial markets and the economy. Yield curve may be upward-sloping, flat, downward-sloping or any other shape in-between. Different shapes appear under different economic conditions. They are used to explain or predict an economic condition. A typical yield curve is shown in Figure 5.1. Interest rate is 5 percent on 1-year maturity, 6 percent on 2-year maturity, and 7 percent on 3-year maturity.

Figure 5.1: A Normal Yield Curve

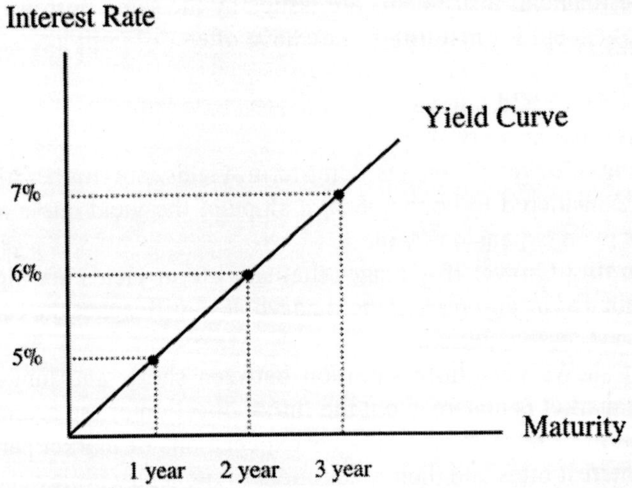

5.3 Three Theories to Explain Yield Curve

Why does a yield curve have different shapes? Why does it change from time to time?

There are three theories for different interest rates among financial instruments with different maturities.

1. Liquidity premium theory.

2. Segmented market theory.
3. Expectations theory.

5.3.1 Liquidity Premium Theory: Normally, the yield curve is upward-sloping. Interest rates on short-term securities are normally lower than interest rates on long-term securities. Securities include shares, scrips, stocks, bonds, debentures, debenture stocks, or other marketable securities of a like nature in or of any incorporated company or other body corporate. Liquidity of an asset means how easily it can be converted into cash and at what loss of its capital value. If an asset cannot be converted into cash easily (i.e. at short notice) or at minimum loss of its value, it is less liquid.

One important difference between short-term securities and long-term securities is their liquidities. In this context, following general rules are noteworthy:

1. Liquidity of short-term securities is higher than liquidity of long-term securities.
2. Even if one cannot sell them, short-term securities will mature sooner than long-term securities and owners of short-term securities will receive full payment sooner.
3. Savers (lenders) prefer liquidity.
4. Demand for short-term securities is higher than demand for long-term securities.
5. Interest rate on short-term securities is lower than interest rates on long-term securities.

Although the liquidity premium theory can explain the yield curve most of the time, it cannot explain why a yield curve becomes sometimes flat, downward-sloping or any shape in-between. Segmented market and expectations theories complement the liquidity premium theory.

5.3.2 Segmented Market Theory: It assumes that the interest rate on each instrument is determined in a separate market with a separate market demand and supply. A short-term interest rate is determined by demand for and supply of short-term securities in the short-term security market. Similarly, a long-term interest rate is determined by demand for and supply of long-term securities in the long-term security market.

In fact, markets of securities can be divided into three different maturities: short-term, mid-term, and long-term. Then, depending on relative demand and supply in each market, a yield curve may have a particular shape.

Although the segmented market theory can explain any shapes of yield curve, based on relative demand and supply of each maturity security, it cannot explain why demands and supplies differ among markets. In reality, demand for each maturity securities is not completely independent of each other. The expectations theory considers this interdependency among securities and provides a reason for different demands.

5.3.3 Expectations Theory: Expectations mean how professional traders and other interested persons in the market anticipate future economic conditions, inflation rate and other macroeconomic variables in an economy. If they expect, for example, the Indian economy to be in an expansion phase of business cycle, then they will expect interest rates to rise in the future. Hence, the yield curve of today should be upward-sloping. Reverse will hold if they expect recessionary tendencies in the future. Similarly, if they expect the inflation rate to rise in the Indian economy, then they will again expect interest rates to rise in the future. So the yield curve of today should again be upward-sloping. Thus, an upward-sloping yield curve of today may indicate expectations of market players of either an expansion or inflation in the Indian economy in the near future.

The three theories of the shape of yield curve explained above are complimentary. While interpreting an actual yield curve, one must apply all the three theories.

5.4 Fixed Income Securities

5.4.1 What is a Fixed-Income Security? A fixed-income security is an investment that provides a return in the form of fixed periodic interest payments and the eventual return of principal at maturity. Unlike variable-income securities, where payments change based on some underlying measure—such as short-term interest rates—the payments of a fixed-income security are known in advance. Bonds are the most common form of fixed-income securities. Companies raise capital by issuing fixed-income products to investors.

A bond is an investment product that is issued by corporations and governments to raise funds to finance projects and fund operations. Bonds are mostly comprised of corporate bonds and government bonds and can have various maturities and face value amounts. The face value is the amount the investor will receive when the bond matures. Corporate and government bonds trade on major exchanges.

5.4.2 Credit Rating Fixed Income Securities: Not all bonds are created equal, i.e. they have different credit ratings assigned to them based on the financial viability of the issuer. Credit ratings are part of a grading system performed by credit-rating agencies. These agencies measure the creditworthiness of corporate and government bonds and the entities ability to repay these loans. Credit ratings are helpful to investors since they indicate the risks involved in investing.

Bonds can either be investment grade or non-investment grade bonds. Investment grade bonds are issued by stable companies with a low risk of default and therefore have lower interest rates than non-investment grade bonds. Non-investment grade bonds, also known as junk bonds or high-yield bonds, have very low credit ratings due to a high probability of the corporate issuer defaulting on its interest payments. As a result, investors typically require a higher rate of interest from junk bonds to compensate them for taking on the higher risk posed by these debt securities.

5.4.3 Types of Fixed Income Securities: Although there are many types of fixed income securities, below are outlined a few of the most popular in addition to corporate bonds.

Treasury notes (T-notes) are issued by the U.S. Treasury and are intermediate-term bonds that mature in two, three, five, or 10 years. T-Notes usually have a face value of US$ 1,000 and pay semi-annual interest payments at fixed coupon rates or interest rates. The interest payment and principal repayment of all Treasurys are backed by the full faith and credit of the U.S. government, which issues these bonds to fund its debts.

A municipal bond is a government bond issued by states, cities, and counties to fund capital projects, such as building roads, schools, and hospitals. The interest earned from these bonds is generally tax exempt.

A bank issues a certificate of deposit (CD). In return for depositing money with the bank for a predetermined period, the bank pays interest to the account holder. CDs have maturities of less than five years and typically pay lower rates than bonds, but higher rates than traditional savings accounts.

Companies issue preferred stocks that provide investors with a fixed dividend, set as a dollar amount or percentage of share value on a predetermined schedule. Interest rates and inflation influence the price of preferred shares, and these shares have higher yields than most bonds due to their longer duration.

5.4.4 Advantages of Fixed Income Securities: Fixed income securities provide steady interest income to investors throughout the life of the bond. Fixed income securities can also reduce the overall risk in an investment portfolio and protect against volatility or wild fluctuations in the market. Equities are traditionally more volatile than bonds meaning their price movements can lead to bigger capital gains but also larger losses. As a result, many investors allocate a portion of their portfolios to bonds to reduce the risk of volatility that comes from stocks.

It is important to note that the prices of bonds and fixed income securities can increase and decrease as well. Although the interest payments of fixed income securities are steady, their prices are not guaranteed to remain stable throughout the life of the bonds. For example, if investors sell their securities before maturity, there could be gains or losses due to the difference between the purchase price and sale price. Investors receive the face value of the bond if it is held to maturity, but if it is sold beforehand, the selling price will likely be different from the face value.

However, fixed income securities typically offer more stability of principal than other investments. Corporate bonds are more likely than other corporate investments to be repaid if a company declares bankruptcy. For example, if a company is facing bankruptcy and must liquidate its assets, bondholders will be repaid before common stockholders.

Fixed income securities are easily traded through a broker and are also available in mutual funds and exchange-traded funds (ETFs). Mutual funds and ETFs contain a blend of many securities in their funds so that investors can buy into many types of bonds or equities.

The advantages of fixed income securities can be listed as under:

1. Fixed income securities provide steady interest income to investors throughout the life of the bond.
2. Fixed income securities are rated by credit rating agencies allowing investors to choose bonds from financially-stable issuers.
3. Although stock prices can fluctuate wildly over time, fixed income securities usually have less price volatility risk.
4. Fixed income securities such as government guaranteed bonds provide a safe return for investors.

5.4.5 Disadvantages of Fixed Income Securities: These are as under:

1. Fixed income securities have credit risk meaning the issuer can default on making the interest payments or paying back the principal.
2. Fixed income securities typically pay a lower rate of return than other investments such as equities.
3. Inflation risk can be an issue if prices rise by a faster rate than the interest rate on the fixed income security.
4. If interest rates rise at a faster rate than the rate on a fixed income security, investors lose out by holding the lower yielding security.
5. The principal amount invested is tied up for a long time, particularly in the case of long-term bonds with maturities greater than 10 years. As a result, investors do not have access to the cash.

Although there are many benefits to fixed income securities, there are also some risks associated with them. Investors must way the pros and cons before investing in fixed income securities.

6

Portfolio of Assets

6.1 Portfolio Defined

People are accustomed to thinking about their savings in terms of goals: retirement, education, marriage or a vacation. But as you build and manage your asset allocation regardless of which goal you are pursuing, there are two important things to consider. The first is the number of years until you expect to need the money also known as your *time horizon*. The second is your attitude toward risk also known as your *risk tolerance*.

A portfolio can be defined as different investment instruments namely stocks, shares, mutual funds, bonds, and cash etc., all combined together depending specifically on the investor's income, budget, risk appetite and the holding period. It is formed in such a way that it stabilizes the risk of non-performance of different pools of investment.

Diversification is a technique that reduces risk by allocating investments among various financial instruments, industries, and other categories. It aims to maximize returns by investing in different areas that would each react differently to the same event. Most investment professionals agree that, although it does not guarantee against loss, diversification is the most important component of reaching long-range financial goals while minimizing risk.

Portfolio theory is a sub-category of the capital market theory that deals with the behaviour of investors in capital markets. Asset managers base their investment decisions on modern portfolio theory. Its creator, Harry Max Markowitz, was an American economist and Nobel laureate for economics.

6.2 Portfolio Manager

A portfolio manager is a professional responsible for making investment decisions and carrying out investment activities on behalf of vested individuals or institutions.

Portfolio managers are primarily responsible for creating and managing investment allocations for private clients. A portfolio manager determines a client's appropriate level of risk based on the client's time horizon, risk preferences, return expectations and market conditions.

The investors invest their money into the portfolio manager's investment policy for future fund growth such as a retirement fund, endowment fund, education fund, or for other purposes. Portfolio managers work with a team of analysts and researchers, and are responsible for establishing an investment strategy, selecting appropriate investments, and allocating each investment properly towards an investment fund or asset management vehicle. Services of portfolio managers are meant for those who want to invest their funds but have limited knowledge of financial dealings. Similarly, people who are from a different work profile and do not have time may also avail the services of portfolio managers. These services are availed in the following manner:

1. Potential investors who lack financial literacy and awareness approach portfolio managers for their financial services.
2. An agreement is reached between an investor and a portfolio manager regarding fee, time frame, risk exposure etc.
3. Portfolio manager carries out a market survey in terms of different schemes and their performance in the past.
4. He uses his experiences and accordingly selects the funds in which money should be invested.
5. The portfolio is structured on the basis of the agreed terms.
6. The report of the performance of the portfolio is periodically sent to the investors.
7. The fund manager takes decisions on the basis of the hardcore research related to financial markets.

6.3 Portfolio Management

Portfolio Management is the art and science of making decisions about investment mix and policy, matching investments to objectives, asset allocation for individuals and institutions, and balancing risk against performance. Portfolio management includes a range of professional services to manage an individual's and company's securities, such as stocks and bonds, and other assets, such as real estate.

Portfolio management refers to managing an individual's investments in the form of bonds, shares, cash, mutual funds etc so that he earns the maximum profits within the stipulated time frame. It is the art of managing the money of an individual under the expert guidance of portfolio managers.

6.3.1 Types of Portfolio Management: There are mainly four types of portfolio management methods:

A. Discretionary Portfolio Management: In this form, the individual authorizes the portfolio manager to take care of his financial needs on his behalf.

B. Non-discretionary Portfolio Management: Here, the portfolio manager can merely advise the client what is good or bad, correct/incorrect for him, but the client reserves the full right to take his own decisions.

C. Passive Portfolio Management: It is the form which involves only tracking the index.

D. Active Portfolio Management: This includes a team of members who take active decisions based on hard core research before investing the corpus into any investment avenue (e.g. close ended funds). The aim of the active portfolio manager is to make better returns than what the market dictates.

6.3.2 Objectives of Portfolio Management: These are as under:

1. It ensures customization of the investment needs of the investors.
2. It helps in providing the best options for investments to individuals as per the defined criterions of their income, budget, age, holding period and risk taking capacity.

3. It is done by portfolio managers who understand an investor's financial needs and accordingly suggest the investment policy that would bring maximum returns with minimum risks involved.
4. Some of the portfolio management schemes are also done for tax saving purposes.
5. It helps the investors maintain the purchasing power.

In the current scenario where there are competitive and complex financial instruments, portfolio management is indeed a preferred method of making investments. With the range of products available across different schemes, there is something to offer for every individual as per the different criterions defined. Portfolio managers understand the financial needs of their clients design a suitable investment plan as per their income and risk-taking abilities. After understanding the financial goals and objectives of an investor, the portfolio manager provides the appropriate investment solution. The role played by the portfolio manager is indeed a challenging, responsible and answerable one.

With the increasing integration of various segments of financial markets, the distinctions between banks and other financial intermediaries are also getting increasingly blurred. There is increased participation of financial institutions, especially banks, in the capital market. These factors have led to increased inter-linkages across financial institutions and markets. While increased inter-linkages are expected to lead to increased efficiency in the resource allocation process and the effectiveness of monetary policy, they also increase the risk of contagion from one segment to another with implications for overall financial stability. This would call for appropriate policy responses during times of crisis. Increased inter-linkages also raise the issue of appropriate supervisory framework.

6.4 Diversification of Portfolio

In finance, diversification is the process of allocating capital in a way that reduces the exposure to any one particular asset or risk. A common path towards diversification is to reduce risk or volatility by investing in a variety of assets.

If asset prices do not change in perfect synchrony, a diversified portfolio will have less variance than the weighted average variance of its constituent assets, and often less volatility than the least volatile of its constituents.

Diversification is one of two general techniques for reducing investment risk. The other is hedging. Hedging is often considered an advanced investing strategy.

6.4.1 Components of a Diversified Portfolio: These are as under:

A. Domestic Stocks: Stocks represent the most aggressive portion of portfolio and provide the opportunity for higher growth over the long-term. However, this greater potential for growth carries a greater risk, particularly in the short-term. Because stocks are generally more volatile than other types of assets, investment in a stock could be worth less if and when one decides to sell it.

B. Bonds: Most bonds provide regular interest income and are generally considered to be less volatile than stocks. They can also act as a cushion against the unpredictable ups and downs of the stock market, as they behave differently than stocks. Investors who are more focused on safety than returns often favour government bonds or other high-quality bonds, while reducing their exposure to stocks.

These investors may have to accept lower long-term returns, as many bonds especially high-quality issues generally do not offer returns as high as stocks over the long-term. However, some fixed income investments, like high-yield bonds and certain international bonds, can offer much higher yields, albeit with more risk.

C. Short-Term Investments: These include money market funds and short-term certificates of deposit (CDs). Money market funds are conservative investments that offer stability and easy access to your money, ideal for those looking to preserve principal. In exchange for that level of safety, money market funds usually provide lower returns than bond funds or individual bonds. While money market funds are considered safer and more conservative, they are not insured or guaranteed.

D. Sector Funds: As the name suggests, sector funds focus on a particular segment of the economy. They can be valuable tools for investors seeking opportunities in different phases of the economic cycle. Because of their narrow focus, sector investments tend to be more volatile than investments that diversify across many sectors and companies.

E. Commodity-focused Funds: Only the most experienced investors should invest in commodities, including equity funds that focus on commodity-intensive industries such as oil and gas, mining, and natural resources. Commodity-focused funds can provide a good hedge against inflation. The commodities industry can be significantly affected by commodity prices, world events, import controls, worldwide competition, government regulations, and economic conditions.

F. Real Estate Funds: Real estate funds can also play a role in diversifying your portfolio and providing some protection against the risk of inflation. Changes in real estate values or economic conditions can have a positive or negative effect on issuers in the real estate industry.

G. Asset Allocation Funds: For investors who do not have the time or the expertise to build a diversified portfolio, asset allocation funds can serve as an effective single-fund strategy. These funds include funds that are managed to a specific target date, or in anticipation of specific outcomes, such as inflation.

H. Foreign Investments: These investments involve greater risks than domestic investments, including political and economic risks and the risk of currency fluctuations, all of which may be magnified in emerging markets.

The primary goal of diversification is not to maximize returns. Its primary goal is to limit the impact of volatility on a portfolio. By diversifying, one loses the chance of having invested solely in the single asset that comes out best, but one also avoids having invested solely in the asset that comes out worst. That is the role of diversification: it narrows the range of possible outcomes. Diversifications need not either help or hurt expected returns, unless the alternative non-diversified portfolio has a higher expected return.

Given the advantages of diversification, many experts recommend maximum diversification, also known as *buying the market portfolio*. Unfortunately, identifying that portfolio is not straightforward. The earliest definition comes from the capital asset pricing model which argues the maximum diversification comes from buying a pro rata share of all available assets. This is the idea underlying index funds.

6.5 Efficient Portfolio and Risk Categories

According to Markowitz, an efficient portfolio is a series of capital investments that achieve a maximum return at the lowest possible risk that the investor is willing to take. Efficient portfolios exist in every risk class. There is no standard definition of risk classes, and thus different financial service providers distinguish between different risk classes. As a general rule, the risk classes differentiate between the investor's risk tolerance and match suitable investment objects along these lines. A possible classification is as follows:

1. **Risk Category 1 (Security-oriented):** It includes: (a) fixed-term deposits, (b) saving bank accounts, (c) government bonds, (d) post office deposits and similar safe investments.
2. **Risk Category 2 (Conservative Investments):** It comprises: (a) fixed-interest securities, (b) bonds with a good credit rating, (c) money market-related funds, and (d) endowment policies etc.
3. **Risk Category 3 (Solid Profit Orientation):** It includes: (a) shares of established companies, (b) mutual funds, (c) corporate bonds and (d) deposits with private banks.
4. **Risk Category 4 (Speculative Profit Orientation):** It includes: (a) shares and bonds of medium-rated companies, (b) deposits with non-banking financial companies, and (c) private placements etc.
5. **Risk Category 5 (High Speculation):** It comprises: (a) participation certificates, (b) subordinated saving certificates, (c) warrants, (d) futures, (e) junk bonds, and chit funds.

According to modern portfolio theory, each risk class has its own respective efficient portfolio. These differ drastically in their make-up and are oriented along the investor's risk tolerance. One end of the spectrum is the very speculative investment portfolio and at the other end the security-oriented one. In between, there are efficient portfolios with mixed investments, along which the so-called line of efficiency runs.

6.6 Problems with Diversification

Investors confront two main types of risk when investing. The first is un-diversifiable which is also known as systematic or market risk. This type of risk is associated with every company. Common causes include inflation rates, exchange rate variations, political instability, war or some other emergency. This type of risk is not specific to a particular company or industry, and it cannot be eliminated or reduced through diversification it is just a risk investors must accept.

The second type of risk is diversifiable. This risk is also known as unsystematic risk and is specific to a company, industry, market, or country. It can be reduced through diversification. The most common sources of unsystematic risk are business risk and financial risk.

While there are many benefits of diversification, there may be some downsides as well. It may be somewhat cumbersome to manage a diverse portfolio, especially if you have multiple holdings and investments. Secondly, it can put a dent in your bottom line. Not all investment vehicles cost the same, so buying and selling may be expensive in terms of transaction fees and brokerage charges.

Many synthetic investment products have been created to accommodate risk tolerance levels of investors. However, these products can be very complicated and are not meant to be used by beginner or small investors. For those who have less investment experience, and do not have the financial backing to enter into hedging activities, bonds are the most popular way to diversify against the stock market.

Unfortunately, even the best analysis of a company and its financial statements cannot guarantee it would not be a losing investment. Diversification cannot prevent a loss, but it can reduce the impact of fraud and bad information on your portfolio.

7

Mean-Variance Portfolio Analysis

During his working life, an individual must accumulate sufficient assets not only to live comfortably in both good and bad economic times, but also to live comfortably in retirement. To achieve the goal of maximizing economic welfare over his expected lifetime, an individual consumer/investor should have a sound understanding of the basic economic principles of lifetime portfolio selection.

7.1 Importance of Portfolio Theory

Portfolio theory is concerned with developing general principles and practical models for making sound lifetime portfolio decisions. Much of the current research on portfolio theory emanates from the path-breaking mean-variance portfolio model of Nobel Laureate Harry Markowitz. He recommends that in making investment decisions, investors should explicitly recognize investment risk as measured by variance of return, as well as expected return. He describes how the variance of return on a portfolio of securities depends on the amount invested in each security, the variance of return on each security, and the correlation between the returns on each pair of securities.

He also suggests that investors limit their choices to an efficient set of portfolios that provide the highest mean return for any level of variance and the lowest variance of return for any level of mean. By providing an intuitively appealing measure of portfolio risk and a framework for analyzing the basic risk/return trade-off of portfolio decisions, Markowitz revolutionized both the theory and practice of portfolio management. For that reason, Markowitz is called the father of modern portfolio theory.

The mean-variance analysis is a component of modern portfolio theory (MPT). This theory is based on the assumption that investors make rational decisions when they possess sufficient information. One of the assumptions of the theory is that investors enter the market to maximize their returns while at the same time avoiding unnecessary risk.

When choosing a financial asset to invest in, investors prefer the asset with lower variance when given choosing between two otherwise identical investments. An investor can achieve diversification by investing in securities with varied variances and expected returns. Proper diversification creates a portfolio where a loss in one security is counterbalanced by a gain in another.

7.2 What is Mean-Variance Analysis?

Mean-variance analysis is a technique that investors use to make decisions about financial instruments to invest in, based on the amount of risk that they are willing to accept (risk tolerance). Ideally, investors expect to earn higher returns when they invest in riskier assets. When measuring the level of risk, investors consider the potential variance (which is the volatility of returns produced by an asset) against the expected returns of that asset. Mean-variance analysis essentially looks at the average variance in the expected return from an investment.

Mean-variance analysis is the process of weighing risk, expressed as variance, against expected return. Investors use mean-variance analysis to make decisions about which financial instruments to invest in, based on how much risk they are willing to take on in exchange for different levels of reward. Mean-variance analysis allows investors to find the biggest reward at a given level of risk or the least risk at a given level of return.

Mean-variance analysis is one part of modern portfolio theory, which assumes that investors will make rational decisions about investments if they have complete information. One assumption is that investors want low risk and high reward.

7.3 Investment Strategy

There is no such thing as the perfect investment, but crafting a strategy that offers high returns and relatively low risk is priority for modern investors.

Prior to the development of modern portfolio theory, investing processes were cantered on individual stocks. Investors would look through available assets and find *sure bets*, i.e. assets that would produce decent returns without subjecting the investor to too much risk. Expected net present value (NPV) was used to distinguish these *sure bet* stocks, while securities were valued by discounting their future cash flows. Stocks that were capable of generating more money at a quicker rate were given great value.

When creating an investment strategy, the goal of every investor is to create a portfolio of stocks that offer the highest long-term returns without getting into high levels of risk. Modern portfolio theory, which includes mean-variance analysis, is based on the idea that investors are risk-averse.

Therefore, they focus on creating a portfolio that optimizes the expected return according to a specific level of risk. Investors understand that risk is an inherent part of high-return stocks. The solution for minimizing risk is to diversify the investment portfolio.

A portfolio can be comprised of stocks, bonds, mutual funds etc., which when combined, comes with varying levels of risk. If one security decreases in value, ideally, the loss is compensated by a gain in another security.

A portfolio comprised of various types of securities is considered a better strategic move, as compared to a portfolio comprised of only one type of security. Mean-variance analysis can be an important part of an investment strategy.

Mean-variance analysis allows an investor to mathematically trade off risk tolerance and reward expectations, resulting in the ideal portfolio.

This theory was based on two main concepts:
1. Every investor's goal is to maximize return for any level of risk.
2. Risk can be reduced by diversifying a portfolio through individual, unrelated securities.

Modern portfolio theory works under the assumption that those investors are risk-averse, preferring a portfolio with less risk for a given level of return. Under this assumption, investors will only take on high-risk investments if they can expect a larger reward.

A *rational investor* is asked to choose between two investments: Investment A and Investment B. Both are expected to increase in value by 6 percent each year. However, Investment B is considered twice as volatile as Investment A, meaning its value fluctuates at twice the magnitude of value fluctuations in Investment A.

Mean-variance analysis suggests that a rational investor will always choose the less volatile asset, in this case Investment A, so long as both options provide an equivalent expected return.

Overall risk of a portfolio is computed through a function of the variances of each asset, along with the correlations between each pair of assets. Asset correlations affect the total portfolio risk, formulating a smaller standard deviation than would be found by a weighted sum.

Under the mean-variance analysis, an investor can hold a high-risk asset, mutual fund, or security, so long as this high-risk investment is minimized by all underlying assets. The portfolio itself is balanced in a way that its overall risk is lower than some of its underlying investments. Risk is defined as the range by which an asset's price will vary on average.

7.4 Main Components of Mean-Variance Analysis

Mean-variance analysis is comprised of the following two main components:

7.4.1 Variance: Variance measures how distant or spread the numbers in a data set are from the mean, or average. For example, variance may tell us how spread out the returns of a specific security are on a daily or weekly basis. A large variance indicates that the numbers are further spread out. A small variance indicates a small spread of numbers from the mean.

The variance may also be zero, which indicates no deviation from the mean. When analyzing an investment portfolio, variance can show how the returns of a security are spread out during a given period.

Portfolio variance is a statistical value that assesses the degree of dispersion of the returns of a portfolio. It is an important concept in modern investment theory. Although the statistical measure by itself may not provide significant insights, we can calculate the standard deviation of the portfolio using portfolio variance.

The calculation of portfolio variance considers not only the riskiness of individual assets but also the correlation between each pair of assets in the portfolio. Thus, the statistical variance analyzes how assets within a portfolio tend to move together. The general rule of portfolio diversification is the selection of assets with a low or negative correlation between each other.

7.4.2 Expected Return: The second component of mean-variance analysis is the expected return. This is the estimated return that a security is expected to produce. Since it is based on historical data, the expected rate of return is not 100 percent guaranteed.

If two securities offer the same expected rate of return, but one comes with a lower variance, most investors would prefer that security. Similarly, if two securities show the same variance, but one of the securities offers a higher expected return, investors would opt for the security with the higher return. When trading multiple securities, an investor can choose securities with different variances and expected returns.

In modern portfolio theory, an investor would choose different securities to invest in with different levels of variance and expected return.

For mean-variance analysis,

Total expected return: $\mu_R = \sum_{i=1}^{n} w_i \mu_i$

Variance of total return: $Var[R] = \sum_{i=1}^{n}\sum_{j=1}^{n} w_i w_j cov(i, j)$

7.5 Assumptions of Mean-Variance Analysis
1. The investor can buy any amount of security.
2. The investor cannot affect the price of the security, i.e. he is a price-taker.
3. Price for both long and short positions is the same.
4. There are no transaction costs.

7.6 Calculation of Expected Return and Variance
It is possible to calculate which investments have the greatest variance and expected return. Assume that the following investments are in the portfolio of an investor:

Investment A: Amount = ₹ 1,00,000 and expected return of 5 percent.

Investment B: Amount = ₹ 3,00,000 and expected return of 10 percent.

In a total portfolio value of ₹ 4,00,000, the weight of each asset is as under:

Investment A weight = ₹ 1,00,000/₹ 4,00,000 = 25 percent.

Investment B weight = ₹ 3,00,000/₹ 4,00,000 = 75 percent.

Therefore, the total expected return of the portfolio is the weight of the asset in the portfolio multiplied by the expected return:

Portfolio expected return = (25 percent x 5 percent) + (75 percent x 10 percent) = 8.75 percent.

Portfolio variance is more complicated to calculate, because it is not a simple weighted average of the variances of investments. The correlation between the two investments is 0.65. The standard deviation, or square root of variance, for investment A is 7 percent, and the standard deviation for investment B is 14 percent.

To take another hypothetical example, assume a portfolio comprised of the following two stocks:

Stock A: ₹ 2,00,000 with an expected return of 5 percent.

Stock B: ₹ 3,00,000 with an expected return of 7 percent.

The total value of the portfolio is ₹ 5,00,000, and the weight of each stock is as follows:

Stock A = ₹ 2,00,000/₹ 5,00,000 = 40 percent

Stock B = ₹ 3,00,000/₹ 5,00,000 = 60 percent

Expected rate of return = (40 percent x 5 percent) + (60 percent x 7 percent)

= 2 percent + 4.2 percent = 6.2 percent

7.7 Criticism

Despite its theoretical importance, critics question whether it is an ideal investment tool, because its model of financial markets does not match the real world in many ways.

The risk, return, and correlation measures used by mean-variance theory are based on expected values, which means that they are statistical statements about the future Such measures often cannot capture the true statistical features of the risk and return which often follow highly skewed distributions and can give rise to, besides reduced volatility, inflated growth of return. In practice, investors must substitute predictions based on historical measurements of asset return and volatility. Very often such expected values fail to take account of new circumstances that did not exist when the historical data were generated.

More fundamentally, investors are stuck with estimating key parameters from past market data because mean-variance theory attempts to model risk in terms of the likelihood of losses, but says nothing about why those losses might occur. The risk measurements used are probabilistic in nature, not structural. This is a major difference as compared to many engineering approaches to risk management.

Although the mean–variance model continues to be the most widely used portfolio model in financial practice, economists have devoted considerable effort to research on two additional models of portfolio behaviour, the geometric mean model and the lifetime consumption-investment model. These models offer significant additional insights into optimal portfolio behaviour.

To sum up, mean-variance analysis is a technique that investors use to make decisions about financial instruments to invest in, based on the amount of risk that they are willing to accept (risk tolerance). Ideally, investors expect to earn higher returns when they invest in riskier assets. When measuring the level of risk, investors consider the potential variance (which is the volatility of returns produced by an asset) against the expected returns of that asset. Mean-variance analysis essentially looks at the average variance in the expected return from an investment.

A diversified portfolio is less volatile than the total sum of its individual parts. While each asset itself might be quite volatile, the volatility of the entire portfolio can actually be quite low.

Lower variance is considered to be a better indicator when choosing among two options having the same returns. By combining the stocks with different variances and expected returns in a portfolio, the diversification objective is fulfilled – the loss due to movement of a particular stock is countered by opposite movement of another stock. Thus for an optimal portfolio, an investor must consider the co-movement of individual securities.

8

Markowitz Model

Harry Markowitz, a Nobel Prize-winning economist, is considered a father of modern portfolio theory. His article, "Portfolio Selection", which appeared in the *Journal of Finance* in 1952, interwove the concepts of portfolio returns, risk, variance, and covariance. His findings greatly changed the asset management industry, and his theory is still considered as cutting edge in portfolio management. There are two main concepts in his model which are as under:

1. Any investor's goal is to maximize return for any level of risk.
2. Risk can be reduced by creating a diversified portfolio of unrelated assets.

Markowitz model is a portfolio optimization model. It assists in the selection of the most efficient portfolio by analyzing various possible portfolios of the given securities. By choosing securities that do not *move* exactly together, the Markowitz model shows investors how to reduce their risk. Markowitz model is also called mean-variance model due to the fact that it is based on expected returns (mean) and the standard deviation (variance) of the various portfolios. It is foundational to modern portfolio theory.

To choose the best portfolio from a number of possible portfolios, each with different return and risk, two separate decisions are to be made:

1. Determination of a set of efficient portfolios.
2. Selection of the best portfolio out of the efficient set.

8.1 Assumptions

Markowitz made the following assumptions while developing his model:

1. Risk of a portfolio is based on the variability of returns from the said portfolio.
2. An investor is risk averse.
3. An investor prefers to increase consumption.
4. Utility function of an investor is concave and increasing, due to his risk aversion and consumption preference.
5. Analysis is based on single period model of investment.
6. An investor either maximizes his portfolio return for a *given* level of risk or minimizes his risk for a given return.
7. An investor is rational in nature.

8.2 Markowitz Efficient Set

A portfolio that gives maximum return for a given risk, or minimum risk for given return is an efficient portfolio. Thus, portfolios are selected as follows:

1. From the portfolios that have the same return, the investor will prefer the portfolio

with lower risk, and

2. From the portfolios that have the same risk level, an investor will prefer the portfolio with higher rate of return.

The Markowitz efficient set is a portfolio with returns that are maximized for a given level of risk based on mean-variance portfolio construction. The efficient solution to a given set of mean-variance parameters can be plotted on what is called the Markowitz efficient frontier. It has the following features:

1. Markowitz efficient set was developed by economist Harry Markowitz in 1952.
2. The goal of the Markowitz efficient set is to maximize the returns of a portfolio for a given level of risk.
3. The efficient solution to a portfolio can be plotted on the Markowitz efficient frontier.
4. The efficient frontier is represented with returns on the Y-axis and risk on the X-axis.
5. The Markowitz efficient set highlights the diversification of assets in a portfolio, which lowers the risk of portfolio.

The optimal risk-return combination of a portfolio lies on an efficient frontier of maximum returns for a given level of risk based on mean-variance portfolio construction.

Individuals have different risk tolerance levels, and therefore these portfolio sets are subject to various returns. Moreover, investors cannot assume that if they bear greater amounts of risk, they will be automatically rewarded with extra returns. In fact, the set becomes inefficient when returns decrease at greater levels of risk. At the core of a Markowitz efficient set is diversification of assets, which lowers portfolio risk.

Because different combinations of assets have different levels of return, the Markowitz efficient set is meant to show the best combination of these assets that will maximize returns at a chosen risk level. In this manner, the Markowitz efficient set shows investors how returns vary given the amount of risk assumed.

8.2.1 Diversification in the Markowitz Efficient Set: Different assets respond differently to market factors. Certain assets move in the same direction while other assets move in opposite directions. When assets have a lower covariance, the more they move in opposite directions, i.e. the risk of the portfolio is lower. Because of this, the efficient frontier is a curved representation rather than a linear one. It implies that a diversified portfolio has less risk than a portfolio consisting of one security or a group of securities that move in the same direction when market factors change.

Risk is a welcome factor when investing as it allows us to reap rewards for taking on the possibility of adverse outcomes. Markowitz model, however, shows that a mixture of diverse assets will significantly reduce the overall risk of a portfolio.

Risk, therefore, has to be seen as a cumulative factor for the portfolio as a whole and not as a simple addition of single risks. Assets that are unrelated will also have unrelated risk. This concept is defined as correlation. If two assets are very similar, then their prices will move in a very similar pattern.

Correlation is measured on a scale of -1.0 to +1.0. If two assets have an expected return correlation of 1.0 that means that they are perfectly correlated.

A perfectly negative correlation (-1.0) implies that one asset's gain is proportionally matched by the other asset's loss. A zero correlation has no predictive relationship. The model stresses that investors should look for a consistently uncorrelated (near zero) pool of assets to limit risk.

8.3 Markowitz Efficient Frontier

The concept of efficient frontier was also introduced by Markowitz and is easier to understand than it sounds. It is a graphical representation of all the possible mixtures of risky assets for an optimal level of return given any level of risk, as measured by standard deviation.

In modern portfolio theory, the efficient frontier is an investment portfolio which occupies the 'efficient' parts of the risk-return spectrum. Formally, it is the set of portfolios which satisfy the condition that no other portfolio exists with a higher expected return but with the same standard deviation of return. A combination of assets, i.e. a portfolio, is referred to as "efficient" if it has the best possible expected level of return for its level of risk. Figure 8.1 shows a hyperbola showing all the outcomes for various portfolio combinations of risky assets, where standard deviation is plotted on the X-axis and return is plotted on the Y-axis.

Figure 8.1: Markowitz Efficient Frontier

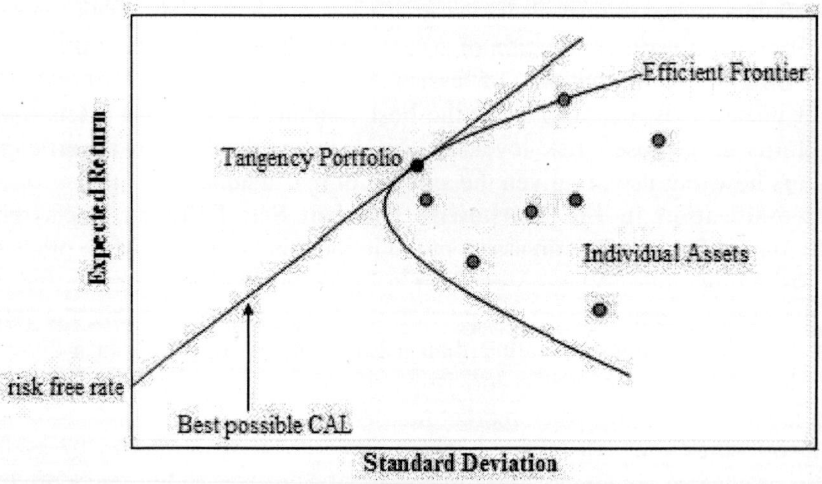

The straight line (capital allocation line or CAL) represents a portfolio of all risky assets and the risk-free asset, which is usually a government bond. Tangency portfolio is the point where the portfolio of only risky assets meets the combination of risky and risk-free assets. This portfolio maximizes return for the given level of risk. Portfolio along the lower part of the hyperbole will have lower return and eventually higher risk.

The hyperbola is sometimes referred to as the *Markowitz Bullet*, and its upward sloped portion is the efficient frontier if no risk-free asset is available. With a risk-free asset, the straight line is the efficient frontier. An efficient portfolio is either a portfolio that offers the highest expected return for a given level of risk, or one with the lowest level of risk for a given expected return. The line that connects all these efficient portfolios is the efficient frontier.

8.4 Limitations of the Markowitz Model

1. One of the major criticisms of Markowitz's initial model was the assumption that the correlation between assets is fixed and predictable. The systematic relationships between different assets do not remain constant in the real world, which means that the model becomes less and less useful during times of uncertainty exactly when investors need the most protection from volatility.

2. Unless positivity constraints are assigned, the Markowitz solution can easily find highly leveraged portfolios, but given their leveraged nature the returns from such a portfolio are extremely sensitive to small changes in the returns of the constituent assets and can therefore be extremely *dangerous*. Positivity constraints are easy to enforce and fix this problem, but if the user wants to *believe* in the robustness of the Markowitz approach, it would be nice if better-behaved solutions were obtained in an unconstrained manner when the set of investment assets is close to the available investment opportunities. However, this is often not the case.

3. Practically more vexing, small changes in inputs can give rise to large changes in the portfolio. Mean-variance optimization suffers from *error maximization*. In the real world, this degree of instability will lead, to begin with, to large transaction costs, but it is also likely to shake the confidence of the portfolio manager in the mode.

4. The amount of information needed to compute a mean-variance optimal portfolio is often intractable and certainly has no room for subjective measurements.

5. Moreover, the presence of illiquid assets, such as human wealth or a family owned business, complicates the problem of portfolio choice.

To sum up, Markowitz model explains as to how risk-averse investors can construct portfolios to optimize or maximize expected return based on a given level of market risk, emphasizing that risk is an inherent part of higher reward.

A Markowitz efficient portfolio is the portfolio that has the highest possible potential return at a given level of risk. It emphasizes that investors can diversify the risk of investment loss by reducing the correlation between the returns from the select securities in their portfolio. The goal is to optimize expected return against a certain level of risk. Hence, investors should measure returns of different assets and strategically select assets that are less likely to lose value at the same time.

Allocating your investments among different asset classes is a key strategy to help minimize risk and potentially increase gains. In short, Markowitz model advises investors not to put all their eggs in one basket.

9

Capital Asset Pricing Model (CAPM)

Capital asset pricing model (CAMP) provides a formula that calculates the expected return on a security based on its level of risk. The formula for CAMP is the risk free rate plus beta times the difference of the return on the market and the risk free rate. There are five principal risk measures, and each measure provides a unique way to assess the risk present in investments that are under consideration. The five measures include the alpha, beta, R-squared, standard deviation, and Sharpe ratio.

Higher risk is associated with greater probability of higher return and lower risk with a greater probability of smaller return. This trade-off which an investor faces between risk and return while considering investment decisions is called the risk return trade-off.

9.1 Risk and Return

Total risk is an assessment that identifies all of the risk factors associated with pursuing a specific course of action. The goal of examining total risk is to make a decision that leads to the best possible outcome.

Risk is the possibility that your investment will lose money. Successful investing is about finding the right balance between risk and return.

Common types of business risks include the following:
1. Competition risk.
2. Operational risk.
3. Legal risk.
4. Compliance risk.
5. Strategy risk.
6. Reputational risk.
7. Risks arising from catastrophic events.
8. Computer hacking.
   Many people grow up with the belief that taking risks is a negative thing.
   Return is what every investor is after. Return on investment is the profit expressed as a percentage of the initial investment. Profit includes income and capital gains.

No matter how much you diversify your investments, some level of risk will always exist. So investors naturally seek a rate of return that compensates for that risk. CAPM helps to calculate investment risk and what return on investment an investor should expect.

9.2 Systematic Risks versus Unsystematic Risks

CAMP was developed by the financial economist (and later Nobel laureate in economics) William Sharpe, set out in his 1970 book *Portfolio Theory and Capital*

Markets. His model starts with the idea that individual investment contains two types of risk:

9.2.1 Systematic Risk: These are market risks, i.e. general perils of investing which cannot be diversified away. These systematic factors include macroeconomic factors such as inflation, interest rates, economic growth, exchange rates, recessions etc.

9.2.2 Unsystematic Risk: Also known as *specific risk*, this risk relates to individual stocks. In more technical terms, it represents the component of a stock's return that is not correlated with general market moves.

Modern portfolio theory shows that specific risk can be removed or at least mitigated through diversification of a portfolio. However, the problem is that diversification still does not solve the problem of systematic risk. Even a portfolio holding all the shares in the stock market cannot eliminate that risk. Therefore, when calculating a deserved return, systematic risk is what most plagues investors.

9.3 Risk-Return Trade-off

The relationship between financial decision making and risk and return is simple. The more risk there is, the more return on the investment is expected. Not all financial managers would view this risk-return trade-off similarly. The risk-return trade-off states that the potential return rises with an increase in risk. Using this principle, individuals associate low levels of uncertainty with low potential returns, and high levels of uncertainty or risk with high potential returns.

There is a positive correlation between risk and return. Generally, a lower risk investment has a lower potential for profit. A higher risk investment has a higher potential for profit but also a potential for a greater loss.

The risk-return trade-off states that the potential return rises with an increase in risk. According to the risk-return trade-off, invested money can render higher profits only if the investor will accept a higher possibility of losses.

As per the trade-off between risk and return, the amount of risk determines the degree of return. If an investor is looking for higher returns, he must invest in the instruments containing higher risk. Higher risk is associated with greater probability of higher return and lower risk with a greater probability of smaller return.

9.4 CAMP Formula

In finance, CAPM is a model used to determine a theoretically appropriate required rate of return of an asset, to make decisions about adding assets to a well-diversified portfolio.

CAPM describes the relationship between systematic risk and expected return for assets, particularly stocks. CAPM is widely used throughout finance for pricing risky securities and generating expected returns for assets given the risk of those assets and cost of capital. CAPM provides investors with a means of estimating the required rate of return for a share based on an assessment of this risk.

CAPM describes the relationship between systematic risk and expected return for assets, particularly stocks. CAPM is widely used throughout finance for pricing risky securities and generating expected returns for assets given the risk of those assets and cost of capital.

CAPM provides a formula that calculates the expected return on a security based on its level of risk. The formula for the capital asset pricing model is the risk free rate plus beta times the difference of the return on the market and the risk free rate.

The formula for calculating the expected return of an asset given its risk is as follows:

$ER_i = R_f + \beta_i (ER_m - R_f)$

ER_i = Expected return of investment

R_f = Risk-free rate

β_i = Beta of the investment

ER_m = Expected return of market

$(ER_m - R_f)$ = Market risk premium

Investors expect to be compensated for risk and the time value of money. The risk-free rate in the CAPM formula accounts for the time value of money. The other components of the CAPM formula account for the investor taking on additional risk.

9.4.1 Beta's Role in CAPM: According to CAPM, beta is the only relevant measure of a stock's risk. It measures a stock's relative volatility, i.e. it shows how much the price of a particular stock jumps up and down compared with how much the entire stock market jumps up and down. If a share price moves exactly in line with the market, then the stock's beta is 1. A stock with a beta of 1.5 would rise by 15 percent if the market rose by 10 percent and fall by 15 percent if the market fell by 10 percent.

Beta is found by statistical analysis of individual, daily share price returns in comparison with the market's daily returns over precisely the same period.

The goal of the CAPM formula is to evaluate whether a stock is fairly valued when its risk and the time value of money are compared to its expected return. For example, imagine an investor is contemplating a stock worth ₹ 100 per share today that pays a 3 percent annual dividend. The stock has a beta compared to the market of 1.3, which means it is riskier than a market portfolio. Also, assume that the risk-free rate is 3 percent and this investor expects the market to rise in value by 8 percent per year. The expected return of the stock based on the CAPM formula is 9.5 percent. 9.5 percent =3 percent + 1.3 (8 percent – 3 percent).

Generally, the capital asset pricing model helps in the pricing of risky securities, such that the implications of risk and the amount of risk premium necessary for the compensation can be ascertained.

Investors who have a portfolio of securities may like to add some more securities to the existing portfolio in order to diversify or reduce the risks. So, it is appropriate to study the extent of risks of a security in terms of its contribution to the riskiness of a portfolio. CAPM measures the risk of a security in relation to the portfolio. It considers the required rate of return of a security in the light of its contribution to total portfolio risk. CAPM holds that only un-diversifiable risk is relevant to the determination of expected return on any asset.

Even though the CAPM is competent to examine the risk and return of any capital asset such as individual security, an investment project or a portfolio asset, we shall be discussing CAPM with reference to risk and return of a security only.

9.5 Assumptions of CAMP

1. Investors are risk averse, i.e. they place funds in the less risky investments.
2. All investors have the same expectations from the market and are well informed.
3. No investor is big enough to influence the price of the securities.
4. The market is perfect: There are no taxes, no transaction costs, securities are completely divisible, and the market is competitive.
5. Investors can borrow and lend unlimited amounts at a risk-free rate (zero bonds).

The model assumes that all active and potential shareholders have access to the same information and agree about the risk and expected return of all assets (homogeneous expectations assumption).

9.6 Limitations of CAPM

There are several assumptions behind the CAPM formula that have been shown not to hold in reality. Despite these issues, the CAPM formula is still widely used because it is simple and allows for easy comparisons of investment alternatives.

Including beta in the formula assumes that risk can be measured by a stock's price volatility. However, price movements in both directions are not equally risky. The look-back period to determine a stock's volatility is not standard because stock returns (and risk) are not normally distributed.

The market portfolio that is used to find the market risk premium is only a theoretical value and is not an asset that can be purchased or invested in as an alternative to the stock. Most of the time, investors will use a major stock index, like the S&P 500, to substitute for the market, which is an imperfect comparison.

The most serious critique of the CAPM is the assumption that future cash flows can be estimated for the discounting process. If an investor could estimate the future return of a stock with a high level of accuracy, the CAPM would not be necessary.

9.7 Consumption Capital Asset Pricing Model (CCAPM)

CCAPM is an extension of CAPM that uses a consumption beta instead of a market beta to explain expected return premiums over the risk-free rate. The beta component of both the CCAPM and CAPM formulas represents risk that cannot be diversified away. The consumption beta is based on the volatility of a given stock or portfolio.

CCAPM predicts that an asset's return premium is proportional to its consumption beta. The model is credited to Douglas Breeden, a finance professor at Fuqua School of Business at Duke University, and Robert Lucas, an economics professor at the University of Chicago who won the Nobel Prize in Economics in 1995.

The formula for the CCAMP is as under:

$R = Rf + \beta c \ (Rm - Rf)$

where,

R = expected return on a security

Rf = risk-free rate

βc = consumption beta

Rm = return on the market

CCAPM provides a fundamental understanding of the relationship between wealth and consumption and an investor's risk aversion. CCAPM works as an asset valuation model to tell you the expected premium investors require in order buying a given stock, and how that return is affected by the risk that comes from consumption-driven stock price volatility.

The quantity of risk related to the consumption beta is measured by the movements of the risk premium (return on asset-risk-free rate) with consumption growth. The CCAPM is useful in estimating how much stock market returns change relative to consumption growth. A higher consumption beta implies a higher expected return on risky assets. For instance, a consumption beta of 2.0 would imply an increased asset return requirement of 2 percent if the market increased by 1 percent.

CCAPM incorporates many forms of wealth beyond stock market wealth and provides a framework for understanding variation in financial asset returns over many time periods. This provides an extension of the CAPM, which only takes into account one-period asset returns.

9.8 Inter-temporal Capital Asset Pricing Model (ICAMP)

ICAPM is a consumption-based capital asset pricing model (CCAPM) that assumes that investors hedge risky positions. ICAPM is an extension of CAPM and was introduced by Nobel laureate Robert Merton in 1973.

ICAPM is a consumption-based asset-pricing model. Whereas CAPM uses market movement to predict a stock's return, CCAPMs explain the market's movement or a security's movement by its relationship to aggregate consumption. In CAPM, a security's return will be proportional to its risk, or market beta. In CCAPM, a stock's return will occur in relation to aggregate consumption, indicated by consumption beta.

Like CAPM and CCAPM, ICAPM also predicts the expected return on a security. It offers further precision by taking into account how investors participate in the market. Most investors participate in markets for multiple years, and over longer time periods, investment opportunities might shift as expectations of risk change, resulting in situations in which investors may wish to hedge. For example, an investment may perform better in bear markets, and an investor may consider holding that asset if a downturn in the business cycle is expected. The ICAPM model, therefore, accounts for one or more hedging portfolios that an investor may use to address these risks. ICAPM covers multiple time periods, so multiple beta coefficients are used.

To sum up, CAPM uses the principles of Modern Portfolio Theory to determine if a security is fairly valued. It relies on assumptions about investor behaviours, risk and return distributions, and market fundamentals that don't match reality. However, the underlying concepts of CAPM and the associated efficient frontier can help investors understand the relationship between expected risk and reward as they make better decisions about adding securities to a portfolio.

Considering the critiques of the CAPM and the assumptions behind its use in portfolio construction, it might be difficult to see how it could be useful. However, using the CAPM as a tool to evaluate the reasonableness of future expectations or to conduct comparisons can still have some value.

This model presents a simple theory that delivers a simple result. The theory says that the only reason an investor should earn more, on average, by investing in one stock rather than another is that one stock is riskier. Not surprisingly, the model has come to dominate modern financial theory. But does it really work?

It is not entirely clear. CAMP is by no means a perfect theory. But the spirit of CAPM is correct. It provides a useful measure that helps investors determine what return they deserve on an investment, in exchange for putting their money at risk on it.

10

Capital Market Line (CML) and Security Market Line (SML)

10.1 Capital Market Line (CML)

CML represents portfolios that optimally combine risk and return. Capital asset pricing model (CAPM) depicts the trade-off between risk and return for efficient portfolios. It is a theoretical concept that represents all the portfolios that optimally combine the risk-free rate of return and the market portfolio of risky assets. Under CAPM, all investors will choose a position on CML by borrowing or lending at the risk-free rate, since this maximizes return for a given level of risk.

Portfolios that fall on CML optimize the risk-return relationship, thereby maximizing performance. CML is a special case of the capital allocation line (CAL) where the risk portfolio is the market portfolio. CAL makes up the allotment of risk-free assets and risky portfolios for an investor.

As an investor moves up the CML, the overall portfolio risk and return increases. Risk adverse investors will select portfolios close to the risk-free asset, preferring low variance to higher returns. Less risk adverse investors will prefer portfolios higher up on the CML, with a higher expected return, but more variance. By borrowing funds at the risk-free rate, they can also invest more than 100 percent of their investable funds in the risky market portfolio, increasing both the expected return and the risk beyond that offered by the market portfolio. Therefore,

1. The capital market line (CML) represents portfolios that optimally combine risk and return.
2. CML is a special case of the CAL where the risk portfolio is the market portfolio.
3. The intercept point of CML and efficient frontier would result in the most efficient portfolio called the tangency portfolio.

CML equation is as follows:

$$R_p = r_f + \frac{R_T - r_f}{\sigma_T} \sigma_p$$

Where:

R_p = Portfolio return

r_f = Risk free rate

R_T = Market return

σ_p = Standard deviation of portfolio returns

σ_T = Standard deviation of market returns

In Figure 10.1, R_1 is the risk-free return, or the return from government securities, as those securities are considered to have no risk for modeling purposes. R_1PX is drawn so that it is tangent to the efficient frontier. Any point on the line R_1PX shows a combination of different proportions of risk-free securities and efficient portfolios.

R_1PX is known as the capital market line (CML). This line represents the risk-return trade off in the capital market. The CML is an upward sloping line, which means that the investor will take higher risk if the return of the portfolio is also higher. The portfolio P is the most efficient portfolio, as it lies on both the CML and Efficient Frontier, and every investor would prefer to attain this portfolio, P. The P portfolio is known as the Market Portfolio and is also the most diversified portfolio. It consists of all shares and other securities in the capital market.

In the market for portfolios that consists of risky and risk-free securities, the CML represents the equilibrium condition. The Capital Market Line says that the return from a portfolio is the risk-free rate *plus* risk premium. Risk premium is the product of the market price of risk and the quantity of risk, and the risk is the standard deviation of the portfolio.

Figure 10.1: Combination of Risk-Free Securities with the Efficient Frontier and CML

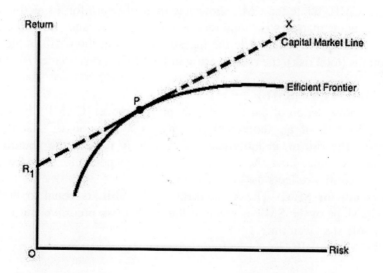

10.1.1 Characteristic Features of CML: These are as under:
1. Tangent point, i.e. portfolio *P*, is the optimum combination of risky investments and the market portfolio.
2. Only efficient portfolios that consist of risk free investments and the market portfolio P lie on the CML.
3. CML is always upward sloping as the price of risk has to be positive. A rational investor will not invest unless they know they will be compensated for that risk.

Thus, capital market line (CML) is a graph that reflects the expected return of a portfolio consisting of all possible proportions between the market portfolio and a risk-free asset. The market portfolio is completely diversified, carries only systematic risk, and its expected return is equal to the expected market return as a whole.

10.1.2 Limitations of CML: The key problem of CML in real market conditions is that it is based on the same assumptions as capital asset pricing model (CAPM).

1. There are taxes and transaction costs, which can significantly differ for various investors.
2. It is supposed that any investor can either lend or borrow unlimited amount at risk-free rate. In real market conditions investors can lend at lower rate than borrow.
3. Real markets do not have strong form of efficiency, so investors have unequal to information.
4. Not all investors are rational and risk-averse.
5. Standard deviation is not the only risk measurement, because real markets are subject to inflation risk, reinvestment risk, currency risk etc.
6. There are no risk-free assets.

Thus, CML in real market condition looks like a fuzzy area rather than a precise line.

The CML is sometimes confused with the security market line (SML). The SML is derived from the CML. While the CML shows the rates of return for a specific portfolio, the SML represents the market's risk and return at a given time, and shows the expected returns of individual assets. And while the measure of risk in the CML is the standard deviation of returns (total risk), the risk measure in the SML is systematic risk, or beta.

10.2 Security Market Line (SML)

SML is the representation of the capital asset pricing model (CAMP). It displays the expected rate of return of an individual security as a function of systematic, non-diversifiable risk. The risk of an individual risky security reflects the volatility of the return from security rather than the return of the market portfolio. The risk in these individual risky securities reflects the systematic risk.

10.2.1 Formula for SLM: The Y-intercept of the SML is equal to the risk-free interest rate. The slope of the SML is equal to the market risk premium and reflects the risk return trade-off at a given time.

SML: $E(R_i) = R_f + \beta_i [E(R_m) - R_f]$

Where

$E(R_i)$ is an expected return on security.

$E(R_M)$ is an expected return on market portfolio M.

β is a non-diversifiable or systematic risk.

R_M is a market rate of return.

R_f is a risk-free rate

SML is a line drawn on a chart that serves as a graphical representation of the capital asset pricing model (CAPM)—which shows different levels of systematic, or market risk, of various marketable securities, plotted against the expected return of the entire market at any given time.

Also known as the *characteristic line*, SML is a visualization of the CAPM, where the x-axis of the chart represents risk (in terms of beta), and the y-axis of the chart represents expected return. The market risk premium of a given security is determined by where it is plotted on the chart relative to the SML.

When used in portfolio management, SML represents the investment's opportunity cost (investing in a combination of the market portfolio and the risk-free asset). All the correctly priced securities are plotted on the SML. In Figure 10.2, the assets above the line are undervalued because for a given amount of risk (beta), they yield a higher return. The assets below the line are overvalued because for a given amount of risk, they yield a lower return.

The assets which are above the SML are undervalued as they give the higher expected return for a given amount of risk. The assets which are below the SML are overvalued as they have lower expected returns for the same amount of risk.

Figure 10.2: Security Market Line

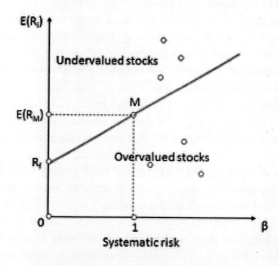

There is a question about what the SML looks like when beta is negative. A rational investor will accept these assets even though they yield sub-risk-free returns, because they will provide "recession insurance" as part of a well-diversified portfolio. Therefore, the SML continues in a straight line whether beta is positive or negative. A different way of thinking about this is that the absolute value of beta represents the amount of risk associated with the asset, while the sign explains when the risk occurs.

10.2.2 Features of SML: The security market line is an investment evaluation tool derived from the CAPM—a model that describes risk-return relationship for securities— and is based on the assumption that investors need to be compensated for both the time value of money (TVM) and the corresponding level of risk associated with any investment, referred to as the risk premium.

1. SML is a line drawn on a chart that serves as a graphical representation of the capital asset pricing model (CAPM).

2. SML can help to determine whether an investment product would offer a favorable expected return compared to its level of risk.

3. The formula for plotting the SML is required return = risk-free rate of return + beta (market return - risk-free rate of return).

Together, SML and CAPM formulas are useful in determining if a security being considered for an investment offers a reasonable expected return for the amount of risk taken on. If a security's expected return versus its beta is plotted above the security market line, it is undervalued given the risk-return trade-off. Conversely, if a security's expected return versus its systematic risk is plotted below the SML, it is overvalued because the investor would accept a smaller return for the amount of systematic risk associated.

For example, suppose an analyst plots the SML. The risk-free rate is 1 percent, and the expected market return is 11 percent. The beta of stock ABC is 2.2, meaning it carries more volatility and more systematic risk. The expected return of stock ABC is 23 percent: 1 percent + [2.2 × (11 percent − 1 percent)] = 23 percent.

If the current return of stock A is 33 percent, it is undervalued, because investors expect a higher return given the same amount of systematic risk. Conversely, say the expected return of stock B is 11 percent, and the current return is 8 percent and is below the SML. The stock is overvalued: investors are accepting a lower return for the given amount of risk, which is a bad risk-return tradeoff.

10.2.3 Role of Beta: The concept of beta is central to the CAPM and the SML. The beta of a security measures the systematic risk and its sensitivity relative to changes in the market. A security with a beta of 1 has a perfect positive correlation with its market. This indicates that when the market increases or decreases, the security increases or decreases in time with the market. A security with a beta greater than 1 carries more systematic risk and volatility than the market, and a security with a beta less than 1 carries less systematic risk and volatility than the market.

10.2.4 Uses of SML: SML is commonly used by money managers and investors to evaluate an investment product that they're thinking of including in a portfolio. SML is useful in determining whether the security offers a favorable expected return compared to its level of risk.

SML is frequently used in comparing two similar securities that offer approximately the same return, in order to determine which of them involves the least amount of inherent market risk relative to the expected return. SML can also be used to compare securities of equal risk to see which one offers the highest expected return against that level of risk.

Although the SML can be a valuable tool for evaluating and comparing securities, it should not be used in isolation, as the expected return of an investment over the risk-free rate of return is not the only thing to consider when choosing investments.

To sum up, SML is the representation of the capital asset pricing model. It displays the expected rate of return of an individual security as a function of systematic, non-diversifiable risk. The risk of an individual risky security reflects the volatility of the return from security rather than the return of the market portfolio. The risk in these individual risky securities reflects the systematic risk.

Part III
Derivatives, Forwards, Futures and Options

Financial Derivatives: Emergence and Popularity

11.1 Emergence of Complex Financial Products

In recent years, complex financial products such as asset-backed securities, derivatives, credit-default swaps (CDSs) and collateralised debt obligations (CDOs) have proliferated in developed countries. These products have become highly popular with banks and financial institutions as they allow them to hedge their risks and manage their regulatory and economic capital more efficiently.

Although various structured products have enabled the transfer of risks and enhanced the liquidity of instruments, the recent turmoil in the US sub-prime mortgage market and related developments connected with complex derivatives have also brought to the fore the risks posed by these instruments.

The emergence of the market for derivative products, most notably forwards, futures and options, can be traced back to the willingness of risk-averse economic agents to guard themselves against uncertainties arising out of fluctuations in asset prices. By their very nature, the financial markets are marked by a very high degree of volatility. Through the use of derivative products, it is possible to partially or fully transfer price risks by locking-in asset prices. As instruments of risk management, derivatives generally do not influence the fluctuations in the underlying asset prices. However, by locking-in asset prices, derivative products minimize the impact of fluctuations in asset prices on the profitability and cash flow situation of risk-averse investors.

Derivative products initially emerged as hedging devices against fluctuations in commodity prices and commodity-linked derivatives remained the sole form of such products for a long time. The financial derivatives came into spotlight in post-1970 period due to growing instability in the financial markets. However, since their emergence, financial derivatives have become very popular and by 1990s, they accounted for about two-thirds of total transactions in derivative products. In recent years, the market for financial derivatives has grown tremendously both in terms of variety of instruments available, their complexity and also turnover.

In India also financial products such as mortgage-backed securities (MBS) and asset-backed securities (ABS) are in existence. Besides the securitised products, the Indian forex and rupee derivative markets have also developed significantly over the years.

In respect of forex derivatives involving rupee, residents have access to foreign exchange forward contracts, foreign currency-rupee swap instruments and currency options—both cross currency and foreign currency-rupee. As stated in the Annual Policy Statement for the year 2008-09, the Reserve Bank of India (RBI) announced the introduction of currency futures in the eligible exchanges for which the broad framework was announced in August 2008. In future, some more innovative and complex products might emerge. These products may pose several regulatory and supervisory challenges.

11.2 Meaning of Derivatives

Derivative in mathematics means a variable derived from another variable. The term *derivative* indicates that it has no independent value, i.e. its value is entirely *derived* from the value of the underlying asset. The underlying asset can be security, commodity, bullion, currency, live stock or anything else. In other words, derivative means a forward, future, option or any other hybrid contract of pre-determined fixed duration, linked for the purpose of contract fulfilment to the value of a specified real or financial asset of an index of securities. Similarly, in the financial sense, a derivative is a financial product, which has been derived from a market for another product. Without the underlying product, derivatives do not have any independent existence in the market.

Derivative instruments are defined by the Indian Securities Contracts (Regulation) Act, 1956 to include: (i) a security derived from a debt instrument, share, secured and unsecured loan, risk instrument or contract for differences, or any other form of security, and (ii) a contract that derives its value from the prices/index of prices of underlying securities.

In other words, derivatives are financial instruments/contracts whose value depends upon the value of an underlying. Since their value is essentially derived out of an underlying, they are financial abstractions whose value is derived mathematically from the changes in the value of the underlying.

The International Monetary Fund (IMF) defines derivatives as, "financial instruments that are linked to a specific financial instrument or indicator or commodity and through which specific financial risks can be traded in financial markets in their own right. The value of a financial derivative derives from the price of an underlying item, such as an asset or index. Unlike debt securities, no principal is advanced to be repaid and no investment income accrues".

Derivatives have come into being because of the existence of risks in business. Thus, derivatives are means of managing risks. The parties managing risks in the market are known as *hedgers*. Some people/organizations are in the business of taking risks to earn profits. Such entities represent the *speculators*. The third players in the market, known as the *arbitragers,* take advantage of the market mistakes.

In recent years, derivatives have become increasingly important in the field of finance. While futures and options are now actively traded on many exchanges, forward contracts are popular on the over-the-counter (OTC) market.

11.3 Reasons for the Popularity of Derivatives

Financial derivatives have become popular due to the following reasons:
1. Increased volatility in asset prices in financial markets.
2. Increased integration of national financial markets with the international markets.
3. Marked improvement in communication facilities and sharp decline in their costs.

4. Development of more sophisticated risk management tools, providing economic agents a wider choice of risk management strategies.
5. Innovations in the derivatives markets, which optimally combine the risks and returns over a large number of financial assets, leading to higher returns, reduced risk as well as transaction costs as compared to individual financial assets.

In the class of equity derivatives, futures and options on stock indices have gained more popularity than on individual stocks, especially among institutional investors, who are major users of index-linked derivatives. Even small investors find these useful due to high correlation of the popular indices with various portfolios and ease of use. The lower costs associated with index derivatives vis-à-vis derivative products based on individual securities is another reason for their growing use.

11.4 Variants (or Types) of Derivative Contracts

Derivative contracts have several variants. The most common variants are forwards, futures, options and swaps.

11.4.1 Forwards (or Forward Contracts): A forward contract is a customised contract between two entities, where settlement takes place on a specific date in the future at today's pre-agreed price. A forward contract is an agreement to buy or sell an asset on a specified date for specified price. One of the parties to the contract assumes a long position and agrees to buy the underlying asset on a certain specified future date, for a certain specified price. The other party assumes a short position and agrees to sell the asset on the same date for the same price. Other contract details like delivery date, price and quantity are negotiated bilaterally by the parties to the contract.

Forward contracts are normally traded outside stock exchanges. They are popular on the over-the-counter (OTC) market.

The salient features of forward contracts are as follows:
1. They are bilateral contracts and hence exposed to counter party risk.
2. Each contract is customer designed, and, hence, is unique in terms of contract size, expiration date and the asset type and quality.
3. The contract price is generally not available in public domain.
4. On the expiration date, the contract has to be settled by delivery for the asset.
5. If a party wishes to reverse the contract, it has to compulsorily go to the same counterparty, which often results in a high price being charged.

Forward contracts are very useful in hedging and speculation. A typical hedging application may pertain to an exporter who expects to receive payment in US dollars, 2 months later. He is exposed to the risk of exchange rate fluctuations. By using the currency forward market to sell dollars forward, he can lock-on a rate today and reduce his uncertainty. Likewise, an importer who is required to make a payment in US dollars 2 months hence can reduce his exposure to exchange rate fluctuations by buying dollars forward.

11.4.2 Futures (or Future Contracts): Future contracts are special types of forward contracts in the sense that the former are standardised exchange-traded contracts. Future contract markets are designed to solve the problems that exist in forward markets. A future contract is an agreement between two parties to buy or sell an asset at a certain time in future, at a certain price. However, unlike forward contracts, future contracts are standardized and stock exchange-traded. To facilitate liquidity in the future contracts, the exchange specifies certain standard features for the contract. It is a standardized contract with a standard underlying instrument, a standard quantity and quality of the underlying instrument that can be delivered, and a standard timing of such settlement. A future contract may be offset prior to maturity by entering into an equal and opposite transaction. The standardized items in a future contract are the following:

1. Quantity of the underlying.
2. Quality of the underlying.
3. Date/month of delivery.
4. Units of price quotation and minimum price change.
5. Location of settlement.

11.4.3 Options: Options are fundamentally different from forward and future contracts. An option gives the holder of the option the right to do something. The holder does not have to necessarily exercise this right. In contrast, in a forward or future contract, the two parties commit themselves to doing something. Whereas it costs nothing (except margin requirements) to enter into a future contract, the purchase of an option requires an up front payment.

Options are of two types: calls options and put options. Calls options give the buyer the right but not the obligation to buy a given quantity of the underlying asset, at a given price on or before a given future date. Put options give the buyer the right, but not the obligation to sell a given quantity of the underlying asset at a given price on or before a given date.

A. Warrants: Options generally have lives of up to 1 year, the majority of options traded on options exchanges having maximum maturity of 9 months. Longer-dated options are called *warrants* and are generally traded over-the-counter.

B. LEAPS: The acronym LEAPS means long-term equity anticipation securities. These are options having a maturity of up to 3 years.

C. Baskets: Basket options are options on portfolios of underlying assets. The underlying asset is usually a moving average or a basket of assets. Equity index options are a form of basket options.

11.4.4 Swaps: Swaps are private agreements between two parties to exchange cash flows in the future according to a pre-arranged formula. They can be regarded as portfolios of forward contracts. Following are the two commonly used swaps:

A. Interest Rate Swaps: These entail swapping of only the interest-related cash flows between the parties in the same currency.

B. Currency Swaps: These entail swapping of both principal and interest between the parties, with the cash flows in one direction being in a different currency than those in the opposite direction.

11.4.5 Swaptions: Swaptions are options to buy or sell a swap that will become operative at the expiry of the options. Thus, swaption is an option on a forward swap. Rather than have call options and put options, the swaptions market has receiver swaptions and payer swaptions.

11.5 Participants in the Derivatives Market

The following three broad categories of participants, viz. hedgers, speculators, and arbitrageurs trade in the derivatives market.

11.5.1 Hedgers: Hedgers face risk associated with the price of an asset. They use future or option markets to reduce or eliminate this risk. In other words, hedgers are those who wish to protect their existing exposures and essentially are safety-driven.

11.5.2 Speculators: They bet on future movements in the price of an asset. Future and option contracts can give them an extra leverage; that is, they can increase both the potential gains and potential losses in a speculative venture. Speculators are willing risk takers who are expectation-driven.

11.5.3 Arbitrageurs: They are in business to take advantage of a discrepancy between prices in two different markets. If, for example, they see the futures price of an asset getting out of line with the cash price, they will take offsetting positions in the two markets to lock-in a profit. Arbitragers are traders and market-makers who deal in buying and selling derivatives contracts hoping to profit from price-differentials between different markets. A market maker is one who provides two-way quotes for a given product and thereby runs a position in that product.

11.6 Economic Role of Derivatives

Derivative markets perform three essential economic functions:
1. Risk management.
2. Price discovery.
3. Transactional efficiency.

The first function refers to the ability of traders to offset financial risks through derivatives. The principal benefit of the derivatives market is that it provides the opportunity for risk management through hedging. [1] Derivatives are innovations in risk management not in risk itself.

The second refers to the better allocation of resources in an economy that is created by the wide availability of an equilibrium price which serves as a measure of value.

The third function alludes to increased efficiency of transacting through derivatives. Derivative markets reduce the costs of trading and raising capital, thereby enhancing their risk management and price discovery functions.

Derivatives have played a major role in the development of financial markets and their integration across several economies, especially in developed countries. Derivatives serve to achieve a more complete financial system because previously fixed combinations of the risk properties of loans and financial assets can be bundled and unbundled into new synthetic assets. For instance, structured products or synthetic derivatives could be created by adding elementary assets or underlying assets such as bonds, equities and borrowing and lending instruments with a combination of derivative products such as put and call options. Repackaging risk properties in this way can provide a more perfect match between an investor's risk preferences and the effective risk of the portfolio or cash-flow. Derivatives allow individual risk elements of an asset to be priced and traded individually, thus ensuring an efficient price system in the asset markets.

The economic functions performed by derivatives market can be summarised as under:

1. Derivatives market helps to increase savings and investment in the long-run. Transfer of risk enables market participants to expand their volume of activity.
2. Derivatives trading acts as a catalyst for new entrepreneurial activity. Derivatives have a history of attracting many bright, creative, well educated people with an entrepreneurial attitude.
3. Prices in an organized derivatives market reflect the perception of the market participants about the future and lead the prices of underlying to the perceived future level.
4. Prices of derivatives converge with the prices of the underlying at the expiration of the derivatives contract. In fact, derivatives help in the discovery of the future as well as current prices.
5. Derivatives market helps to transfer risks from those who have them but may not like them to those who have an appetite for them.
6. Derivatives, due to their inherent nature are linked to the underlying cash markets. With the introduction of derivatives, the underlying market witnesses higher trading volumes because of participation by more players who would not otherwise participate for lack of an arrangement to transfer risk.
7. Speculative trades shift to a more controlled environment of derivatives market. In the absence of an organized derivatives market, speculators trade in the underlying cash markets. Margining, monitoring and surveillance of the activities of various participants become extremely difficult in these kinds of mixed markets.

11.7 History of Derivatives

The first future contracts are generally traced to the Yodoya rice market in Osaka, Japan around 1650. These were evidently standardized contracts, which made them much like today's futures, although it is not known if the contracts were marked to market daily and/or had credit guarantees.

Probably the next major event, and the most significant as regards the history of US future markets, was the creation of the Chicago Board of Trade in 1848. Due to its prime location on Lake Michigan, Chicago was developing as a major centre for the storage, sale, and distribution of Midwestern grain. Due to the seasonality of grain, Chicago's storage facilities were unable to accommodate the enormous increase in supply that occurred following the harvest.

Similarly, its facilities were underutilized in the spring. Chicago spot prices rose and fell drastically. A group of grain traders created the *to-arrive* contract, which permitted farmers to lock-in the price and deliver the grain later. This allowed the farmer to store the grain either on the farm or at a storage facility nearby and deliver it to Chicago months later. These *to-arrive* contracts proved useful as a device for hedging and speculating on price changes. Farmers and traders soon realized that the sale and delivery of the grain itself was not as important as the ability to transfer the price risk associated with the grain. The grain could always be sold and delivered anywhere else at any time. These contracts were eventually standardized around 1865, and in 1925 the first future clearing house was formed. From that point on, future contracts were pretty much of the form we know them today.

In the early 19th century, famed New York financier Russell Sage began creating synthetic loans using the principle of put-call parity. Sage would buy the stock and a put from his customer and sell the customer a call. By fixing the put, call, and strike prices, Sage was creating a synthetic loan with an interest rate significantly higher than usury laws allowed.

Interestingly, futures/options/derivatives trading was banned numerous times in Europe and Japan and even in the US in the state of Illinois in 1867 though the law was quickly repealed. In 1874, the Chicago Mercantile Exchange predecessor, the Chicago Produce Exchange, was formed. It became the modern day Merc in 1919. Other exchanges had been popping up around the country and continued to do so.

In 1922, the US Federal Government made its first effort to regulate the futures market with the Grain Futures Act. In 1936, options on futures were banned in the US. All the while options, futures and various derivatives continued to be banned from time to time in other countries.

The 1950s marked the era of two significant events in the futures market. In 1955, the US Supreme Court ruled in the case of Corn Products Refining Company that profits from hedging were treated as ordinary income. This ruling stood until it was challenged by the 1988 ruling in the Arkansas Best case. The Best decision denied the deductibility of capital losses against ordinary income and effectively gave hedging a tax disadvantage. Fortunately, this interpretation was overturned in 1993.

In 1972 the Chicago Mercantile Exchange, responding to the now-freely floating international currencies, created the International Monetary Market, which allowed trading in currency futures. These were the first future contracts that were not on physical commodities. In 1975, the Chicago Board of Trade created the first interest rate futures contract, one based on Ginnie Mae (GNMA) mortgages. While the contract met with initial success, it eventually died. In 1975, the Merc responded with the Treasury bill futures contract. This contract was the first successful pure interest rate futures. In 1982, the Kansas City Board of Trade launched the first stock index futures, a contract on the Value Line Index. The Chicago Mercantile Exchange quickly followed with their highly successful contract on the S&P 500 index.

1973 marked the creation of both the Chicago Board Options Exchange and the publication of perhaps the most famous formula in finance, the option pricing model of Fischer Black and Myron Scholes. These events revolutionized the investment world in ways no one could imagine at that time. The Black-Scholes model, as it came to be known, set up a mathematical framework that formed the basis for an explosive revolution in the use of derivatives. In 1983, the Chicago Board Options Exchange decided to create an option on an index of stocks. Though originally known as the CBOE 100 Index, it was soon turned over to Standard and Poor's and became known as the S&P 100, which remains the most actively traded exchange-listed option.

The 1980s marked the beginning of the era of swaps and other over-the-counter (OTC) derivatives. Although OTC options and forwards had previously existed, the generation of corporate financial managers of that decade was the first to come out of business schools with exposure to derivatives. Soon virtually every large corporation, and even some that were not so large, were using derivatives to hedge, and in some cases, speculate on interest rate, exchange rate and commodity risk. New products were rapidly created to hedge the now-recognized wide varieties of risks. As the problems became more complex, Wall Street turned increasingly to the talents of mathematicians and physicists, offering them new and quite different career paths and unheard-of money. The instruments became more complex and were sometimes even referred to as *exotic*.

In 1994, the derivatives world was hit with a series of large losses on derivatives trading announced by some well-known and highly experienced firms, such as Procter and Gamble and Metallgesellschaft. One of America's wealthiest localities, Orange County, California, declared bankruptcy, allegedly due to derivatives trading, but more accurately, due to the use of leverage in a portfolio of short-term Treasury securities. England's venerable Barings Bank declared bankruptcy due to speculative trading in future contracts by a 28 year old clerk in its Singapore office. These and other large losses led to a huge outcry, sometimes against the instruments and sometimes against the firms that sold them. While some minor changes occurred in the way in which derivatives were sold, most firms simply instituted tighter controls and continued to use derivatives.

11.8 International Experience of Derivatives

As we watch efforts going into the creation of India's exchange-traded derivatives industry, comparisons with other countries are useful. In all Organisation for Economic Cooperation and Development (OECD) countries, derivatives are a crucial and vibrant part of the financial system.

The most interesting and important experience is that of China, a fascinating case study of the merits and demerits of a relatively unregulated start of derivatives trading. In the early 1990s, a plethora of unregulated derivatives exchanges came up in China. Many of these exchanges lacked the key institution of the clearing house as counterparty, and most of them featured rampant market manipulation where insiders in the exchange management earned abnormal profits at the expense of outside market participants.

Many observers have cited China's experience with 50 exchanges as an example of how poorly-regulated and hasty growth of derivatives markets may be problematic. However, the other side of the picture is now clear: the experience with these 50 exchanges got the Chinese markets off the ground, and generated the necessary know-how amongst exchange staff, regulators and users. In the end, China has derivatives exchanges which have significant trading volumes on a world scale.

Another important example is that of Mexico, which is in the same time zone as Chicago: the derivatives exchanges of Chicago have done a thorough job of launching numerous derivative products based on Mexican underlying. This has made the creation of exchanges in Mexico much harder.

Taiwan is another interesting case. Taiwan is like India in terms of enormous delays which have beset the creation of a domestic derivatives exchange. In January 1997, markets in Chicago and Singapore started trading futures on a Taiwanese market index.

Exchanges such as the Chicago Mercantile Exchange (CME), Chicago Board of Trade (CBOT), Chicago Board Options Exchange (CBOE), American Stock Exchange, Sydney Futures Exchange, Hong Kong Futures Exchange and Singapore International Monetary Exchange (SIMEX) have all launched emerging market initiatives, whereby they aim to trade derivatives of underlying from emerging markets.

The US is an example of a clumsy regulatory approach, where an agency named the CFTC regulates futures while the traditional securities markets regulator, the SEC, regulates options on securities. This artificial distinction has no economic rationale, and has served to distort the development of the markets.

What are the problems which bedevil the growth of derivative markets across emerging markets in general? One source of difficulty is poor infrastructure, particularly in clearing and settlement.

In India, a major initiative in clearing for derivatives was National Securities Clearing Corporation (NSCC) which was created by National Stock Exchange (NSE). NSCC was the first effort in clearing where the clearing corporation becomes the *legal counterparty* to both legs of every transaction, and thus eliminates counterparty risk.

To sum up, derivatives is an area where a *unified* picture of the entire securities industry—spanning equity, debt, foreign exchange, commodities and real estate—is enormously useful. The functioning of the derivatives industry emphasizes that a futures is a futures, regardless of the underlying on which the futures is being traded. The great derivatives exchanges of the world simultaneously trade derivatives on all of equity, debt, foreign exchange, commodities and real estate. In this sense, the basic policy issues faced in the derivatives area (market manipulation, strength of the clearing house and competition between exchanges worldwide) are universal to all major markets.

Endnote

1. Hedging is the process of stabilizing the value (including cash flows) of a given portfolio by neutralizing adverse market movements.

12

Forward Contracts (or Forwards)

A deal for the purchase or sale of a commodity, security or other asset can be in the spot or forward markets. A spot (or current) market is the most commonly used for trading. A majority of day-to-day transactions are in the spot market, where we make the payment and get the delivery of goods and services. In addition to a spot purchase, another way to acquire or sell assets is by entering into a forward contract.

12.1 What is a Forward Contact?

A forward contract is an agreement to buy or sell an asset on a specified date for a specified price. One of the parties to the contract assumes a long position and agrees to buy the underlying asset on a certain specified future date for a certain specified price. The other party assumes a short position and agrees to sell the asset on the same date for the same price. Other contract details like delivery date, price and quantity are negotiated bilaterally by the parties to the contract. The forward contracts are normally traded outside the exchanges. A forward contract is a particularly simple derivative.

Usually no money changes hands when forward contracts are entered into, but sometimes one or both the parties to a contract may like to ask for some initial, good-faith deposits to insure that the contract is honoured by the other party.

A forward contract is settled at maturity. The holder of the short position delivers the asset to the holder price. A forward contract is worth zero when it is first entered into. Later it can have position or negative value, depending on movements in the price of the asset.

However, forward contracts in certain markets have become much standardised, as in the case of foreign exchange, thereby reducing transaction costs and increasing transaction volumes. This process of standardisation reaches its limit in the organised futures market.

Unlike standard future contracts, a forward contract can be customized to a commodity, amount and *delivery date*. Commodities traded can be grains, precious metals, natural gas, oil, or even poultry. A forward contract settlement can occur on a cash or delivery basis.

Forward contracts do not trade on a centralized exchange and are therefore regarded as over-the-counter (OTC) instruments. While their OTC nature makes it easier to customize terms, the lack of a centralized clearinghouse also gives rise to a higher degree of default risk. As a result, forward contracts are not as easily available to the retail investor as futures contracts.

Forward contracts have been in existence for quite some time. The organized commodity exchanges, on which forward contracts are traded, probably started in Japan in the early 18th century, while the establishment of the Chicago Board of Trade (CBOT) in 1848 led to the start of a formal commodity exchange in the US.

12.2 Salient Features of Forward Contracts

These are as under:

1   They are bilateral contracts and hence exposed to counter party risk.
2   Each contract is custom designed, and hence is unique in terms of contract size, expiration date and the asset type and quality.
3   Contract price is generally not available in public domain.
4   On the expiration date, the contract has to be settled by delivery of the asset.
5   If the party wishes to reverse the contract, it has to compulsorily go to the same counterparty, which often results in high prices being charged.
6   A forward contract is a customizeable derivative contract between two parties to buy or sell an asset at a specified price on a future date. Forward contracts can be tailored to a specific commodity, amount and delivery date. Forward contracts do not trade on a centralized exchange and are considered over-the-counter (OTC) instruments.
7   Since the final value (at maturity) of a forward position depends on the spot price which will then be prevailing, this contract can be viewed, from a purely financial point of view, as *a bet on the future spot price.*

12.3 Example of a Forward Contract

Consider the following example of a forward contract. Assume that a potato grower farmer, averse to price fluctuations, wants to sell his produce 6 months from now. At the same time, suppose that a company producing potato chips wishes to buy potatoes 6 months from now. Both parties can enter into a forward contract with each other. Assume that they both agree that the farmer will sell to the company 20 quintals of a specified variety of potatoes at a price of ₹ 2,000 per quintal (called contract price or delivery price) after 6 month with settlement on a cash basis. The total consideration of the contract is ₹ 40,000.

At the end of 6 months (i.e. the time of delivery), the spot price (or current price) of potatoes has three possibilities:

1.   It is exactly ₹ 2,000 per quintal. In this case, no party is a loser or gainer.
2.   It is higher than the contract price, say ₹ 2,500 per quintal. The farmer is a loser by ₹ 10,000 which *ipso facto* means that the company is a gainer by ₹ 10,000.
3.   It is lower than the contract price, say ₹ 1,500 per quintal. The farmer is a gainer by ₹ 10,000.

The similar situation works among currency forwards, in which one party opens a forward contract to buy or sell a currency (e.g. a contract to buy US dollars) to expire/settle at a future date, as they do not wish to be exposed to exchange rate/currency risk over a period of time. As the exchange rate between US dollars and Indian rupee fluctuates between the trade date and the earlier of the date at which the contract is closed or the expiration date, one party gains and the counterparty loses as one currency strengthens against the other. Sometimes, the buy forward is opened because the investor will actually need US dollars at a future date such as to pay a debt owed that is denominated in US dollars. Other times, the party opening a forward does so, not because they need US dollars nor because they are hedging currency risk, but because they are speculating on the currency, expecting the exchange rate to move favourably to generate a gain on closing the contract.

12.4 Advantages of Forwards

Forward contracts are very useful in hedging and speculation. A typical hedging application would be that of an exporter who expects to receive payment in US dollars 3 months later. He is exposed to the risk of exchange rate fluctuations. By using the currency forward market to sell dollars forward, he can lock-on to a rate today and reduce his uncertainty. Similarly, an importer who is required to make a payment in US dollars 2 months hence can reduce his exposure to exchange rate fluctuations by buying dollars forward.

In a forward contract the price at which the underlying commodity or assets will be traded, is decided at the time of entering into the contract. The essential idea of entering into the forward contract is to peg the price and thereby avoid the price risk. Thus, by entering in the forward contract, one is assured of the price at which one can buy/sell goods or other assets. Manufacturers using a certain raw material whose price is subject to variation, can avoid the risk of price moving adversely by entering into a forward contract and plan their operations better. Similarly, by entering into a forward contract, a farmer can ensure the price he can get for his crops and not worry about what price would prevail at the time of maturity of the contract. Of course, at the time of maturity of contract, if the market price of the commodity is greater than the price agreed, then the buyer stands to gain. The opposite would hold when the market price is lower than the agreed price.

If a speculator has information or analysis, which forecasts an upturn in a price, then he can go long on the forward market instead of the current market. The speculator would go long on the forward, wait for the price to rise, and then take a reversing transaction to book profits. Speculators may well be required to deposit a margin upfront. However, this is generally a relatively small proportion of the value of the assets underlying the forward contract.

Having no upfront cash flows is one of the advantages of a forward contract compared to its futures counterpart. Especially when the forward contract is denominated in a foreign currency, not having to post (or receive) daily settlements, simplifies cash flow management.

12.5 Problems of Forward Contracts

Forward markets world-wide are afflicted by several problems:

A forward contract is evidently a good method of avoiding price risk, but it entails elements of risk in that a party to the contract may not honour its part of the obligation. Thus, each party is at risk of default. There is another problem. Once a position of buyer and seller takes in a forward contract, an investor cannot retreat except through mutual consent with the party or by entering into an identical contract and taking a position that is the reverse of earlier position. Alternatives are by no means easy. With forward contract entered on a one-to-one basis and with no standardization, the forward contract has virtually no liquidity. This problem of credit risk and no liquidity associated with forward contracts led to the emergence of future contracts. Future contracts are the refined version of forward contracts.

The basic problem is that of too much flexibility and generality. The forward market is like a real estate market in that any two consenting adults can form contracts against each other. This often makes them design terms of the deal which are very convenient in that specific situation, but makes the contract non-tradable. Counter party risk arises from the possibility of default by any one party to the transaction. When one of the two sides to the transaction declares bankruptcy, the other suffers. Even when forward markets trade standardised contracts, and hence avoid the problem of illiquidity, still the counterparty risk remains a very serious issue.

12.6 Risks with Forward Contracts

The market for forward contracts is huge since many of the world's biggest corporations use it to hedge currency and interest rate risks. However, since the details of forward contracts are restricted to the buyer and seller—and are not known to the general public—the size of this market is difficult to estimate.

The large size and unregulated nature of the forward contracts market mean that it may be susceptible to a cascading series of defaults in the worst-case scenario. While banks and financial corporations mitigate this risk by being very careful in their choice of counterparty, the possibility of large-scale default does exist.

Another risk that arises from the non-standard nature of forward contracts is that they are only settled on the settlement date and are not marked-to-market like futures. What if the forward rate specified in the contract diverges widely from the spot rate at the time of settlement?

In this case, the financial institution that originated the forward contract is exposed to a greater degree of risk in the event of default or non-settlement by the client than if the contract were marked-to-market regularly.

12.7 Forward Markets Commission (FMC) of India

FMC was merged with SEBI in September 2015. FMC was the chief regulator of forwards and futures markets in India. Headquartered in Mumbai, it was overseen by the Ministry of Consumer Affairs, Food and Public Distribution, Government of India.

Established in 1953 under the provisions of the Forward Contracts (Regulation) Act, 1952, it consisted of 2 to 4 members, all appointed by the Government of India. The Commission allowed commodity trading in 22 exchanges in India, of which 6 were national.

Responsibilities and functions of Forward Markets Commission (FMC) were as follows:

1. To advise the Central Government in respect of the recognition or the withdrawal of recognition from any association or in respect of any other matter arising out of the administration of the Forward Contracts (Regulation) Act, 1952.

2. To keep forward markets under observation and to take such action in relation to

them, as it may consider necessary, in exercise of the powers assigned to it by or under the Act.

3. To collect and, whenever the Commission thinks it necessary, publish information regarding the trading conditions in respect of goods to which any of the provisions of the Act is made applicable, including information regarding supply, demand and prices, and to submit to the Central Government, periodical reports on the working of forward markets relating to such goods.

4. To make recommendations generally with a view to improving the organization and working of forward markets.

5. To undertake the inspection of the accounts and other documents of any recognized association or registered association or any member of such association whenever it considers it necessary.

To conclude, a forward contract is a customized contract between two parties to buy or sell an asset at a specified price on a future date. A forward contract can be used for hedging or speculation, although its non-standardized nature makes it particularly apt for hedging. A forward contract or simply a forward is a non-standardized contract between two parties to buy or sell an asset at a specified future time at a price agreed on at the time of conclusion of the contract, making it a type of derivative instrument. The party agreeing to buy the underlying asset in the future assumes a long position, and the party agreeing to sell the asset in the future assumes a short position. The price agreed upon is called the *delivery price*, which is equal to the forward price at the time the contract is entered into.

The price of the underlying instrument, in whatever form, is paid before control of the instrument changes. This is one of the many forms of buy/sell orders where the time and date of trade is not the same as the value date where the securities themselves are exchanged. Forwards, like other derivative securities, can be used to hedge risk (typically currency or exchange rate risk), as a means of speculation, or to allow a party to take advantage of a quality of the underlying instrument which is time-sensitive.

13

Future Contracts (or Futures)

13.1 What is a Future Contract?

A future contract is an agreement between two parties to buy or sell an asset at a certain time in future at a certain price. However, unlike forward contracts, the future contracts (or simply futures) are standardised and exchange traded. To facilitate liquidity in the future contracts, the exchange specifies certain standard features of the contract. It is a standardised contract with standard underlying instrument, a standard quantity and quality of the underlying instrument that can be delivered and a standard timing of such settlement.

A future contract may be offset prior to maturity by entering into an equal and opposite transaction. The standardised items in a future contract are as under:

1. Quantity of the underlying.
2. Quality of the underlying.
3. Date and the month of delivery.
4. Units of price quotation and minimum price change.
5. Location of settlement.

Future contracts are normally traded on an exchange. To make trading possible, the exchange specifies certain standardized features of the contract. As the two parties to the contract do not necessarily know each other the exchange also provides a mechanism, which gives the two parties a guarantee that the contract will be honoured. Future markets are designed to solve the problems that exist in forward markets.

Where the underlying asset happens to be a commodity, the futures contract is termed as *commodity futures* whereas in cases where the underlying happens to be a financial asset or instrument, the resultant futures contract is referred to as *financial futures*.

A currency futures contract, also called an FX future, is a type of financial futures contract where the underlying is an exchange rate. In other words, it is a futures contract to exchange one currency for another at a specified date in the future at a price (exchange rate) that is fixed on the last trading date. The buyer or seller in a futures market locks into an exchange rate for a specific value date or delivery date. In other words, currency futures are used primarily as a price setting mechanism rather than for physical exchange of currencies.

13.2 History of Futures

Future contracts, especially those which involve agricultural commodities, have been traded for long. The origin of futures can be traced back to 1851 when the Chicago Board of Trade (CBOT) introduced standardized forward contracts which were being traded in non-standard bilateral form for the preceding three years. Subsequently, contracts began to trade on commodities involving precious metals like gold, silver etc. However, significant changes have taken place in recent years with the development of financial future contracts. They represent a very significant financial innovation. Such contracts encompass a variety of underlying asset-security, stock indices, and interest rates and so on. The beginnings of financial futures were made with the introduction of foreign currency future contracts on the International Monetary Markets (IMM) in 1972. Subsequently, interest rate futures—where a contract is on an asset whose price is dependent solely on the level of interest rates—were introduced.

An important development took place in the world of future contracts in 1982 when stock index futures were introduced in US, after strong initial opposition to such contracts. A future contract on a stock index has been a revolutionary and novel idea because it represents a contract based not on a readily deliverable physical commodity or currency or other negotiable instrument. It is instead based on the concept of a mathematically measurable index that is determined by the market movements of a pre-determined set of equity stocks. Such contracts are now very widely traded the world over.

13.3 How Do Future Contracts Work?

Futures are derivative financial contracts that obligate the parties to transact an asset at a predetermined future date and price. Here, the buyer must purchase or the seller must sell the underlying asset at the set price, regardless of the current market price at the expiration date. Underlying assets include physical commodities or other financial instruments. Futures contracts detail the quantity of the underlying asset and are standardized to facilitate trading on a futures exchange. Futures can be used for hedging or trade speculation.

Future contracts are standardized, unlike forward contracts. Forwards are similar types of agreements that lock in a future price in the present, but forwards are traded over-the-counter (OTC) and have customizable terms that are arrived at between the counterparties. Futures contracts, on the other hand, will each have the same terms regardless of who is the counterparty.

Future contracts are used by two categories of market participants: hedgers and speculators. Producers or purchasers of an underlying asset hedge or guarantee the price at which the commodity is sold or purchased, while portfolio managers and traders may also make a bet on the price movements of an underlying asset using futures.

13.3.1 Example of Future Contract: A crude oil producer, averse to volatility of oil prices, wants to sell his produce 1 year from now. At the same time, a refinery needs crude oil to produce different types of petroleum products (petrol, diesel, kerosene etc.). It plans ahead and always needs crude oil coming periodically. Both parties can enter into a future contract with each other.

Assume that they both agree that crude oil producer will sell to the refinery 1 million barrel of oil at a price of US$ 45 per barrel (called contract price or delivery price) after 1 year.

At the end of 1 year (i.e. the time of delivery), the spot price (or current price) of crude oil has three possibilities:

1. It is exactly US$ 45 per barrel. In this case, no party is a loser or gainer.
2. It is higher than the contract price, say US$ 50 per barrel. The crude oil producer is a loser which *ipso facto* means that the refinery is a gainer.
3. It is lower than the contract price, say US$ 40 per barrel. The crude oil producer is a gainer.

Contracts are standardized. For example, one oil contract on the Chicago Mercantile Exchange (CME) is for 1,000 barrels of oil. Therefore, if someone wanted to lock-in a price (selling or buying) on 10,000 barrels of oil, he would need to buy/sell 10 contracts.

In the US, the futures markets are regulated by the Commodity Futures Trading Commission (CFTC). The CFTC is a federal agency created by Congress in 1974 to ensure the integrity of futures market pricing, including preventing abusive trading practices, fraud, and regulating brokerage firms engaged in futures trading.

The original use of future contracts was to mitigate the risk of price or exchange rate movements by allowing parties to fix prices or rates in advance for future transactions. This can be advantageous when a party expects to receive payment in foreign currency in the future, and wishes to guard against an unfavourable movement of the currency in the interval before payment is received.

However, future contracts also offer opportunities for speculation in that a trader who predicts that the price of an asset will move in a particular direction can contract to buy or sell it in the future at a price which (if the prediction is correct) will yield a profit. In particular, if the speculator is able to profit, then the underlying commodity that the speculator traded would have been saved during a time of surplus and sold during a time of need, offering the consumers of the commodity a more favourable distribution of commodity over time.

13.4 Hedgers and Speculators

Hedgers typically include producers and consumers of a commodity or the owner of an asset or assets subject to certain influences such as an interest rate. For example, in traditional commodity markets, farmers often sell future contracts for the crops and livestock they produce to guarantee a certain price, making it easier for them to plan. Similarly, livestock producers often purchase futures to cover their feed costs, so that they can plan on a fixed cost for feed. In modern (financial) markets, *producers* of interest rate swaps or equity derivative products will use financial futures or equity index futures to reduce or remove the risk on the swap.

Investment fund managers at the portfolio and the fund sponsor level can use financial asset futures to manage portfolio interest rate risk, or duration, without making cash purchases or sales using bond futures. Investment firms that receive capital calls or capital inflows in a different currency than their base currency could use currency futures to hedge the currency risk of that inflow in the future.

Speculators typically fall into three categories: position traders, day traders, and swing traders (swing trading), though many hybrid types and unique styles exist. With many investors pouring into the futures markets in recent years, controversy has risen about whether speculators are responsible for increased volatility in commodities like oil, and experts are divided on the matter.

13.5 Role of Clearing House

Future contracts are traded on commodity exchanges or other future exchanges. People can buy or sell futures like other commodities. When an investor buys a future contract on an organized future exchange, he is in fact assuming the right and obligation of taking the delivery of the specified underlying item on a specified date. Similarly, when an investor sells a contract, to take a short position, one assumes the right and obligation to make the delivery of the underlying asset. There is no risk of non-performance in the case of trading in the future contracts. This is because a clearing house or a clearing corporation is associated with the futures exchange, which plays a pivotal role in the trading of futures. A clearing house takes the opposite in each trade, so that it becomes the buyer to the seller and vice versa. When a party takes a short position in a contract, it is obliged to sell the underlying commodity in question at the stipulated price to the clearing house on maturity of the contract. Similarly, an investor who takes a long position on the contract can seek its performance through the clearing house only.

13.5.1 Margin Requirement: It is noteworthy that while a clearing house guarantees the performance of the future contracts, the parties in the contracts are required to keep margins with it. The margins are taken to ensure that each party to a contract performs its part. The margins are adjusted on a daily basis to account for the gains or losses, depending upon the situation. This is known as marking-to-market and involves giving a credit to the buyer of the contract, if the price of the contract rises, debiting the seller's account by an equal amount. Similarly, the buyer's balance is reduced when the contract price declines and the seller's account is accordingly updated.

13.6 Currency Futures

The birth of currency futures is of a recent origin and was a sequel to the breakdown of the Bretton Woods system. The resultant currency volatility provided a business opportunity for launching futures contracts in foreign currencies. The Chicago Mercantile Exchange (CME) first conceived the idea of a currency futures exchange and it launched the same in 1972 amidst considerable scepticism, since traditionally futures market had traded agricultural commodities and not financial instruments. The CME commissioned Professor Milton Friedman to write a paper on currency futures in order to gain credibility in the market. Professor Milton Friedman stated, "Changes in the international financial structure will create a great expansion in the demand for foreign cover. It is highly desirable that this demand be met by as broad, as deep, as resilient a futures market in foreign currencies as possible in order to facilitate foreign trade and investment. Such a wider market is almost certain to develop in response to the demand. The major open question is where. The US is a natural place and it is very much in the interests of the US that it should develop here". The CBOT saw this as a competitive challenge, as also an opportunity to launch other financial futures and proposed trading options and futures on stocks.

13.6.1 The Rationale: The rationale for establishing currency futures market is manifold. Both residents and non-residents are exposed to currency risk when residents purchase foreign currency assets and non-residents purchase domestic currency assets. If the exchange rate remains unchanged from the time of the purchase of the asset to its sale, no gains and losses are made out of currency exposures. But if domestic currency depreciates (appreciates) against the foreign currency, the exposure would result in gain (loss) for residents purchasing foreign assets and loss (gain) for non-residents purchasing domestic asset. In this backdrop, unpredicted movements in exchange rates expose investors to currency risks. Currency futures enable them to hedge these risks. Nominal exchange rates are often random walks with or without drift, while real exchange rates over long-run are mean reverting. As such, it is possible that over a long-run, the incentive to hedge currency risk may not be large.

However, financial planning horizon is much smaller than the long-run, which is typically inter-generational in the context of exchange rates. As such, there is a strong need to hedge currency risk and this need has grown manifold with fast growth in cross-border trade and investments flows. The argument for hedging currency risks appear to be natural in case of assets, and applies equally to trade in goods and services, which result in income flows with leads and lags and get converted into different currencies at the market rates. Empirically, changes in exchange rate are found to have very low correlations with foreign equity and bond returns. This in theory should lower portfolio risk. Therefore, sometimes argument is advanced against the need for hedging currency risks. But there is strong empirical evidence to suggest that hedging reduces the volatility of returns and indeed considering the episodic nature of currency returns, there are strong arguments to use instruments to hedge currency risks.

Currency risks could be hedged mainly through forwards, futures, swaps and options. Each of these instruments has its role in managing the currency risk. The main advantage of currency futures over its closest substitute product, viz., forwards which are traded over-the-counter (OTC) lies in price transparency, elimination of counterparty credit risk and greater reach in terms of easy accessibility to all. Currency futures are expected to bring about better price discovery and also possibly lower transaction costs. Apart from pure hedgers, currency futures also invite arbitrageurs, speculators and noise traders who may take a bet on exchange rate movements without an underlying or an economic exposure as a motivation for trading.

From an economy-wide perspective, currency futures contribute to hedging of risks and help traders and investors in undertaking their economic activity. There is a large body of empirical evidence which suggests that exchange rate volatility has an adverse impact on foreign trade. Since there are first order gains from trade which contribute to output growth and consumer welfare, currency futures can potentially have an important impact on real economy. Gains from international risk sharing through trade in assets could be of relatively smaller magnitude than gains from trade. However, in a dynamic setting these investments could still significantly impact capital formation in an economy and as such currency futures could be seen as a facilitator in promoting investment and aggregate demand in the economy, thus promoting growth.

13.7 Distinction between Forwards and Futures

Both forward and future contracts involve the agreement to buy or sell a commodity at a set price in the future. But there are differences between the two. While a forward contract does not trade on an exchange, a future contract does. Settlement for the forward contract takes place at the end of the contract, while the future contract settles on a daily basis. Most importantly, future contracts exist as standardized contracts that are not customized between counterparties. Forwards also typically have no interim partial settlements or *true-ups* in margin requirements like futures, i.e. the parties do not exchange additional property securing the party at gain and the entire unrealized gain or loss builds up while the contract is open. Therefore forward contracts have a significant counterparty risk which is also the reason why they are not readily available to retail investors. However, being traded over-the-counter (OTC), forward contracts specification can be customized and may include mark-to-market and daily margin calls.

Forward and future contracts are different in following respects.

13.7.1 Standardization: A forward contract is a tailor-made contract between the buyer and the seller where the terms are settled in mutual agreement between the parties. On the other hand, a future contract is standardized in regards to the quality, quantity, place of delivery of the asset etc. Only the price is negotiated. Forwards are popular on the over-the-counter (OTC) market. Futures are traded on an organised stock exchange. Exchange-traded derivatives tend to be more standardised and offer greater liquidity than OTC contracts, which are negotiated between counterparties and tailored to meet the needs of the parties to the contract. Exchange-traded derivatives also offer centralised limits on individual positions and have formal rules for risk and burden sharing.

13.7.2 Liquidity: There is no secondary market for forward contracts while future contracts are traded on organized exchanges. Accordingly, future contracts are usually much more liquid than the forward contracts. Forwards have customised contract terms, and therefore they are less liquid. Futures have standardised contract terms, and hence they are more liquid.

It is not necessary to hold on to a future contract until maturity and one can easily close out a position. Either of the parties may reverse their position by initiating a reverse trade, so that the original buyer of a contract can sell an identical contract at a later date, cancelling, in effect, the original contract. Thus, the exchange facilitates subsequent selling (buying) of a contract so that a party can offset its position and eliminate the obligation. The fact that the buyer as well as the seller of a contract is free to transfer his interest in the contract to another party makes such contracts highly liquid in nature. In fact, most of the future contracts are cancelled by the parties, by engaging into reverse trades: the buyers cancel a contract by selling another contract, while the seller does so by buying another contract. Only a very small portion of them is held for actual delivery.

13.7.3 Conclusion of Contract: A forward contract is generally concluded with a delivery of the asset in question whereas the future contracts are settled sometimes with delivery of the asset and generally with the payment of the price differences. One who holds a contract can always eliminate his/her obligation by subsequently selling a contract for the same asset and same delivery date, before the conclusion of contract one holds. In the same manner, the seller of a future contract can buy a similar contract and offset his/her position before maturity of the first contract. Each one of these actions is called offsetting a trade.

13.7.4 Margins: A forward contract has zero value for both the parties involved so that no collateral is required for entering into such a contract. There are only two parties involved. But in a futures contract, a third party called Clearing Corporation is also involved with which margin is required to be kept by both parties. In other words, forwards require no margin payments. Futures require margin payments.

13.7.5 Profit/Loss Settlement: The settlement of a forward contract takes place on the date of maturity so that the profit/loss is booked on maturity only. On the other hand, the future contracts are marked-to-market daily so that the profits or losses are settled daily. In other words, in the case of forwards, settlement happens at the end of the period. Futures follow daily settlement.

Thus, future contracts are a significant improvement over forward contracts as they eliminate counterparty risk and offer more liquidity.

Future contracts represent an improvement over the forward contracts in terms of standardization, performance guarantee and liquidity. A future contract is a standardized contract between two parties where one of the parties commits to sell, and the other to buy, a stipulated quantity of a commodity, currency, security, index or some other specified item at an agreed price on a given date in the future.

13.8 Introduction of Futures in India

The first derivative product introduced in the Indian securities market was *index futures* in June 2000. In India, the *stock futures* were first introduced on November 9, 2001.

The Indian capital market has grown quite well since the early 1990s. In the boom period of 1992 and thereafter, even the common man was attracted to the stock market. The stock market was considered a profitable investment opportunity. Before July 2001, various stock exchanges including the Bombay Stock Exchange (BSE), National Stock Exchange (NSE) and Delhi Stock Exchange, provided carry forward facilities through the traditional *badla* system. By means of this system the purchase or sale of a security was not postponed till a particular future date; instead the system only provided for the carry forward of a transaction from one settlement period (seven days) to the next settlement period for the payment of a fee known as *badla* charges.

In the *badla* system, due to limited settlement period and no future price discovery, a speculator could manipulate prices, thus causing loss to small investors and ultimately eroding investors' confidence in the capital market. Hence, the necessity of futures trading in the capital market was emphasized. In the absence of an efficient futures market, there was no price discovery and therefore prices could be moved in any desired direction. Recent developments in the capital market culminated in a ban on *badla* from July 2001.

In the absence of futures trading, certain operators—either on their own or in collusion with corporate management teams—at times manipulated prices in the secondary market, causing irreparable damage to the growth of the market. The small and medium investors, who are the backbone of the market and whose savings come to the market via primary or secondary routes shied away. As the small investors avoided the capital market, the downturn in the secondary market ultimately affected the primary market because people stopped investing in share for fear of loss or liquidity. Introducing futures in major shares along with index futures helped to revive the capital market. This not only provided liquidity and efficiency to the market, but also helped in future price discovery.

13.8.1 Currency Futures: Globalisation and integration of financial markets, coupled with the progressively increasing cross-border flow of funds, have transformed the intensity of market risk, which, in turn, has made the issues relating to hedging of such risk exposures very critical. The economic agents in India currently have a menu of over-the-counter (OTC) products, such as forwards, swaps and options, available to them for hedging their currency risk and the markets for these are quite deep and liquid. However, in the context of growing integration of the Indian economy with the rest of the world, as also the continued development of financial markets, a need has been felt to make available a wider choice of hedging instruments to the market participants to enable them to cope better with their currency risk exposures.

To sum up, a futures contract is a legal agreement to buy or sell a particular commodity asset, or security at a predetermined price at a specified time in the future. Future contracts are standardized for quality and quantity to facilitate trading on an exchange. The buyer of a futures contract is taking on the obligation to buy and receive the underlying asset when the futures contract expires. The seller of the futures contract is taking on the obligation to provide and deliver the underlying asset at the expiration date.

Thus, both the parties of the futures contract must fulfil their contractual obligations on the settlement date. However, such contracts do provide options to deliver the underlying asset or settle the difference in cash. The holder of a contract could exit from his commitment prior to the settlement date by either selling a long position or buying back a short position (offset or reverse trade). The futures contracts are exchange traded derivatives and the exchange's clearing house acts as counterparty to all contracts, sets margin requirements etc.

14

Options

14.1 What is an Option?

An option is a contract which gives the buyer the right, but not the obligation, to buy or sell specified quantity of the underlying assets, at a specific (strike) price on or before a specified time (expiration date). The underlying may be a commodity like wheat or rice or financial instrument like equity stock or bonds etc.

Like forwards and futures, options represent another derivative instrument and provide a mechanism by which one can acquire a certain commodity or other asset in order to make profit or cover risk for a price. The options are similar to the future contracts in the sense that they are also standardized but are different from them in many ways. Options, in fact, represent the rights.

An option is the right, but not the obligation, to buy or sell a specified amount (and quality) of a commodity, currency, index, or financial instrument, or to buy or sell a specified number of underlying future contracts, at a specific price on or before a given date in future.

Similar to other contracts, there are two parties to an option contract: the buyer who takes a long position and the seller or writer, who takes a short position. The option contract gives the owner a right to buy/sell a particular commodity or other asset at a specific pre-destined price by a specified date. The price involved is called exercise or strike price and the date involved is known as expiration. It is important to understand that such a contract gives its holder the right, and not the obligation to buy/sell. The option writer, on the other hand, undertakes upon himself the obligation to sell/buy the underlying asset if that suits the option holder. There is a wide variety of underlying assets including agricultural commodities, metals, shares, indices and so on, on which options are written.

Further, like future contracts, options are also tradable on exchanges. The exchange-traded options are standardized contracts and their trading is regulated by the exchanges that ensure the honouring of such contracts. Thus, in case of options as well, a clearing corporation takes the other side in every contract so that the party with the long position has a claim against the clearing corporation and the one with short position is obliged to it. However, buying or selling of future contracts does not require any price to be paid, called premium. The writer of an option receives the premium as a compensation of the risk that he takes upon himself. The premium belongs to the writer and is not adjusted in the price if the holder of the option decides to exercise it. This price is determined on the exchange, like the price of a share, by the forces of demand and supply. Further, like the share prices, the option prices also keep on changing with passage of time as trading takes place.

One difference between future and option trading may be noted. Whereas both parties to a future contract are required to deposit margins to the exchange, only the party with the short position is called upon to pay margin in case of options trading. The party with the long position does not pay anything beyond the premium.

14.2 Options in Historical Perspective

Options were traded in the US and UK during the 19th century but confined mainly to the agricultural commodities. Earlier, they were declared illegal in UK in 1733 and remained so until 1860 when the Act declaring them illegal was repealed. In the US, options on equity stocks of the companies were available on the over-the-counter (OTC) market only, until April 1973. They were not standardized and involved the intra-party risk. In India, options on stocks of companies, though illegal, were traded for many years on a limited scale in the form of *teji* and *mandi*, and related transactions. As such, this trading was a very risky proposition to undertake.

In spite of the long time that has elapsed since the inception of options, they were, until not very long ago, looked down upon as mere speculative tools and associated with corrupt practices. Things changed dramatically in the 1970s when options were transformed from relative obscurity to a systematically traded asset which is an integral part of financial portfolios.

In fact, the year 1973 witnessed some major developments. Black and Scholes published a seminal paper explaining the basic principal of options pricing and hedging. In the same year, the Chicago Board Options Exchange was created. It was the first registered securities exchange dedicated to options trading. While trading in options existed for long, it experienced a gigantic growth with the creation of this exchange. The listing of options meant orderly and thicker markets for this kind of securities. Options trading is now undertaken widely in many countries besides the US and UK. In fact, options have become an integral part of the large and developed financial markets.

Options are basically of two types: call options and put options.

14.3 Call Options

A call option is an option to buy a stock at a specific price on or before a certain date. In this way, call options are like security deposits. If, for example, Mr. Wilson wants to rent a certain property, and leaves a security deposit for it, the money would be used to insure that he would, in fact, rent that property at the price agreed upon when he returns. If Mr. Wilson never returns, he would lose his security deposit, but he would have no other liability.

Call options usually increase in value as the value of the underlying instrument rises. When you buy a call option, the price you pay for it, called the option premium, secures your right to buy that certain stock at a specified price called the strike price. If you decide not to use the option to buy the stock, and you are not obligated to, your only cost is the *option premium*.

14.3.1 Risk and Profits from Buying Call Options: Call options let the holder buy an underlying security at the stated strike price by the expiration date called the expiry. The holder has no obligation to buy the asset if he does not want to purchase the asset. The risk to the call option buyer is limited to the premium paid. Fluctuations of the underlying stock have no impact.

Call options buyers are bullish on a stock and believe the share price will rise above the strike price before the option's expiry. If the investor's bullish outlook is realized and the stock price increases above the strike price, the investor can exercise the option, buy the stock at the strike price, and immediately sell the stock at the current market price for a profit.

Their profit on this trade is the market share price less the strike share price plus the expense of the option—the premium and any brokerage commission to place the orders. The result would be multiplied by the number of option contracts purchased, then multiplied by 100—assuming each contract represents 100 shares.

However, if the underlying stock price does not move above the strike price by the expiration date, the option expires worthlessly. The holder is not required to buy the shares but will lose the premium paid for the call.

14.3.2 Risk and Profits from Selling Call Options: Selling call options is known as writing a contract. The writer receives the premium fee. In other words, an option buyer will pay the premium to the writer (or seller) of an option. The maximum profit is the premium received when selling the option. An investor who sells a call option is bearish and believes that the underlying price of the stock will fall or remain relatively close to the option's strike price during the life of the option.

If the prevailing market share price is at or below the strike price by expiry, the option expires worthlessly for the call buyer. The option seller pockets the premium as their profit. The option is not exercised because the option buyer would not buy the stock at the strike price higher than or equal to the prevailing market price.

However, if the market share price is more than the strike price at expiry, the seller of the option must sell the shares to an option buyer at that lower strike price. In other words, the seller must either sell shares from their portfolio holdings or buy the stock at the prevailing market price to sell to the call option buyer. The contract writer incurs a loss. How large of a loss depends on the cost basis of the shares they must use to cover the option order, plus any brokerage order expenses, but less any premium they received.

It is clear that the risk to the call writers is far greater than the risk exposure of call buyers. The call buyer only loses the premium. The writer faces infinite risk because the stock price could continue to rise increasing losses significantly.

14.4 Put Options

Put options are options to sell a stock at a specific price on or before a certain date. In this way, put options are like insurance policies. If you buy a new car, and then buy auto insurance on the car, you pay a premium and are, hence, protected if the asset is damaged in an accident. If this happens, you can use your policy to regain the insured value of the car. In this way, the put option gains in value as the value of the underlying instrument decreases. If all goes well and the insurance is not needed, the insurance company keeps your premium in return for taking on the risk.

With a put option, you can *insure* a stock by fixing a selling price. If something happens which causes the stock price to fall, and thus, *damages* your asset, you can exercise your option and sell it at its *insured* price level. If the price of your stock goes up, and there is no *damage*, then you do not need to use the insurance, and, once again, your only cost is the premium.

Buying put options is buying insurance. To buy a put option on Nifty [1] is to buy insurance which reimburses the full extent to which Nifty drops below the strike price of the put option. This is attractive to many people, and to mutual funds creating *guaranteed return products*. The Nifty index fund industry will find it very useful to make a bundle of a Nifty index fund and a Nifty put option to create a new kind of a Nifty index fund, which gives the investor protection against extreme drops in Nifty. Selling put options is selling insurance, so anyone who feels like earning revenues by selling insurance can set himself up to do so on the index options market.

14.4.1 Risk and Profits from Buying Put Options: Put options are investments where the buyer believes that the market price of underlying stock will fall below the strike price on or before the expiration date of the option. Once again, the holder can sell shares without the obligation to sell at the stated strike per share price by the stated date.

Since buyers of put options want the stock price to decrease, the put option is profitable when the price of underlying stock is below the strike price. If the prevailing market price is less than the strike price at expiry, the investor can exercise the put. He will sell shares at the option's higher strike price. Should he wish to replace his holding of these shares he may buy them on the open market.

His profit on this trade is the strike price less the current market price, plus expenses—the premium and any brokerage commission to place the orders. The result would be multiplied by the number of option contracts purchased, then multiplied by 100—assuming each contract represents 100 shares.

The value of holding a put option will increase as the underlying stock price decreases. Conversely, the value of the put option declines as the stock price increases. The risk of buying put options is limited to the loss of the premium if the option expires worthlessly.

14.4.2 Risk and Profits from Selling Put Options: Selling put options is also known as writing a contract. A put option writer believes the underlying stock's price will stay the same or increase over the life of the option—making them bullish on the shares. Here, the option buyer has the right to make the seller, buy shares of the underlying asset at the strike price on expiry.

If the underlying stock's price closes above the strike price by the expiration date, the put option expires worthlessly. The writer's maximum profit is the premium. The option is not exercised because the option buyer would not sell the stock at the lower strike share price when the market price is more.

However, if the stock's market value falls below the option strike price, the put option writer is obligated to buy shares of the underlying stock at the strike price. In other words, the put option will be exercised by the option buyer. The buyer will sell their shares at the strike price since it is higher than the stock's market value.

The risk for the put option writer happens when the market's price falls below the strike price. Now, at expiration, the seller is forced to purchase shares at the strike price. Depending on how much the shares have appreciated, the put writer's loss can be significant.

The put writer (the seller) can either hold on to the shares and hope the stock price rises back above the purchase price or sell the shares and take the loss. However, any loss is offset somewhat by the premium received.

14.5 Example of an Option

Suppose that Facebook shares are trading at US$ 108 per share and Mr. Wilson believes that they are going to increase in value. He decides to buy a call option to benefit from the perceived increase in the price of the stock.

He purchases one call option with a strike price of US$ 115 for 1 month in the future for 37 cents per share. His total cash outlay is US$ 37 for the position (0.37 x 100 = US$ 37). One option contract represents 100 shares.

If the stock rises to US$ 116, his option will be worth US$ 1, because he can exercise the option to acquire the stock for US$ 115 per share and immediately resell it for US$ 116 per share. The profit on the option position would be 170.3 percent since he paid 37 cents and earned US$ 1, i.e. much higher than the 7.4 percent increase in the underlying stock price from US$ 108 to US$ 116 at the time of expiry.

In other words, the profit in dollar terms would be a net of 63 cents per share or US$ 63 for the option contract (US$ 1 – 0.37 x 100 = US$ 63).

If the stock fell to US$ 100, his option would expire worthlessly, and he would be out US$ 37 premium. The upside is that he did not buy 100 shares at US$ 108, which would have resulted in an US$ 8 per share, or US$ 800, total loss. As is evident, options helped Mr. Wilson limit his downside risk.

14.5.1 Option Spreads: Option spreads are strategies that use various combinations of buying and selling different options for a desired risk-return profile. Spreads are constructed using vanilla options, and can take advantage of various scenarios such as high- or low-volatility environments, up- or down-moves, or anything in-between. Spread strategies, can be characterized by their payoff or visualizations of their profit-loss profile, such as bull call spreads or iron condors.

14.6 Advantages of Option Trading

14.5.1 Risk Management: Put options allow investors holding shares to hedge against a possible fall in their value. This can be considered similar to taking out insurance against a fall in the share price.

14.6.2 Time to Decide: By taking a call option the purchase price for the shares is locked-in. This gives the call option holder until the expiry day to decide whether or not to exercise the option and buy the shares. Likewise, the taker of a put option has time to decide whether or not to sell the shares.

14.6.3 Speculation: The ease of trading in and out of an option position makes it possible to trade options with no intention of ever exercising them. If an investor expects the market to rise, he may decide to buy call options. If expecting a fall, he may decide to buy put options. Either way the holder can sell the option prior to expiry to take a profit or limit a loss. Trading options has a lower cost than shares, as there is no stamp duty payable unless and until options are exercised.

14.6.4 Leverage: Leverage provides the potential to make a higher return from a smaller initial outlay than investing directly. However, leverage usually involves more risks than a direct investment in the underlying shares. Trading in options can allow investors to benefit from a change in the price of the share without having to pay the full price of the share.

14.6.5 Income Generation: Shareholders can earn extra income over and above dividends by writing call options against their shares. By writing an option they receive the option premium upfront. While they get to keep the option premium, there is a possibility that they could be exercised against and have to deliver their shares to the taker at the exercise price.

14.6.6 Strategies: By combining different options, investors can create a wide range of potential profit scenarios.

14.7 Forms of Option Trading

14.7.1 Exchange-traded Options: Also called *listed options*, these are a class of exchange-traded derivatives. Exchange-traded options have standardized contracts, and are settled through a clearing house with fulfillment guaranteed by the Options Clearing Corporation (OCC). Since the contracts are standardized, accurate pricing models are often available. Exchange-traded options include the following:

1. Stock options.
2. Bond options and other interest rate options.
3. Stock market index options.
4. Options on futures contracts.
5. Callable bull/bear contract.

As an intermediary to both sides of the transaction, the benefits the exchange provides to the transaction include the following:

1. Fulfillment of the contract is backed by the credit of the exchange, which typically has the highest rating (AAA).
2. Counterparties remain anonymous.
3. Enforcement of market regulation to ensure fairness and transparency.
4. Maintenance of orderly markets, especially during fast trading conditions.

14.7.2 Over-the-counter Options: Over-the-counter options (OTC options, also called *dealer options*) are traded between two private parties, and are not listed on an exchange. The terms of an OTC option are unrestricted and may be individually tailored to meet any business need. In general, the option writer is a well-capitalized institution (in order to prevent the credit risk). Option types commonly traded over the counter include:

1. Interest rate options
2. Currency cross rate options, and
3. Options on swaps or swaptions.

By avoiding an exchange, users of OTC options can narrowly tailor the terms of the option contract to suit individual business requirements. In addition, OTC option transactions generally do not need to be advertised to the market and face little or no regulatory requirements. However, OTC counterparties must establish credit lines with each other, and conform to each other's clearing and settlement procedures.

14.8 Valuation Models

The value of the option is estimated using a variety of quantitative techniques, all based on the principle of risk-neutral pricing, and using stochastic calculus in their solution. In general, standard option valuation models depend on the following factors:

1. Current market price of the underlying security.
2. Strike price of the option, particularly in relation to the current market price of the underlying.
3. Cost of holding a position in the underlying security, including interest and dividends.
4. Estimate of the future volatility of the underlying security's price over the life of the option.

The following are some of the principal valuation techniques used in practice to evaluate option contracts.

14.8.1 Black-Scholes Model: There are various models which help us get close to the true price of an option. Most of these are variants of the celebrated Black-Scholes model for pricing European options. By employing the technique of constructing a risk neutral portfolio that replicates the returns of holding an option, Black and Scholes produced a closed-form solution for a European option's theoretical price. At the same time, the model generates hedge parameters necessary for effective risk management of option holdings.

While the ideas behind the Black-Scholes model were ground-breaking, the application of the model in actual options trading is clumsy because of the assumptions of continuous trading, constant volatility, and a constant interest rate. Nevertheless, the Black-Scholes model is still one of the most important methods and foundations for the existing financial market in which the result is within the reasonable range.

For details, see chapter 15 of this book.

14.8.2 Binomial Tree Pricing Model: Closely following the derivation of Black-Scholes, John Cox, Stephen Ross and Mark Rubinstein developed the original version of the binomial options pricing model. It models the dynamics of the option's theoretical value for discrete time intervals over the option's life. The model starts with a binomial tree of discrete future possible underlying stock prices. By constructing a riskless portfolio of an option and stock (as in the Black-Scholes model) a simple formula can be used to find the option price at each node in the tree. This value can approximate the theoretical value produced by Black-Scholes, to the desired degree of precision.

However, the binomial model is considered more accurate than Black-Scholes because it is more flexible; e.g., discrete future dividend payments can be modeled correctly at the proper forward time steps, and American options can be modeled as well as European ones. Binomial models are widely used by professional option traders.

For details, see chapter 16 of this book.

14.9 Options Risk Metrics: The Greeks

The *Greeks* is a term used in the options market to describe the different dimensions of risk involved in taking an options position, either in a particular option or a portfolio of options. These variables are called Greeks because they are typically associated with Greek symbols. Each risk variable is a result of an imperfect assumption or relationship of the option with another underlying variable. Traders use different Greek values, such as delta, theta, and others, to assess options risk and manage option portfolios.

Delta (Δ) represents the rate of change between the option's price and a US$ 1 change in the underlying asset's price. In other words, it signifies the price sensitivity of the option relative to the underlying. Delta of a call option has a range between 0 and 1, while the delta of a put option has a range between 0 and negative 1.

Theta (Θ) represents the rate of change between the option price and time, or time sensitivity, sometimes known as an option's time decay. Theta indicates the amount an option's price would decrease as the time to expiration decreases, all else equal.

Gamma (Γ) represents the rate of change between an option's delta and the underlying asset's price. This is called second-order (second-derivative) price sensitivity. Gamma indicates the amount the delta would change given a US$ 1 move in the underlying security. Gamma is used to determine how stable an option's delta is: higher gamma values indicate that delta could change dramatically in response to even small movements in the underlying's price.

Vega (V) represents the rate of change between an option's value and the underlying asset's implied volatility. This is the option's sensitivity to volatility. Vega indicates the amount an option's price changes given a 1 percent change in implied volatility.

Rho (p) represents the rate of change between an option's value and a 1 percent change in the interest rate. This measures sensitivity to the interest rate.

Some other Greeks, with are not discussed as often, are lambda, epsilon, vomma, vera, speed, zomma, color, ultima.

To conclude, options are financial instruments that are derivatives based on the value of underlying securities such as stocks. An options contract offers the buyer the opportunity to buy or sell—depending on the type of contract they hold—the underlying asset. Unlike futures, the holder is not required to buy or sell the asset if they choose not to.

Call options allow the holder to buy the asset at a stated price within a specific timeframe. Put options allow the holder to sell the asset at a stated price within a specific timeframe.

Each option contract will have a specific expiration date by which the holder must exercise their option. The stated price on an option is known as the strike price. Options are typically bought and sold through online or retail brokers.

Endnote

1. Nifty is a market index introduced by the National Stock Exchange (NSE) in India. It is a blended word—National Stock Exchange Fifty—coined by NSE. Nifty is one of the two national indices, the other being SENSEX, a product of the Bombay Stock Exchange.

15

Black-Scholes-Merton Option Pricing Model

15.1 What is Black-Scholes Model?

The Black-Scholes model, also known as the Black-Scholes-Merton (BSM) model, is a mathematical model for pricing an options contract. In particular, the model estimates the variation over time of financial instruments. It assumes these instruments (such as stocks or futures) will have a lognormal distribution of prices. Using this assumption and factoring in other important variables, the equation derives the price of a call option.

The formula, developed by three economists—Fischer Black, Myron Scholes and Robert Merton—is perhaps the world's most well-known options pricing model. The initial equation was introduced in Black and Scholes' 1973 paper, "The Pricing of Options and Corporate Liabilities", published in the *Journal of Political Economy*. Black passed away two years before Scholes and Merton were awarded the 1997 Nobel Prize in economics for their work in finding a new method to determine the value of derivatives However, the Nobel committee acknowledged Black's role in the Black-Scholes model. The committee cited their discovery of the risk neutral dynamic revision as a breakthrough that separates the option from the risk of the underlying security.

The key idea behind the model is to hedge the option by buying and selling the underlying asset in just the right way and, as a consequence, to eliminate risk. This type of hedging is called *continuously revised delta hedging* and is the basis of more complicated hedging strategies such as those engaged in by investment banks and hedge funds.

15.2 Basics of the Black-Scholes Model

It is the first widely used model for option pricing. It is used to calculate the theoretical value of options using current stock prices, expected dividends, the option's strike price, expected interest rates, time to expiration and expected volatility.

The Black-Scholes formula has only one parameter that cannot be directly observed in the market: the average future volatility of the underlying asset, though it can be found from the price of other options. Since the option value (whether put or call) is increasing in this parameter, it can be inverted to produce a *volatility surface* that is then used to calibrate other models, e.g. for OTC derivatives.

The model assumes the price of heavily traded assets follows a geometric Brownian motion with constant drift and volatility. When applied to a stock option, the model incorporates the constant price variation of the stock, the time value of money, the option's strike price, and the time to the option's expiry.

The Black-Scholes model is mainly used to calculate the theoretical value of European-style options and it cannot be applied to the American-style options due to their feature to be exercised before the maturity date.

The Black-Scholes model was designed to value options that can be exercised only at expiration. Options with this characteristic are called European options. In contrast, most options that we encounter in practice can be exercised any time until expiration. These options are called American options. The possibility of early exercise makes American options more valuable than otherwise similar European options. In general, though, with traded options, it is almost always better to sell the option to someone else rather than exercise early because options have a time premium, i.e., they sell for more than their exercise value.

Black-Scholes pricing model is largely used by option traders who buy options that are priced under the formula calculated value, and sell options that are priced higher than the Black-Scholes calculated value.

There are two important models for option pricing, Binomial Model and Black-Scholes Model. The model is used to determine the price of a European call option, which simply means that the option can only be exercised on the expiration date. While Black-Scholes model is mathematically complicated, there is a simpler binomial model for valuing options that draws on the same logic.

15.3 Assumptions of Black-Scholes Model

The model operates under the certain assumptions regarding the distribution of the stock price and the economic environment.

1. The option is European and can only be exercised at expiration.
2. No dividends are paid out during the life of the option.
3. Markets are efficient (i.e. market movements cannot be predicted).
4. There are no transaction costs in buying the option.
5. The risk-free rate and volatility of the underlying are known and constant.
6. The returns on the underlying asset are normally distributed.

The model's assumptions have been relaxed and generalized in many directions, leading to a plethora of models that are currently used in derivative pricing and risk management. It is the insights of the model, as exemplified in the Black-Scholes formula, that are frequently used by market participants, as distinguished from the actual prices. These insights include no-arbitrage bounds and risk-neutral pricing. Further, the Black-Scholes equation, a partial differential equation that governs the price of the option, enables pricing using numerical methods when an explicit formula is not possible.

While the original Black-Scholes model did not consider the effects of dividends paid during the life of the option, the model is frequently adapted to account for dividends by determining the ex-dividend date value of the underlying stock.

15.4 Black-Scholes Formula

The mathematics involved in the formula is complicated. Call option formula is calculated by multiplying the stock price by the cumulative standard normal probability distribution function. Thereafter, the net present value (NPV) of the strike price multiplied by the cumulative standard normal distribution is subtracted from the resulting value of the previous calculation.

In mathematical notation:

$C = S_t N (d_1) - K_e^{-rt} N (d_2)$

Where

$d_1 = \ln \dfrac{S_t}{K} + (r + \sigma^2 p) t \div \sigma s \sqrt{t}$

and

$d_2 = d_1 - \sigma s \sqrt{t}$

Where

C = Call option price.

S = Current stock price.

K = Strike price.

r = Risk-free interest rate.

t = Time to maturity.

N = A normal distribution.

What does the Black-Scholes Model tell? Black Scholes model is one of the most important concepts in modern financial theory. It was developed in 1973 by Fischer Black, Robert Merton, and Myron Scholes and is still widely used today. It is regarded as one of the best ways of determining fair prices of options. The Black-Scholes model requires the following 5 input variables:

1.   The strike price of an option.
2.   The current stock price.
3.   The time to expiration.
4.   Risk-free rate.
5.   Volatility.

The model assumes that stock prices follow a lognormal distribution because asset prices cannot be negative (they are bounded by zero). This is also known as a Gaussian distribution. Often, asset prices are observed to have significant right skewness and some degree of kurtosis (fat tails). This means high-risk downward moves often happen more often in the market than a normal distribution predicts.

The assumption of lognormal underlying asset prices should thus show that implied volatilities are similar for each strike price according to the Black-Scholes model. However, since the market crash of 1987, implied volatilities for at the money options have been lower than those further out of the money or far in the money. The reason for this phenomenon is the market is pricing in a greater likelihood of a high volatility move to the downside in the markets.

This has led to the presence of the volatility skew. When the implied volatilities for options with the same expiration date are mapped out on a graph, a smile or skew shape can be seen.

Thus, the Black-Scholes model is not efficient for calculating implied volatility.

15.5 Limitations of the Black-Scholes Model

As stated earlier, the Black Scholes model is only used to price European options. Moreover, the model assumes dividends and risk-free rates are constant, but this may not be true in reality. The model also assumes volatility remains constant over the option's life, which is not the case because volatility fluctuates with the level of supply and demand.

Further, the model assumes that there are no transaction costs or taxes; that the risk-free interest rate is constant for all maturities; that short selling of securities with use of proceeds is permitted; and that there are no risk-less arbitrage opportunities. These assumptions can lead to prices that deviate from the real world where these factors are present.

The model is based upon the assumption that exercising an option does not affect the value of the underlying asset. This may be true for listed options on stocks, but it is not true for some other types of options.

The Black-Scholes model was designed to value options that can be exercised only at maturity and on underlying assets that do not pay dividends. In addition, options are valued based upon the assumption that option exercise does not affect the value of the underlying asset. In practice, assets do pay dividends, options sometimes get exercised early and exercising an option can affect the value of the underlying asset. Adjustments exist. While they are not perfect, adjustments provide partial corrections to the Black-Scholes model.

To sum up, Black-Scholes model is a mathematical model for the dynamics of a financial market containing derivative investment instruments. From the partial differential equation in the model, known as the Black–Scholes equation, one can deduce the Black-Scholes formula, which gives a theoretical estimate of the price of European-style options and shows that the option has a *unique* price regardless of the risk of the security and its expected return (instead replacing the security's expected return with the risk-neutral rate). The formula led to a boom in options trading and provided mathematical legitimacy to the activities of the Chicago Board Options Exchange and other options markets around the world. It is widely used, although often with some adjustments, by options market participants.

Black-Scholes is a pricing model used to determine the fair price or theoretical value for a call or a put option based on variables such as volatility, type of option, underlying stock price, time, strike price, and risk-free rate. The quantum of speculation is more in case of stock market derivatives, and hence proper pricing of options eliminates the opportunity for any arbitrage.

16

Binomial Option Pricing Model

16.1 What is Binomial Option Pricing Model (BOPM)?

BOPM is an options valuation method developed in 1979. It uses an iterative procedure, allowing for the specification of nodes, or points in time, during the time span between the valuation date and the option's expiration date.

In finance, BOPM provides a generalizable numerical method for the valuation of options. Essentially, the model uses a *discrete-time* (lattice based) model of the varying price over time of the underlying financial instrument, addressing cases where the closed-form Black-Scholes formula is wanting.

The binomial model was first proposed by William Sharpe in the 1978 and formalized by Cox, Ross and Rubinstein in 1979 and by Rendleman and Bartter in that same year.

BOPM is a risk-neutral method for valuing path-dependent options (e.g., American options). It is a popular tool for stock options evaluation, and investors use the model to evaluate the right to buy or sell at specific prices over time. Under this model, the current value of an option is equal to the present value of the probability-weighted future payoffs.

In contrast to the Black-Scholes model, which provides a numerical result based on inputs, the binomial model allows for the calculation of the assets and the option for multiple periods along with the range of possible results for each period. Binomial model is different from the Black-Scholes model, which is more suitable for path-independent options, which cannot be exercised before their due date.

16.2 Basics of the BOPM

BOPM values options using an iterative approach utilizing multiple periods to value American options. In this model, there are two possible outcomes with each iteration—a move up or a move down that follows a binomial tree. The model is intuitive and is used more frequently in practice than the well-known Black-Scholes model. The model reduces possibilities of price changes and removes the possibility for arbitrage.

A binomial tree (Figure 16.1) is a graphical representation of possible intrinsic values that an option may take at different nodes or time periods.

BOPM assumes that there are two possible outcomes, hence the binomial part of the model. With a pricing model, the two outcomes are a move up, or a move down. The major advantage of a binomial option pricing model is that it is mathematically simple.

For a US-based option, which can be exercised at any time before the expiration date, the binomial model can provide insight as to when exercising the option may be advisable and when it should be held for longer periods. By looking at the binomial tree of values, a trader can determine in advance when a decision on an exercise may occur. If the option has a positive value, there is the possibility of exercise whereas if the option has a value less than zero, it should be held for longer periods.

Figure 16.1: Binomial Trees B$_0$, B$_1$, ...B$_4$

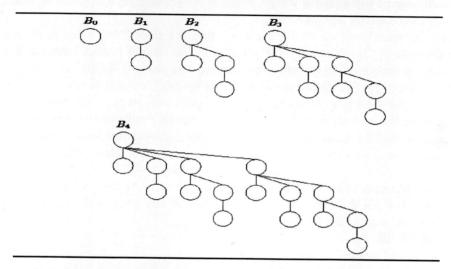

16.3 Assumptions of BOPM

When setting up a binomial option pricing model, we need to be aware of the underlying assumptions, to understand the limitations of this approach better.

1. At every point in time, the price can go to only two possible new prices, one up and one down (this is in the name, binomial).
2. The underlying asset pays no dividends.
3. The interest rate (discount factor) is a constant throughout the period.
4. The market is frictionless, and there are no transaction costs and no taxes.
5. Investors are risk-neutral, indifferent to risk.
6. The risk-free rate remains constant.

It is mostly useful for American-style options, which investors can exercise at any given time. The model also assumes that there is no arbitrage, meaning there is no buying while selling at a higher price. Having no-arbitrage ensures the value of the asset remains the same, which is a requirement for the Binomial Option Pricing model to work.

16.4 Calculating Price with the Binomial Model

The basic method of calculating the binomial option model is to use the same probability each period for success and failure until the option expires. However, a trader can incorporate different probabilities for each period based on new information obtained as time passes.

A binomial tree is a useful tool when pricing American options and embedded options. Its simplicity is its advantage and disadvantage at the same time. The tree is easy to model out mechanically, but the problem lies in the possible values the underlying asset can take in one period time. In a binomial tree model, the underlying asset can only be worth exactly one of two possible values, which is not realistic, as assets can be worth any number of values within any given range.

For example, there may be a 50/50 chance that the underlying asset price can increase or decrease by 30 percent in one period. For the second period, however, the probability that the underlying asset price will increase may grow to 70/30.

Thus, if an investor is evaluating an oil well, that investor is not sure what the value of that oil well is, but there is a 50/50 chance that the price will go up. If oil prices go up in Period 1 making the oil well more valuable and the market fundamentals now point to continued increases in oil prices, the probability of further appreciation in price may now be 70 percent. The binomial model allows for this flexibility; the Black-Scholes model does not.

A simplified example of a binomial tree has only one step. Assume there is a stock that is priced at ₹ 100 per share. In one month, the price of this stock will go up by ₹ 10 or go down by ₹ 10, creating the following situation:

Stock price = ₹ 100

Stock price in one month (up state) = ₹ 110

Stock price in one month (down state) = ₹ 90

Next, assume there is a call option available on this stock that expires in one month and has a strike price of ₹ 100. In the up state, this call option is worth ₹ 10, and in the down state, it is worth ₹ 0. The binomial model can calculate what the price of the call option should be today.

16.5 Option Valuation

Valuation is performed iteratively, starting at each of the final nodes (those that may be reached at the time of expiration), and then working backwards through the tree towards the first node (valuation date). The value computed at each stage is the value of the option at that point in time.

Option valuation using this method is a three-step process:

1. Price tree generation.
2. Calculation of option value at each final node.
3. Sequential calculation of the option value at each preceding node.

Step 1: Create the binomial price tree.

The tree of prices is produced by working forward from valuation date to expiration. At each step, it is assumed that the underlying instrument will move up or down by a specific factor (or) per step of the tree.

Step 2: Find option value at each final node.

At each final node of the tree, i.e. at expiration of the option, the option value is simply its intrinsic, or exercise, value:

Max $[(S_n - K), 0]$, for a call option

Max $[(K - S_n), 0]$, for a put option,

Where K is the strike price and S is the spot price of the underlying asset at the nth period.

Step 3: Find option value at earlier nodes

Once the above step is complete, the option value is then found for each node, starting at the penultimate time step, and working back to the first node of the tree (the valuation date) where the calculated result is the value of the option.

16.6 Advantages and Disadvantages of BOPM

Due to its simple and iterative structure, the binomial option pricing model presents certain unique advantages. For example, since it provides a stream of valuations for a derivative for each node in a span of time, it is useful for valuing derivatives such as American options—which can be executed anytime between the purchase date and expiration date. It is also much simpler than other pricing models such as the Black–Scholes model.

The BOPM approach has been widely used since it is able to handle a variety of conditions for which other models cannot easily be applied. This is largely because the BOPM is based on the description of an underlying instrument over a period of time rather than a single point. As a consequence, it is used to value American options that are exercisable at any time in a given interval. Being relatively simple, the model is readily implementable in computer software (including a spreadsheet).

A significant advantage is a multi-period view the model provides for the underlying asset's price and the transparency of the option's value over time.

Although computationally slower than the Black–Scholes formula, it is more accurate, particularly for longer-dated options on securities with dividend payments. For these reasons, various versions of the binomial model are widely used by practitioners in the options markets.

For options with several sources of uncertainty (e.g. real options) and for options with complicated features (e.g. Asian options), binomial methods are less practical due to several difficulties, and Monte Carlo option models are commonly used instead.

The most significant limitation of the model is the inherent necessity to predict future prices. Binomial Option Pricing is useful for American options, where the holder has the right to exercise at any time up until expiration.

The binomial model provides insight into the determinants of option value. The value of an option is not determined by the expected price of the asset but by its current price, which, of course, reflects expectations about the future. This is a direct consequence of arbitrage. If the option value deviates from the value of the replicating portfolio, investors can create an arbitrage position, i.e., one that requires no investment, involves no risk, and delivers positive returns.

While the binomial model provides an intuitive feel for the determinants of option value, it requires a large number of inputs, in terms of expected future prices at each node.

To sum up, binomial pricing model traces the evolution of the option's key underlying variables in discrete-time. This is done by means of a binomial lattice (tree), for a number of time steps between the valuation and expiration dates. Each node in the lattice represents a possible price of the underlying at a given point in time. In contrast to the Black-Scholes model, which provides a numerical result based on inputs, the binomial model allows for the calculation of the asset and the option for multiple periods along with the range of possible results for each period. The advantage of this multi-period view is that the user can visualize the change in asset price from period to period and evaluate the option based on decisions made at different points in time.

17

Principles of Arbitrage

17.1 What is Arbitrage?

Arbitrage means the simultaneous buying and selling of securities, currency or commodities in different markets in order to take advantage of differing prices for the same asset. Arbitrage is basically the act of buying a security in one market and simultaneously selling it in another market at a higher price, profiting from the temporary difference in prices. This is considered risk-free profit for the investor/trader.

In the context of the stock market, traders often try to exploit arbitrage opportunities. For example, a trader may buy a stock on a foreign exchange where the price has not yet adjusted for the constantly fluctuating exchange rate. The price of the stock on the foreign exchange is therefore undervalued compared to the price on the local exchange and the trader can make a profit from this difference. Differences in prices usually occur because of imperfect dissemination of information.

17.1.1 Price Convergence: Arbitrage has the effect of causing prices in different markets to converge. As a result of arbitrage, the currency exchange rates, the price of commodities, and the price of securities in different markets tend to converge. The speed at which they do so is a measure of market efficiency. Arbitrage tends to reduce price discrimination by encouraging people to buy an item where the price is low and resell it where the price is high (as long as the buyers are not prohibited from reselling and the transaction costs of buying, holding and reselling are small relative to the difference in prices in the different markets).

17.1.2 Arbitrage-Free Market: If the market prices do not allow for profitable arbitrage, the prices are said to constitute an arbitrage equilibrium, or an arbitrage-free market. An arbitrage equilibrium is a precondition for a general economic equilibrium. The "no arbitrage" assumption is used in quantitative finance to calculate a unique risk neutral price for derivatives.

17.2 Conditions for Arbitrage

Arbitrage is possible when one of three conditions is met:
1. The same asset does not trade at the same price on all markets.
2. Two assets with identical cash flows do not trade at the same price.
3. An asset with a known price in the future does not today trade at its future price discounted at the risk-free interest rate (or, the asset has significant costs of storage. This condition holds for grain but not for securities).

Arbitrage is not simply the act of buying a product in one market and selling it in another for a higher price at some later time. The transactions must occur simultaneously to avoid exposure to market risk, or the risk that prices may change on one market before both transactions are complete. In practical terms, this is generally possible only with securities and financial products that can be traded electronically, and even then, when each leg of the trade is executed the prices in the market may have moved. Missing one of the legs of the trade (and subsequently having to trade it soon after at a worse price) is called *execution risk* or more specifically *leg risk*.

In the simplest example, any good sold in one market should sell for the same price in another. Traders may, for example, find that the price of wheat is lower in agricultural regions than in cities, purchase the good, and transport it to another region to sell at a higher price. This type of price arbitrage is the most common, but this simple example ignores the cost of transport, storage, risk, and other factors. *True* arbitrage requires that there is no market risk involved. Where securities are traded on more than one exchange, arbitrage occurs by simultaneously buying in one and selling on the other.

17.3 Risks Involved in Arbitrage

Generally it is impossible to close two or three transactions at the same instant; therefore, there is the possibility that when one part of the deal is closed, a quick shift in prices makes it impossible to close the other at a profitable price. However, this is not necessarily the case. Many exchanges and inter-dealer brokers allow multi legged trades.

Competition in the market place can also create risks during arbitrage transactions. As an example, if one was trying to profit from a price discrepancy between Tata Steel on the Bombay Stock Exchange and Tata Steel on the Kolkata Stock Exchange, he may purchase a large number of shares on the Bombay Stock Exchange and finds that he cannot simultaneously sell on the Kolkata Stock Exchange, it leaves the arbitrageur in an unhedged risk position.

Another risk occurs if the items being bought and sold are not identical and the arbitrage is conducted under the assumption that the prices of the items are correlated or predictable. This is more narrowly referred to as a convergence trade. In the extreme case this is merger arbitrage, described below. In comparison to the classical quick arbitrage transaction, such an operation can produce disastrous losses.

As arbitrages generally involve *future* movements of cash, they are subject to counterparty risk if the counterparty fails to fulfil its side of a transaction. This is a serious problem if one has either a single trade or many related trades with a single counterparty, whose failure thus poses a threat, or in the event of a financial crisis when many counterparties fail. This hazard is serious because of the large quantities one must trade in order to make a profit on small price differences.

Arbitrage trades are necessarily synthetic, *leveraged* trades, as they involve a short position. If the assets used are not identical (so a price divergence makes the trade temporarily lose money), or the margin treatment is not identical, and the trader is accordingly required to post margin (faces a margin call), the trader may run out of capital (if they run out of cash and cannot borrow more) and be forced to sell these assets at a loss even though the trades may be expected to ultimately make money. In effect, arbitrage traders synthesize a put option on their ability to finance themselves.

Prices may diverge during a financial crisis, often termed a "flight to quality"; these are precisely the times when it is hardest for leveraged investors to raise capital (due to overall capital constraints), and thus they will lack capital precisely when they need it most.

17.4 Types of Arbitrage

Following are the main types of arbitrage:

17.4.1 Spatial Arbitrage: Also known as geographical arbitrage, this is the simplest form of arbitrage. In spatial arbitrage, an arbitrageur looks for price differences between geographically separate markets.

17.4.2 Merger Arbitrage: Also called risk arbitrage, merger arbitrage generally consists of buying/holding the stock of a company that is the target of a takeover while shorting the stock of the acquiring company.

Usually the market price of the target company is less than the price offered by the acquiring company. The spread between these two prices depends mainly on the probability and the timing of the takeover being completed as well as the prevailing level of interest rates.

The bet in a merger arbitrage is that such a spread will eventually be zero, if and when the takeover is completed. The risk is that the deal "breaks" and the spread massively widens.

17.4.3 Cross-Border Arbitrage: Cross-border arbitrage exploits different prices of the same stock in different countries. In most cases, the quotation on the local exchanges is done electronically by high-frequency traders, taking into consideration the home price of the stock and the exchange rate.

17.4.4 Regulatory Arbitrage: Regulatory arbitrage is where a regulated institution takes advantage of the difference between its real (or economic) risk and the regulatory position. For example, if a bank, operating under the Basel I accord, has to hold 8 percent capital against default risk, but the real risk of default is lower, it is profitable to securities the loan, removing the low risk loan from its portfolio.

On the other hand, if the real risk is higher than the regulatory risk then it is profitable to make that loan and hold on to it, provided it is priced appropriately. Regulatory arbitrage can result in parts of entire businesses being unregulated as a result of the arbitrage.

In economics, regulatory arbitrage (sometimes, tax arbitrage) may be used to refer to situations when a company can choose a nominal place of business with a regulatory, legal or tax regime with lower costs. For example, an insurance company may choose to locate in Bermuda due to preferential tax rates and policies for insurance companies. This can occur particularly where the business transaction has no obvious physical location. In the case of many financial products, it may be unclear "where" the transaction occurs.

Regulatory arbitrage can include restructuring a bank by outsourcing services such as information technology (IT). The outsourcing company takes over the installations, buying out the bank's assets and charges a periodic service fee back to the bank. This frees up cash flow usable for new lending by the bank. The bank will have higher IT costs, but counts on the multiplier effect of money creation and the interest rate spread to make it a profitable exercise.

17.4.5 Telecom Arbitrage: Telecom arbitrage companies allow phone users to make international calls for free through certain access numbers. Such services are offered in the United Kingdom; the telecommunication arbitrage companies get paid an interconnect charge by the UK mobile networks and then buy international routes at a lower cost. The calls are seen as free by the UK contract mobile phone customers since they are using up their allocated monthly minutes rather than paying for additional calls.

Such services were previously offered in the United States by companies such as FuturePhone.com. These services would operate in rural telephone exchanges, primarily in small towns in the state of Iowa. In these areas, the local telephone carriers are allowed to charge a high "termination fee" to the caller's carrier in order to fund the cost of providing service to the small and sparsely populated areas that they serve. However, Future Phone (as well as other similar services) ceased operations upon legal challenges from AT&T and other service providers.

17.4.6 Statistical Arbitrage: Statistical arbitrage is an imbalance in expected nominal values. A casino has a statistical arbitrage in every game of chance that it offers referred to as the house advantage, house edge, vigorish or house vigorish.

17.4.7 Political Arbitrage: It is a trading strategy which involves using knowledge or estimates of future political activity to forecast and discount security values. For example, the major factor in the values of some foreign government bonds is the risk of default, which is a political decision taken by the country's government. The values of companies in war-sensitive sectors such as oil and arms are affected by political decisions to make war.

Legal trading must be based on publicly available information. However, there is a grey area involving lobbyists and market rumours. Like insider trading there is scope for conflicts of interest when political decision makers themselves are in positions to profit from private investments whose values are linked to their own public political actions.

17.4.8 Triangular Arbitrage: It is the act of exploiting an arbitrage opportunity resulting from a pricing discrepancy among three different currencies in the foreign exchange market. A triangular arbitrage strategy involves three trades, exchanging the initial currency for a second, the second currency for a third, and the third currency for the initial. During the second trade, the arbitrageur locks in a zero-risk profit from the discrepancy that exists when the market cross exchange rate is not aligned with the implicit cross exchange rate. A profitable trade is only possible if there exist market imperfections. Profitable triangular arbitrage is very rarely possible because when such opportunities arise, traders execute trades that take advantage of the imperfections and prices adjust up or down until the opportunity disappears.

17.5 Arbitrage Pricing Theory (APT)

APT is a model of pricing that is based on the concept that an asset can have its returns predicted. To do so, the relationship between the asset and its common risk factors must be analyzed. APT was first created by Stephen Ross in 1976 to examine the influence of macroeconomic factors. It allows for the returns of a portfolio and the returns of specific asset to be predicted by examining the various variables that are independent within the relationship. It is based on the idea that in a well-functioning securities market, there should be no arbitrage opportunities available. That makes it possible to predict the outcome of that security over time.

In finance, APT is a general theory of asset pricing that holds that the expected return of a financial asset can be modelled as a linear function of various factors or theoretical market indices, where sensitivity to changes in each factor is represented by a factor-specific beta coefficient. The model-derived rate of return will then be used to price the asset correctly the asset price should equal the expected end of period price discounted at the rate implied by the model. If the price diverges, arbitrage should bring it back into line. The linear factor model structure of the APT is used as the basis for many of the commercial risk systems employed by asset managers.

APT is an alternate version of the Capital Asset Pricing Model (CAPM). This theory, like CAPM, provides investors with an estimated required rate of return on risky securities. APT considers risk premium basis specified set of factors in addition to the correlation of the price of the asset with expected excess return on the market portfolio.

As per assumptions under Arbitrage Pricing Theory, return on an asset is dependent on various macroeconomic factors like inflation, exchange rates, market indices, production measures, market sentiments, changes in interest rates, movement of yield curves etc.

APT based model aims to do away with the limitations of the one-factor model (CAPM) that different stocks will have different sensitivities to different market factors which may be totally different from any other stock under observation. In layman terms, one can say that not all stocks can be assumed to react to single and same parameter always and hence the need to take multifactor and their sensitivities.

17.5.1 Arbitrage Pricing Theory Formula: It is given below:

$E(R)i = E(R)z + (E(I) - E(R)z) \times \beta n$

Where

$E(R)i$ = Expected return on the asset.

Rz = Risk-free rate of return.

βn = Sensitivity of the asset price to macroeconomic factor n

Ei = Risk premium associated with factor i

If one is able to identify a single factor which singly affects the price, the CAPM model shall be sufficient. If there is more than one factor affecting the price of the asset/stock, one will have to work with a two-factor model or a multi-factor model depending on the number of factors that affect the stock price movement for the company.

To understand APT, it is important for us to learn the underlying assumptions of this theory as given below.

17.5.2 APT Assumptions: These are as under:

1. The theory is based on the principle of capital market efficiency and hence assumes all market participants trade with the intention of profit maximization.
2. It assumes no arbitrage exists and if it occurs participants will engage to benefit out of it and bring back the market to equilibrium levels.
3. It assumes markets are frictionless, i.e. there are no transaction costs, no taxes, short selling is possible and an infinite number of securities are available.

17.5.3 Advantages of APT: These are as follows:

A. It Has Fewer Restrictions: The APT does not have the same requirements about individual portfolios as other predictive theories. It also has fewer restrictions regarding the types of information allowed to perform predictions. Because there is more information available, with fewer overall restrictions, the results tend to be more reliable with the arbitrage pricing theory than with competitive models.

B. It Allows for More Sources of Risk: The APT allows for multiple risk factors to be included within the data set being examined instead of excluding them. This makes it possible for individual investors to see more information about why certain stock returns are moving in specific ways. It eliminates many of the questions on movement that other theories leave behind because there are more sources of risks included within the data set.

C. No Specific Factors: Although APT does not offer specific factors like other pricing models, there are four important factors that are taken into account by the theory. APT looks at changes in inflation, changes in industrial production, shifts in risk premiums, and shifts in the structure of interest rates when creating long-term predictive factors.

D. It Allows for Unanticipated Changes: APT is based on the idea that no surprises are going to happen. That is an unrealistic expectation, so Ross included an equation to support the presence of an unanticipated change. That makes it easier for investors to identify assets which have the strongest potential for growth or the strongest potential for failure, based on the information that is provided by the opportunity itself.

E. It Allows Investors to Find Arbitrage Opportunities: The goal of APT is to help investors find securities in the market that are mis-priced in some way. Once these can be identified, it becomes possible to build a portfolio based on them to generate returns that are better than what the indexes are offering. If a portfolio is then undervalued, the opportunities can be exploited to generate profits because of the changes in the pricing theory.

17.5.4 Disadvantages of APT: These are the following:

A. It Generates a Large Amount of Data: For someone unfamiliar with the arbitrage pricing theory, the amount of data that needs to be sorted through can feel overwhelming. The information is generated by a specific analysis of the various factors involved that create growth or loss, allowing for the predictive qualities to be factors in portfolio decisions. Someone not familiar with the purpose of each data point, will not understand the results APT generates, which makes it a useless tool for them.

B. It Requires Risk Sources to be Accurate: Every portfolio encounters some level of risk. For APT to be useful, it requires investors to have a clear perception of the risk, as well as the source of that risk. Only then, will this theory be able to factor in reasonable estimates with factoring sensitivities with a higher level of accuracy. If there is no clear definition of a risk source, then there will be more potential outcomes that reduce the effectiveness of the predictive qualities that APT provides.

C. It Requires the Portfolio to be Examined Singularly: The APT is only useful when examining a single item for risk. Because of that feature, trying to examine an entire portfolio with diverse investments is virtually impossible to do. That is why the entire portfolio is examined using the arbitrage pricing theory instead. Because it doesn't account for each account, only the portfolio, there are certain assumptions which must be made during the evaluation. That can lead to factors of uncertainty, which reduces the accuracy of the outcomes being analyzed.

D. It is not a Guarantee of Results: The arbitrage pricing theory does not guarantee that profits will happen. There are securities which are undervalued on the market today for reasons that fall outside of the scope of what APT considers. Some risks are not "real" risks, as they are built into the pricing mechanisms by the investors themselves, who have a certain fear of specific securities in certain market conditions.

The advantages and disadvantages of the arbitrage pricing theory are designed to look at the long-term average of returns. There are a handful of systematic influences which can affect this long-term average. By looking at the asset and the risks involved, a prediction of an anticipated return becomes possible. It is a good option for individual securities. When a portfolio of diverse securities is examined, however, APT may not be a suitable tool to use.

17.5.5 Limitations of Arbitrage Pricing Theory: These are as under:
1. The model requires a short listing of factors that impact the stock under consideration. Finding and listing all factors can be a difficult task and runs a risk of some or the other factor being ignored. Also, the risk of accidental correlations may exist which may cause a factor to become substantial impact provider or vice versa.
2. The expected returns for each of these factors will have to be arrived at, which depending on the nature of the factor, may or may not be easily available always.
3. The model requires calculating sensitivities of each factor which again can be an arduous task and may not be practically feasible.
4. The factors that affect the stock price for a particular stock may change over a period of time. Moreover, the sensitivities associated may also undergo shifts which need to be continuously monitored making it very difficult to calculate and maintain.

Arbitrage pricing theory-based models are built on the principle of capital market efficiency and aim to provide decision-makers and participants with estimates of the required rate of return on the risky assets. The required rate of return arrived using the APT model can be used to evaluate, if the stocks are over-priced or under-priced. Empirical tests conducted in the past have resulted from APT as a superior model over CAPM in many cases. However, in several cases, it has arrived at similar results as the CAPM model, which is relatively simpler in use.

Some risks are not *real* risks, as they are built into the pricing mechanisms by the investors themselves, who have a certain fear of specific securities in certain market conditions. The advantages and disadvantages of the arbitrage pricing theory are designed to look at the long-term average of returns.

To sum up, arbitrage is an extremely fast-paced process and its successful performance requires lots of time, experience, dedication and discipline, and especially liquidity.

Part IV
Corporate Finance

18

Patterns of Corporate Financing

Corporate finance is the division of finance that deals with how corporations deal with funding sources, investment decisions and capital structuring. Corporate finance is primarily concerned with maximizing shareholder value through long and short-term financial planning and the implementation of various strategies. Corporate finance activities range from capital investment decisions to investment banking.

Corporate finance departments are charged with governing and overseeing their firms' financial activities and capital investment decisions. Such decisions include whether to pursue a proposed investment and whether to pay for the investment with equity, debt, or both.

18.1 Meaning of Corporate Financing

Corporate financing includes the activities involved with the financing, investment, and capital budgeting decisions of a corporation.

Corporate financing deals with sourcing capital in the form of debt or equity. A company may borrow from commercial banks and other financial intermediaries or may issue debt securities in the capital markets through investment banks. A company may also choose to sell stocks to equity investors, especially when need large amounts of capital for business expansions.

Corporate financing is a balancing act in terms of deciding on the relative amounts or weights between debt and equity. Having too much debt may increase default risk, and relying heavily on equity can dilute earnings and value for early investors. In the end, capital financing must provide the capital needed to implement capital investments.

18.2 Sources of Capital

The sources of financing are, generically, capital self-generated by the firm and capital from external sources, obtained by issuing new debt and equity (and hybrid- or convertible securities).

18.2.1 Ordinary Shares: Corporations can sell shares of the company to investors to raise capital. Investors, or shareholders, expect that there will be an upward trend in value of the company (or appreciate in value) over time to make their investment a profitable purchase. Shareholder value is increased when corporations invest equity capital and other funds into projects (or investments) that earn a positive rate of return for the owners. Investors prefer to buy shares of stock in companies that will consistently earn a positive rate of return on capital in the future, thus increasing the market value of the stock of that corporation. Shareholder value may also be increased when corporations payout excess cash surplus (funds from retained earnings that are not needed for business) in the form of dividends.

Ordinary shares represent ownership capital and their owners—ordinary shareholders—share the reward and risk associated with ownership of corporate enterprises. They are called ordinary shares in contrast with preference shares which carry certain prior rights with regard to income and redemption.

There are certain concepts associated with ordinary shares. Authorised equity represents the maximum amount that a company can raise from the ordinary shareholders. It can be changed in the prescribed manner. The portion of the authorized capital offered by the company to investors is the issued capital. Subscribed share capital is that part of the issued capital which has been subscribed by the investors. The actual amount paid by the shareholders is the paid-up capital. The issued, subscribed and paid-up capitals are generally the same.

Ordinary shares typically have a face value in terms of the price of each share, the most popular denomination being ₹ 10. However, companies are permitted to issue such shares without a face value. The price at which the ordinary shares are issued is the issue price. The issue price for new companies is generally equal to the face value. It may be higher for existing companies, the difference being the share premium. The book value of ordinary shares refers to the paid-up capital plus reserves and surplus (net worth) divided by the number of outstanding shares. The price at which ordinary shares are traded in the stock market is their market value.

Ordinary shares have some special features in terms of the rights and claims of their holders: (a) residual claim to income/assets, (b) right to control, (c) pre-emptive rights, and (d) limited liability.

Ordinary shareholders have a residual claim to the income of the company. They are entitled to the remaining income/profits of the company after all outside claims are met. The amount actually received by the shareholders in the form of dividend depends on the decision of the board of directors. The directors have the right to decide what portion of the earning will be distributed to the shareholders as cash dividend and what portion will be ploughed back as retained earnings, which the shareholders may receive later in the form of capital appreciation/bonus shares.

The ordinary shareholders' claim in the assets of the company is also residual in that their claim would rank after the claims of the creditors and preference shareholders in the event of liquidation. If the liquidation value of assets is insufficient, their claims may remain unpaid.

As owners of the company, ordinary shareholders have the right to control the operations of, participate in the management of, the company. Their control is, however, indirect. The major policies/decisions are approved by the board of directors and the board-appointed management carries out the day-to-day operations. The shareholders have the legal right/power to elect the board of directors as well as vote on every resolution placed in various meetings of the company.

The ordinary shareholders exercise their right to control the company through voting in the meetings of the company. According to the most commonly used system of voting in India, namely majority rule voting, each share carries one vote. As a result, shareholders/groups holding more than 50 percent of the outstanding equity shares are able to elect all the directors of their choice.

The ordinary shareholders of a company enjoy pre-emptive rights in the sense that they have a legal right to be offered, by the company, the first opportunity to purchase additional issues of equity capital in proportion to their existing holdings.

Although ordinary shareholders share the ownership risk, their liability is limited to the extent of their investment in the share capital of the company.

18.2.2 Preference Shares: Preference shares are a unique type of long-term capital market instruments in that they combine some of the features of ordinary shares as well as some features of debentures.

1. As a hybrid form of financial instrument, they are similar to debentures insofar as they carry a fixed rate of dividend.
2. They rank higher than ordinary shares as claimants to the income/assets of the company.
3. Generally, preference shareholders do not have voting rights.
4. They do not have a share in residual earnings/assets.
5. Dividend on preference shares is paid out of divisible/after tax profit.
6. Payment of preference dividend depends on the discretion of the management, i.e. it is not an obligatory payment and non-payment does not force insolvency/liquidation.
7. Irredeemable types of preference shares have no fixed maturity date.

Preference shares have a prior claim over ordinary shares both on the income and assets of the company. In other words, preference dividend must be paid in full before payment of any dividend on ordinary shares. In the event of liquidation, the whole of preference share capital must be paid before anything is paid to the ordinary shareholders. Thus, preference shares stand midway between debentures and ordinary shares as regards claims on the income and assets of the company. Stated in terms of risk perspective, preference shares are less risky than ordinary shares but more risky than debentures.

Preference share holders are senior (i.e. higher ranking) to common stock holders, but subordinate to bonds in terms of claim (or rights to their share of the assets of the company). Terms of the preferred stock are stated in a *certificate of designation.*

Similar to bonds, preferred stocks are rated by the major credit-rating companies. The rating for preferred stock is generally lower, since preferred dividends do not carry the same guarantees as interest payments from bonds and they are junior to all creditors.

18.2.3 Debentures: Debentures represent creditorship securities and debentures holders are long-term creditors of the company. As a secured instrument, it is a promise to pay interest and repay principal at stipulated times.

The payment of interest and repayment of principal is a contractual obligation enforceable by law. Failure/default leads to bankruptcy of the company. The claim of debenture holders on income and assets ranks pari passu with other secured debt and higher than that of shareholders—preference as well as ordinary shares.

Convertible debentures give the holders the right (option) to convert them into equity shares on certain terms. They are entitled to a fixed income till the conversion option is exercised and share the benefits associated with equity shares after the conversion.

18.2.4 Bonds: Corporations may rely on borrowed funds (debt capital or credit) as sources of investment to sustain ongoing business operations or to fund future growth. Debt comes in several forms, such as through bank loans, notes payable, or bonds issued to the public.

A bond is a fixed income investment in which an investor loans money to an entity which borrows the funds for a defined period of time at a variable or fixed interest rate. Bonds are used by companies, municipalities, states and sovereign governments to raise money and finance a variety of projects and activities. Owners of bonds are creditors of the issuer.

Bonds are commonly referred to as fixed-income securities and are one of the three main generic asset classes, along with stocks (equities) and cash equivalents. Many corporate and government bonds are publicly traded on exchanges, while others are traded only over-the-counter (OTC).

When companies or other entities need to raise money to finance new projects, maintain ongoing operations, or refinance existing debts, they may issue bonds directly to investors instead of obtaining loans from a bank. The indebted entity (issuer) issues a bond that contractually states the interest rate that will be paid and the time at which the loaned funds (bond principal) must be returned (maturity date). The interest rate, called the coupon rate or payment, is the return that bondholders earn for loaning their funds to the issuer.

The issuance price of a bond is usually of ₹ 1,000 or ₹ 10,000 face value per individual bond. The actual market price of a bond depends on a number of factors including the credit quality of the issuer, the length of time until expiration, and the coupon rate compared to the general interest rate environment at the time.

Bonds require the corporations to make regular interest payments (interest expenses) on the borrowed capital until the debt reaches its maturity date, therein the firm must pay back the obligation in full. Debt payments can also be made in the form of sinking fund provisions, whereby the corporation pays annual instalments of the borrowed debt above regular interest charges. Corporations that issue callable bonds are entitled to pay back the obligation in full whenever the company feels it is in their best interest to pay off the debt payments. If interest expenses cannot be made by the corporation through cash payments, the firm may also use collateral assets as a form of repaying their debt obligations (or through the process of liquidation).

18.3 Capital Investments

Corporate finance tasks include making capital investments and deploying a company's long-term capital. The capital investment decision process is primarily concerned with capital budgeting. Through capital budgeting, a company identifies capital expenditures, estimates future cash flows from proposed capital projects, compares planned investments with potential proceeds, and decides which projects to include in its capital budget.

Making capital investments is perhaps the most important corporate finance task that can have serious business implications. Poor capital budgeting (e.g., excessive investing or under-funded investments) can compromise a company's financial position, either because of increased financing costs or inadequate operating capacity.

18.3.1 Capital Budgeting: Capital budgeting is concerned with the setting of criteria about which value-adding projects should receive investment funding, and whether to finance that investment with equity or debt capital. Capital budgeting is the planning of value-adding, long-term corporate financial projects relating to investments funded through and affecting the firm's capital structure. Management must allocate the firm's limited resources between competing opportunities (projects).

Capital budgeting is also concerned with the setting of criteria about which projects should receive investment funding to increase the value of the firm, and whether to finance that investment with equity or debt capital. Investments should be made on the basis of value-added to the future of the corporation. Projects that increase a firm's value may include a wide variety of different types of investments, including but not limited to, expansion policies, or mergers and acquisitions. When no growth or expansion is possible by a corporation and excess cash surplus exists and is not needed, then management is expected to pay out some or all of those surplus earnings in the form of cash dividends or to repurchase the company's stock through a share buyback program.

18.3.2 Alternative Theories: Economists have developed a set of alternative theories about how managers allocate a corporation's finances.

One of the main alternative theories of how firms manage their capital funds is the Pecking Order Theory (Stewart Myers), which suggests that firms avoid external financing while they have internal financing available and avoid new equity financing while they can engage in new debt financing at reasonably low interest rates.

Also, the Capital Structure Substitution Theory hypothesizes that management manipulates the capital structure such that earnings per share (EPS) are maximized. An emerging area in finance theory is right-financing whereby investment banks and corporations can enhance investment return and company value over time by determining the right investment objectives, policy framework, institutional structure, source of financing (debt or equity) and expenditure framework within a given economy and under given market conditions.

One of the more recent innovations in this area from a theoretical point of view is the Market Timing Hypothesis. This hypothesis, inspired in the behavioural finance literature, states that firms look for the cheaper type of financing regardless of their current levels of internal resources, debt and equity.

19

Capital Structure and the Cost of Capital

Firms rationally invest and seek financing in a manner compatible with their short- and long-term objectives.

19.1 Capital Structure Defined

In corporate finance, capital structure is the way a corporation finances its assets through some combination of equity, debt, or hybrid securities. It refers to the make up of capitalisation of a firm. It is the mix of different sources of long-term funds such as equity shares, preference shares, long-term debt, retained profits etc. To put it differently, capital structure is the *composition* or *structure* of the liabilities of a firm. For example, a firm that has ₹ 30 crore in equity and ₹ 70 crore in debt is said to be 30 percent equity-financed and 70 percent debt-financed. The firm's ratio of debt to total financing (70 percent in this example) is referred to as the firm's leverage. Leverage ratio represents the proportion of a firm's capital that is obtained through debt which may be either bank loans or bonds. In the real world, capital structure may be highly complex and include dozens of sources of capital.

In the event of bankruptcy, the seniority of the capital structure comes into play. A typical company has the following seniority structure listed from most senior to least:
1. Debt.
2. Preferred stock.
3. Common stock.

19.1.1 Debt versus Equity: Both debt and equity can be found on the balance sheet of a company. Company assets, also listed on the balance sheet, are purchased with this debt and equity. Capital structure can be a mixture of a company's long-term debt, short-term debt, common stock, and preferred stock. A company's proportion of short-term debt versus long-term debt is considered when analyzing its capital structure.

When analysts refer to capital structure, they are most likely referring to a debt-to-equity ratio of a firm, which provides insight into how risky a company's borrowing practices are. Usually, a company that is heavily financed by debt has a more aggressive capital structure and therefore poses greater risk to investors. This risk, however, may be the primary source of the firm's growth.

Debt is one of the two main ways a company can raise money in the capital markets. Companies benefit from debt because of its tax advantages. Interest payments made as a result of borrowing funds are generally tax deductible. Debt also allows a company or business to retain ownership, unlike equity. Additionally, in times of low interest rates, debt is abundant and easy to access.

Equity allows outside investors to take partial ownership in the company. Equity is more expensive than debt, especially when interest rates are low. However, unlike debt, equity does not need to be paid back. This is a benefit to the company in the case of declining earnings. On the other hand, equity represents a claim by the owner on the future earnings of the company.

Companies that use more debt than equity to finance their assets and fund operating activities have a high leverage ratio and an aggressive capital structure. A company that pays for assets with more equity than debt has a low leverage ratio and a conservative capital structure. That said, a high leverage ratio and an aggressive capital structure can also lead to higher growth rates, whereas a conservative capital structure can lead to lower growth rates.

It is the goal of company management to find the ideal mix of debt and equity, also referred to as the optimal capital structure, to finance operations.

Analysts use the debt-to-equity ratio to compare capital structure. It is calculated by dividing total liabilities by total equity. Savvy companies have learned to incorporate both debt and equity into their corporate strategies. At times, however, companies may rely too heavily on external funding, and debt in particular. Investors can monitor a firm's capital structure by tracking the debt-to-equity ratio and comparing it against the company's industry peers.

19.1.2 Modigliani-Miller Theorem and Capital Structure: Modigliani-Miller theorem, proposed by Franco Modigliani and Merton Miller in 1958, forms the basis for modern thinking on capital structure, though it is generally viewed as a purely theoretical proposition since it disregards many important factors in the capital structure process such as fluctuations and uncertain situations that may occur in the course of financing a firm. The theorem states how, in a perfect market, a firm is financed is irrelevant to its value. This result provides the base with which to examine real world reasons why capital structure is relevant, i.e. a company's value is affected by the capital structure it employs. Some other reasons include bankruptcy costs, agency costs, taxes, and information asymmetry. This analysis can then be extended to look at whether there is in fact an optimal capital structure, the one which maximizes the value of the firm.

Consider a perfect capital market with no transaction or bankruptcy costs and perfect information. Firms and individuals can borrow at the same interest rate. There are no taxes and investment returns are not affected by financial uncertainty. Assuming perfection in the capital market is a mirage and unattainable as suggested by Modigliani and Miller.

Modigliani and Miller made two findings under these conditions. Their first proposition was that the value of a company is independent of its capital structure. Their second proposition stated that the cost of equity for a leveraged firm is equal to the cost of equity for an unleveraged firm, plus an added premium for financial risk. It means as leverage increases, risk is shifted between different investor classes, while the total risk of the firm is constant, and hence no extra value created.

Their analysis was extended to include the effect of taxes and risky debt. Under a classical tax system, the tax-deductibility of interest makes debt financing valuable, i.e. the cost of capital decreases as the proportion of debt in the capital structure increases.

The optimal structure would be to have virtually no equity at all, i.e. a capital structure consisting of 99.99 percent debt.

For details, see chapter 22 of this book.

19.1.3 Theories Related to Imperfections in the Capital Market: The theories explained below try to address some of the imperfections in the capital market by relaxing assumptions made in the Modigliani-Miller theorem.

A. Trade-off Theory: Trade-off theory of capital structure allows bankruptcy cost to exist as an offset to the benefit of using debt as tax shield. It states that there is an advantage to financing with debt, namely the tax benefits of debt and that there is a cost of financing with debt the bankruptcy costs and the financial distress costs of debt. This theory also refers to the idea that a company chooses how much equity finance and how much debt finance to use by considering both costs and benefits. Empirically, this theory may explain differences in debt-to-equity ratios between industries, but it doesn't explain differences within the same industry.

B. Pecking Order Theory: Pecking order theory tries to capture the costs of asymmetric information. It states that companies prioritize their sources of financing (from internal financing to equity) according to the law of least effort, or of least resistance, preferring to raise equity as a financing means *of last resort.* Hence, internal financing is used first and when that is depleted, debt is issued; and when it is no longer sensible to issue any more debt, equity is issued. This theory maintains that businesses adhere to a hierarchy of financing sources and prefer internal financing when available, and debt is preferred over equity if external financing is required. Equity requires issuing shares which means *bringing external ownership* into the company. Thus, the form of debt a firm chooses can act as a signal of its need for external finance.

The pecking order theory argues that equity is a less preferred means to raise capital, because when managers issue new equity, investors believe that managers think the firm is overvalued, and managers are taking advantage of the assumed over-valuation. As a result, investors may place a lower value to the new equity issuance.

C. Capital Structure Substitution Theory: This theory is based on the hypothesis that company management may manipulate capital structure such that earnings per share (EPS) are maximized. The model is not normative. It does not state that management should maximize EPS. It simply hypothesizes they do so.

19.1.4 Agency Costs and Capital Structure: Three types of agency costs can help explain the relevance of capital structure.

A. Asset Substitution Effect: As debt-to-equity ratio increases, management has an incentive to undertake risky, even negative net present value (NPV) projects. This is because if the project is successful, share holders earn the benefit, whereas if it is unsuccessful, debtors experience the downside.

B. Underinvestment Problem: If debt is risky, the gain from the project will accrue to debt holders rather than shareholders. Thus, management has an incentive to reject positive NPV projects, even though they have the potential to increase firm value.

C. Free Cash Flow: Unless free cash flow is given back to investors, management has an incentive to destroy firm value through empire building and perks etc. Increasing leverage imposes financial discipline on management.

19.1.5 Arbitrage: A capital structure arbitrageur seeks to profit from differential pricing of various instruments issued by one corporation. Consider, for example, traditional bonds, and convertible bonds. The latter are bonds that are, under contracted-for conditions, convertible into shares of equity. The stock-option component of a convertible bond has a calculable value in itself. The value of the whole instrument *should* be the value of the traditional bonds *plus* the extra value of the option feature. If the spread (the difference between the convertible and the non-convertible bonds) grows excessively, then the capital-structure arbitrageur will bet that it will converge.

To sum up, capital structure is the particular combination of debt and equity used by a company to finance its overall operations and growth. Debt comes in the form of bond issues or loans, while equity may come in the form of common stock, preferred stock, or retained earnings. Short-term debt is also considered to be part of the capital structure. Capital structure is how a company funds its overall operations and growth. Debt consists of borrowed money that is due back to the lender, commonly with interest expense. Equity consists of ownership rights in the company, without the need to pay back any investment. The debt-to-equity ratio is useful in determining the riskiness of a company's borrowing practices.

Variation in capital structures is primarily determined by factors that remain stable for long periods of time. These stable factors are unobservable.

19.2 Cost of Capital

For an investment to be worthwhile, the expected return on capital has to be higher than the cost of capital. Given a number of competing investment opportunities, investors are expected to put their capital to work in order to maximize the return. In other words, the cost of capital is the rate of return that capital could be expected to earn in the best alternative investment of equivalent risk. This is the opportunity cost of capital. If a project is of similar risk to a company's average business activities it is reasonable to use the company's average cost of capital as a basis for the evaluation or cost of capital is a firm's cost of raising funds. However, for projects outside the core business of the company, the current cost of capital may not be the appropriate yardstick to use, as the risks of the businesses are not the same.

Every company has to chart out its financing strategy at an early stage. The cost of capital becomes a critical factor in deciding which financing track to follow—debt, equity, or a combination of the two.

19.2.1 What is Cost of Capital? Cost of capital is the required return necessary to make a capital budgeting project, such as building a new factory, worthwhile. Capital budgeting is a process a business uses to evaluate potential major projects or investments. It allows a comparison of estimated costs versus rewards. When analysts and investors discuss the cost of capital, they typically mean the weighted average of a firm's cost of debt and cost of equity blended together.

The cost of capital metric is used by companies internally to judge whether a capital project is worth the expenditure of resources, and by investors who use it to determine whether an investment is worth the risk compared to the return. The cost of capital depends on the mode of financing used. It refers to the cost of equity if the business is financed solely through equity, or to the cost of debt if it is financed solely through debt. Many companies use a combination of debt and equity to finance their businesses and, for such companies, the overall cost of capital is derived from the weighted average cost of all capital sources, widely known as the weighted average cost of capital (WACC).

Cost of capital, from the perspective on an investor, is the return expected by whoever is providing the capital for a business. In other words, it is an assessment of the risk of a company's equity. In doing this an investor may look at the volatility (beta) of a company's financial results to determine whether a certain stock is too risky or would make a good investment.

19.2.2 Significance of Cost of Capital: The cost of capital concept is also widely used in economics and accounting. Another way to describe the cost of capital is the opportunity cost of making an investment in a business. Wise company management will only invest in initiatives and projects that will provide returns that exceed the cost of their capital.

The new debt-holders and shareholders who have decided to invest in the company to fund a new machinery or plant will expect a return on their investment. Debt-holders require interest payments and shareholders require dividends (or capital gain from selling the shares after their value increases). The idea is that some of the profit generated by this new project will be used to repay the debt and satisfy the new shareholders.

Suppose a company considers taking on a project or investment of some kind, for example installing a new piece of machinery in one of their factories. Installing this new machinery will cost money; paying the technicians to install the machinery, transporting the machinery, buying the parts and so on. This new machinery is also expected to generate new profit. So the company will finance the project with two broad categories of finance: issuing debt, by taking out a loan or other debt instrument such as a bond; and issuing equity, usually by issuing new shares.

Cost of capital represents a *hurdle rate* that a company must overcome before it can generate value, and it is used extensively in the capital budgeting process to determine whether a company should proceed with a project.

Early-stage companies seldom have sizable assets to pledge as collateral for debt financing, so equity financing becomes the default mode of funding for most of them. Less-established companies with limited operating histories will pay a higher cost for capital than older companies (with solid track records) because lenders and investors will demand a higher risk premium from the former.

19.2.3 Weighted Average Cost of Capital (WACC): WACC is a calculation of a firm's cost of capital in which each category of capital is proportionately weighted. A firm's cost of capital is typically calculated using the weighted average cost of capital formula that considers the cost of both debt and equity capital. Each category of the firm's capital is weighted proportionately to arrive at a blended rate, and the formula considers every type of debt and equity on the company's balance sheet, including common and preferred stock, bonds and other forms of debt.

A. Cost of Debt: The cost of debt is merely the interest rate paid by the company on its debt. However, since interest expense is tax-deductible, the debt is calculated on an after-tax basis as follows:

$$\text{Cost of debt} = \frac{\text{Interest expense}}{\text{Total debt}} \times (1 - T)$$

Where,

Interest expense = Interest paid on the current debt of the firm.

T = Marginal tax rate of the company.

The cost of debt can also be estimated by adding a credit spread to the risk-free rate and multiplying the result by $(1 - T)$.

B. Cost of Equity: The cost of equity is more complicated since the rate of return demanded by equity investors is not as clearly defined as it is by lenders. The cost of equity is approximated by the capital asset pricing model as follows:

$$\text{CAPM (cost of equity)} = R_f + \beta (R_m - R_f)$$

Where

R_f = Risk-free rate of return.

R_m = Market rate of return.

Beta is used in the CAPM formula to estimate risk, and the formula would require a public company's own stock beta. For private companies, a beta is estimated based on the average beta of a group of similar, public firms. Analysts may refine this beta by calculating it on an unlevered, after-tax basis. The assumption is that a private firm's beta will become the same as the industry average beta.

The firm's overall cost of capital is based on the weighted average of these costs. For example, consider an enterprise with a capital structure consisting of 70 percent equity and 30 percent debt; its cost of equity is 10 percent and the after-tax cost of debt is 7 percent.

Therefore, its WACC would be:

$(0.7 \times 10 \text{ percent}) + (0.3 \times 7 \text{ percent}) = 9.1 \text{ percent}$.

This is the cost of capital that would be used to discount future cash flows from potential projects and other opportunities to estimate their net present value (NPV) and the ability to generate value.

Companies strive to attain the optimal financing mix based on the cost of capital for various funding sources. Debt financing has the advantage of being more tax efficient than equity financing since interest expenses are tax deductible and dividends on common shares are paid with after-tax dollars. However, too much debt can result in dangerously high leverage, resulting in higher interest rates sought by lenders to offset the higher default risk.

Calculation of WACC is an iterative procedure which requires estimation of the fair market value of equity capital if the company is not listed. The adjusted present value method (APV) is much easier to use in this case as it separates the value of the project from the value of its financing program.

To conclude, cost of capital represents the return a company needs in order to take on a capital project, such as purchasing new equipment or constructing a new building. Cost of capital typically encompasses the cost of both equity and debt, weighted according to the company's preferred or existing capital structure, known as the weighted-average cost of capital (WACC). A company's investment decisions for new projects should always generate a return that exceeds the firm's cost of the capital used to finance the project—otherwise, the project will not generate a return for investors.

A company's securities typically include both debt and equity, one must therefore calculate both the cost of debt and the cost of equity to determine a company's cost of capital. Importantly, both cost of debt and equity must be forward looking, and reflect the expectations of risk and return in the future. This means that the past cost of debt is not a good indicator of the actual forward looking cost of debt.

20

Corporate Debt

Companies obtain debt both to meet their working capital requirements and long-term investments.

20.1 What is Debt?

Debt is the money borrowed by one party from another to serve a financial need that otherwise cannot be met outright. Many organizations use debt to procure goods and services that they cannot manage to pay for with cash.

Under a debt agreement, the borrower obtains authorization to get whatever amount of money is needed on condition it will be repaid on an agreed date. In most cases, the amount owed is serviced with some interest.

Based on the amount borrowed, debt can be an asset or a complication. Knowing the best way to manage debt is tricky, particularly for a borrower who is finding it hard to make scheduled payments.

There are many types of debt, but the most common ones are auto loans, mortgages, and credit card debt. Based on the terms agreed, the borrower must repay the outstanding amount by the set date. Also, the terms usually specify what interest the loan will accrue over the period it is being serviced, as a percentage of the principal amount. Interest is an essential element of the loan as it ensures that lenders are repaid for the risks they take and encourages borrowers to make payments quickly to limit interest-based expenses.

20.2 Need for Corporate Debt

Other than credit card and loans, companies wanting to borrow money can resort to other functional options. Corporate bodies can explore other debt types such as commercial paper and bonds, which are not available to an individual.

In the field of corporate finance, a lot of attention goes to the amount of debt an entity owes. If, for one reason or another, sales drop, and a company is no longer as profitable as it once was, then it may not be able to repay its loans. Such a company suffers the risk of going bankrupt. However, an entity that does not take out loans may be limiting its expansion potential.

There are many industries in the market, and each interacts with debt uniquely. Thus, each company defines the right amount of debt using scales unique to its industry. When evaluating a company's financials, a variety of metrics come into play to assess whether its debt level is within an acceptable range.

Prudent debt policy lets an individual or company manage finances effectively so that it becomes easy to build on existing wealth, purchase what is needed, and prepare well for uncertainties. This includes mortgages, buying goods and services that save the buyer money, education loans, and debt consolidation.

Corporate bonds are a form of debt financing. They are a major source of capital for many businesses, along with equity, bank loans, and lines of credit. They often are issued to provide the ready cash for a particular project the company wants to undertake. Debt financing is sometimes preferable to issuing stock (equity financing) because it is typically cheaper for the borrowing firm and does not entail giving up any ownership stake or control in the company.

Generally speaking, a company needs to have consistent earnings potential to be able to offer debt securities to the public at a favourable coupon rate. If a company's perceived credit quality is higher, it can issue more debt at lower rates.

20.2.1 Secured versus Unsecured Debt: Secured debts involve a repayment promise, as well as collateral. Securing a debt means providing an asset so that in the event a borrower defaults, it can be sold to recover the money that was lent out. Real-life examples of secured loans include mortgages and auto loans because the item under financing is the collateral. For example, if the borrower is purchasing a car, and defaults on payment, the loaner can sell the vehicle to recover the remaining amount. Also, if an entity takes a mortgage, the property is used as collateral. The lender maintains interest, financially, over the asset until the borrower clears the mortgage.

Unsecured debt, on the other hand, does not involve collateral. However, if a borrower does not repay the loan, the lender can institute charges at a court of law to recover the amount loaned. Lenders use creditworthiness to assess a borrower's repayment potential.

20.3 Corporate Bonds

A corporate bond is a type of debt security that is issued by a firm and sold to investors. The company gets the capital it needs and in return the investor is paid a pre-established number of interest payments at either a fixed or variable interest rate. When the bond expires, or reaches maturity, the payments cease and the original investment is returned. The backing for the bond is generally the ability of the company to repay, which depends on its prospects for future revenues and profitability. In some cases, the company's physical assets may be used as collateral.

Bonds allow companies to raise funds by selling a repayment promise to interested investors. Institutions and individual investment organizations can procure bonds that typically come with a predefined interest rate, or coupon. For example, if an entity wants to raise ₹ 1 crore to purchase new machinery, it can provide the public with 10,000 bonds each worth ₹ 1,000. Once individuals or other companies purchase the bonds, the holders are guaranteed a face value on a given date, commonly known as the maturation date. This amount is in addition to regular interest on the bond throughout the period the bond is active. Bonds work on a similar principle to that of conventional loans. However, a company is the one borrowing while investors are either creditors or lenders.

The highest quality (and safest, lower yielding) bonds are commonly referred to as Triple-A bonds, while the least creditworthy are termed junk. In the investment hierarchy, high-quality corporate bonds are considered a relatively safe and conservative investment. Investors building balanced portfolios often add bonds in order to offset riskier investments such as growth stocks. Over a lifetime, these investors tend to add more bonds and fewer risky investments in order to safeguard their accumulated capital. Retirees often invest a larger portion of their assets in bonds in order to establish a reliable income supplement.

In general, corporate bonds are considered to have a higher risk than government bonds. As a result, interest rates are almost always higher on corporate bonds, even for companies with top-flight credit quality. The difference between the yields on highly-rated corporate bonds and government bonds is called the credit spread.

Corporate bonds sometimes have call provisions to allow for early prepayment if prevailing interest rates change so dramatically that the company deems it can do better by issuing a new bond. Investors may also opt to sell bonds before they mature. If a bond is sold, the owner gets less than face value. The amount it is worth is determined primarily by the number of payments that still are due before the bond matures.

Investors may also gain access to corporate bonds by investing in any number of bond-focused mutual funds.

20.3.1 Contingency Provisions: Corporate bonds sometimes have contingency provisions such as a call, put and conversion options:

A. Callable Bond: A callable bond entitles the issuer to retire the debt before maturity. This feature enables a company to refinance a debt when interest rates decline or to eliminate restrictive covenants. They must pay a relatively higher yield than a plain-vanilla bond.

B. Putable Bond: A putable bond entitles the bondholder to sell the bond to the issuer if its price falls. This feature is valuable when interest rates increase. Since the put option is value for bondholders, these bonds pay a lower yield.

C. Convertible Bond: A convertible bond contains a straight-bond and conversion option which entitles the bondholder to convert the debt to equity. Common issuers are early-stage companies who do not have established presence in capital markets. Established issuers may also issue convertible bonds to take advantage of lower coupon rates. However, they may result in equity dilution.

Standardized issuance, trading, and settlement processes have been developed in the international bond market. Most bond prices are quoted in basis points in the over-the-counter (OTC) market.

20.3.2 Role of Corporate Bond Market: A liquid corporate bond market can play a critical role in supporting economic development in the following ways:

1. It supplements the banking system to meet the requirements of the corporate sector for long-term capital investment and asset creation.
2. It provides a stable source of finance when the equity market is volatile.
3. With the decline in the role of specialised financial institutions, there is an increasing realisation of the need for a well-developed corporate debt market as an alternative source of finance.
4. Corporate bond markets can also help firms reduce their overall cost of capital by

allowing them to tailor their asset and liability profiles to reduce the risk of maturity and currency mismatches.

5. Corporate bond market is important for nurturing a credit culture and market discipline.
6. The existence of a well-functioning bond market can lead to the efficient pricing of credit risk as expectations of all bond market participants are incorporated into bond prices.

Apart from providing a channel for financing investments, the corporate bond markets also contribute towards portfolio diversification for holders of long-term funds. Effective asset management requires a balance of asset alternatives. In view of the underdeveloped state of the corporate bond markets, there would be an overweight position in government securities and even equities. The existence of a well-functioning corporate bond market widens the array of asset choices for long-term investors such as pension funds and insurance companies and allows them to better manage the maturity structure of their balance sheets.

20.3.3 Bond Rating: Before being issued to investors, bonds are reviewed for the creditworthiness of the issuer by one or more of three U.S. rating agencies: Standard & Poor's Global Ratings, Moody's Investor Services, and Fitch Ratings. Each has its own ranking system, but the highest-rated bonds are commonly referred to as Triple-A rated bonds. The lowest rated corporate bonds are called high-yield bonds due to their greater interest rate applied to compensate for their higher risk. These are also known as junk bonds.

Bond ratings are vital to altering investors to the quality and stability of the bond in question. These ratings consequently greatly influence interest rates, investment appetite, and bond pricing.

20.3.4 Difference between Corporate Bonds and Stocks: An investor who buys a corporate bond is lending money to the company. An investor who buys stock is buying an ownership share of the company.

The value of a stock rises and falls, and the investor's stake rises or falls with it. The investor may make money by selling the stock when it reaches a higher price, or by collecting dividends paid by the company, or both.

By investing in bonds, an investor is paid in interest rather than profits. The original investment can only be at risk if the company collapses. One important difference is that even a bankrupt company must pay its bondholders and other creditors first. Stock owners may be reimbursed for their losses only after all of those debts are paid in full. Companies may also issue convertible bonds, which are able to be turned into shares of the company if certain conditions are met.

20.4 Emergence of Private Placement Market

In private placement, resources are raised privately through arrangers (merchant banking intermediaries) who place securities with a limited number of investors such as financial institutions, corporates and high net worth individuals. Under Section 81 of the Companies Act, 1956, a private placement is defined as 'an issue of shares or of convertible securities by a company to a select group of persons'. An offer of securities to more than 50 persons is deemed to be a public issue under the Act. Corporates access the private placement market because of its following advantages:

1.   It is a cost and time-effective method of raising funds.
2.   It can be structured to meet the needs of the entrepreneurs.

Private placement does not require detailed compliance of formalities as required in public or rights issues.

The emergence of private placement market has provided an easier alternative to the corporates to raise funds. Although the private placement market provides a cost-effective and time-saving mechanism for raising resources, the unbridled growth of this market has raised some concerns. The quality of issues and extent of transparency in the private placement deals remain areas of concern even though privately placed issues by listed companies are now required to be listed and also subject to necessary disclosures. In the case of public issues, all the issues coming to the market are screened for their quality and the investors rely on ratings and other public information for evaluation of risk. Such a screening mechanism is missing in the case of private placements. This increases the risk associated with privately placed securities. Further, the private placement market appears to be growing at the expense of the public issues market, which has some distinct advantages in the form of wider participation by the investors and, thus, diversification of the risk.

The private placement market was not regulated until May 2004. In view of the mushrooming growth of the market and the risk posed by it, SEBI prescribed that the listing of all debt securities, irrespective of the mode of issuance, i.e. whether issued on a private placement basis or through public/rights issue, shall be done through a separate listing agreement. The RBI also issued guidelines to the financial intermediaries under its purview on investments in non-SLR securities, including private placement. In June 2001, boards of banks were advised to lay down policy and prudential limits on investments in bonds and debentures, including cap on unrated issues and on a private placement basis. The policy laid down by banks should prescribe stringent appraisal of issues, especially by non-borrower customers, provide for an internal system of rating, stipulate entry-level minimum ratings/quality standards and put in place proper risk management systems.

20.5 Other Types of Corporate Debt

20.5.1 Bank Loans: Loans from banks and other financial institutions form a major part of the debt raised by companies. However, recently more and more companies, particularly companies with high-credit quality are issuing bonds.

20.5.2 Bilateral Loan: A bilateral loan is a loan offered to a company by a single financial institution. They form a major funding source for small and medium-sized enterprises and enterprises in countries with under-developed bond markets. Access to loans depends both on the borrower's credit quality and market conditions.

20.5.3 Syndicated Loan: A syndicated loan is a loan advanced by a syndicate, a group of banks (joined sometimes by pension funds, insurance companies etc.) to a single company. One bank acts as a lead (also called originator) and it manages the whole process. Even a secondary market has recently developed in the syndicated loans market in which syndicated loans are securitized and sold to investors.

Most bilateral and syndicated loans are floating-rate loans with reference rates typically LIBOR [1] or a sovereign rate or the prime rate. The prime rate initially referred to a rate that banks offered to its most creditworthy customers but recently it is more influenced by the overnight rate at which banks lend to each other. Further, bank loans have varying structures, some are bullet, others are amortizing.

For companies with high credit quality, bank loans are expensive, hence they have an incentive to issue bonds directly to investors.

20.5.4 Commercial Paper: Commercial paper refers to a short-term unsecured promissory note issued in public market through private placement. It is a low-cost funding source for working capital, seasonal cash flow demand and bridge financing.

Even though the largest issuers of commercial paper are financial institutions, some non-financial institutions including governments, supranational organizations, etc. also issue them. The maturity of commercial paper may range from overnight to 1 year, with 3 months being most common. While issuers of most commercial paper have very high credit quality, some commercial papers have a higher risk and hence higher yield. Credit rating agencies issue credit ratings for commercial paper on a scale different than the bond credit rating scale.

The key to a good commercial paper credit rating is to have backup lines of credit. It is because many commercial papers are rolled over, investors face rollover risk, the risk that an issuer might not be able to issue new commercial paper to pay off the existing commercial paper. Many issuers maintain 100 percent back lines of credit (also called liquidity enhancement or backup liquidity lines).

Default rates on commercial paper are low because of the short maturity. When an issuer's credit quality deteriorates, investors can opt not to invest in the rolled over the commercial paper. This is why funding can dry up quickly in the commercial paper market. Due to short maturity, most institutional investors hold the commercial paper to maturity, hence there is little secondary market trading.

The yield on commercial paper is higher than the yield on short-term sovereign debt because: (a) commercial paper has credit risk, and (b) commercial paper market is less liquid. Yield is typically higher than municipal bonds because municipal bonds have tax advantages.

20.6 Significance of the Corporate Debt Market

There are many reasons why bond markets are important for an emerging economy. Prominent among these is the fact that they lead to more efficient entrepreneurship and greater value creation. When an entrepreneur takes a loan or issues bonds, all additional profit over and above the pre-fixed repayment amount accrues to the entrepreneur. So he or she is better incentivized to take sharper decisions. By having a weak bond market, this efficiency is lost. Further, this efficiency gap may well mean that there is less lending and hence less investment and entrepreneurship in the economy than is feasible.

Corporate debt market provides an alternative means of long-term resources to corporates—alternative to financing by banks and financial institutions. The size and growth of private corporate debt market depends upon several factors, including financing patterns of companies. Among market-based sources of financing, while the equity markets have been largely developed, the corporate bond markets in most developing countries have remained relatively underdeveloped. This has been the result of dominance of the banking system combined with the weaknesses in market infrastructure and inherent complexities. However, credit squeeze following the Asian financial crisis in the mid-1990s drew attention of policy makers to the importance of multiple financing channels in an economy. Alternative sources of finance, apart from banks, need to be actively developed to support higher levels of investment and economic growth. The development of corporate debt market has, therefore, become the prime concern of regulators in developing countries.

20.7 Lessons from East Asian Crisis

In many Asian economies, banks have traditionally been performing the role of financial intermediation. The East Asian crisis of 1997 underscored the limitations of weak banking systems. The primary role of a banking system is to create and maintain liquidity that is needed to finance production within a short-term horizon. The crisis showed that over-reliance on bank lending for debt financing exposes an economy to the risk of a failure of the banking system. Banking systems, therefore, cannot be the sole source of long-term investment capital without making an economy vulnerable to external shocks. In times of financial distress, when banking sector becomes vulnerable, the corporate bond markets act as a buffer and reduce macroeconomic vulnerability to shocks and systemic risk through diversification of credit and investment risks. By contributing to a more diverse financial system, a bond market can promote financial stability. A bond market may also help the banking system in difficult conditions by allowing banks to recapitalise their balance sheets through securitisation.

Presently, when India is endeavouring to sustain its high growth rate, it is necessary that financing constraints in any form are removed and alternative financing channels are developed in a systematic manner for supplementing traditional bank credit. The problem of *missing* corporate bond market, however, is not unique to India alone. Predominantly bank-dominated financial systems in most Asian economies faced this situation. Many Asian economies woke up to meet this challenge in the wake of the Asian financial crisis. During less than a decade, the domestic bond markets of many Asian economies have undergone significant transformation. In the case of India, however, the small size of the private corporate debt market has shrunk further. This trend needs to be reversed soon. India could learn from the experiences of countries that have undertaken the process of reforming their domestic corporate bond markets.

To conclude, in any country, companies face different types of financing choices at different stages of development. Reflecting the varied supplies of different types of capital and their costs, regulatory policies and financial innovations, the financing patterns of firms vary geographically and temporally. While developed countries rely more on market-based sources of finance, the developing countries rely more on bank-based sources.

The development of a corporate bond market, for direct financing of the capital requirements of corporates by investors assumes paramount importance, particularly in a liberalised financial system. A corporate bond is debt issued by a company in order for it to raise capital. An investor who buys a corporate bond is effectively lending money to the company in return for a series of interest payments, but these bonds may also actively trade on the secondary market. Corporate bonds are typically seen as somewhat riskier than government bonds, so they usually have higher interest rates to compensate for this additional risk.

Endnote

1. LIBOR is the acronym for London Inter-bank Offer Rate. It is the global reference rate for unsecured short-term borrowing in the inter-bank market. It acts as a benchmark for short-term interest rates.

21

Dividend Policy Models

Dividends are often part of a company's strategy. However, they are under no obligation to repay shareholders using dividends. Stable, constant, and residual are the three types of dividend policy. Even though investors know companies are not required to pay dividends, many consider it a bellwether of that specific company's financial health.

21.1 Dividend Policy Explained

A dividend policy is the policy a company uses to structure its dividend payout to shareholders. Dividend policy is concerned with financial policies regarding paying cash dividend in the present or paying an increased dividend at a later stage. Whether to issue dividends, and what amount, is determined mainly on the basis of the company's unappropriated profit (excess cash) and influenced by the company's long-term earning power. When cash surplus exists and is not needed by the firm, then management is expected to pay out some or all of those surplus earnings in the form of cash dividends or to repurchase the company's stock through a share buyback programme.

Chalking out the dividend policy is challenging for the directors and financial manager of a company, because different investors have different views on present cash dividends and future capital gains. Another confusion that pops up is regarding the extent of effect of dividends on the share price. Due to this controversial nature of a dividend policy it is often called the *dividend puzzle*.

Financial theory suggests that the dividend policy should be set based upon the type of company and what management determines is the best use of those dividend resources for the firm to its shareholders. As a general rule, shareholders of growth companies would prefer managers to have a share buyback program, whereas shareholders of value or secondary stocks would prefer the management of these companies to payout surplus earnings in the form of cash dividends.

If there are no positive opportunities, i.e. projects where returns exceed the hurdle rate, and excess cash surplus is not needed, then management should return some or all of the excess cash to shareholders as dividends. This is the general case. However there are exceptions. For example, shareholders of a *growth stock*, expect that the company will, almost by definition, retain most of the excess earnings so as to fund future growth internally. By withholding current dividend payments to shareholders, managers of growth companies are hoping that dividend payments will be increased proportionality higher in the future, to offset the retainment of current earnings and the internal financing of present investment projects.

Management must also choose the *form* of the dividend distribution, generally as cash dividends or via a share buyback. Various factors may be taken into consideration:

where shareholders must pay tax on dividends, firms may elect to retain earnings or to perform a stock buyback, in both cases increasing the value of shares outstanding. Alternatively, some companies will pay "dividends" from stock rather than in cash.

21.2 Types of Dividend Policy

Most companies view a dividend policy as an integral part of their corporate strategy. Management must decide on the dividend amount, timing, and various other factors that influence dividend payments. There are three types of dividend policies:

1. A stable dividend policy.
2. A constant dividend policy.
3. A residual dividend policy.

21.2.1 Stable Dividend Policy: A stable dividend policy is the easiest and most commonly used. The goal of the policy is a steady and predictable dividend payout each year, which is what most investors seek. Whether earnings are up or down, investors receive a dividend.

The goal is to align the dividend policy with the long-term growth of the company rather than with quarterly volatility in earnings. This approach gives the shareholder more certainty concerning the amount and timing of the dividend.

21.2.2 Constant Dividend Policy: The primary drawback of the stable dividend policy is that investors may not see a dividend increase in boom years. Under the constant dividend policy, a company pays a percentage of its earnings as dividends every year. In this way, investors experience the full volatility of company earnings.

If earnings are up, investors get a larger dividend. If earnings are down, investors may not receive a dividend. The primary drawback to the method is the volatility of earnings and dividends. It is difficult to plan financially when dividend income is highly volatile.

21.2.3 Residual Dividend Policy: Residual dividend policy is also highly volatile, but some investors see it as the only acceptable dividend policy. With a residual dividend policy, the company pays out what dividends remain after the company has paid for capital expenditures and working capital.

This approach is volatile, but it makes the most sense in terms of business operations. Investors do not want to invest in a company that justifies its increased debt with the need to pay dividends.

21.3 Dividend Irrelevance Theories

Some financial experts suggest the dividend policy is irrelevant, in theory, because investors can sell a portion of their shares or portfolio if they need funds. This is the *dividend irrelevance theory,* which infers that dividend payouts minimally affect a stock's price.

There are two important theories relating to the irrelevance approach:

1. Residuals theory of dividends.
2. Modigliani and Miller approach.

21.3.1 Residuals Theory of Dividends: One of the assumptions of this theory is that external financing to re-invest is either not available, or that it is too costly to invest in any profitable opportunity. If a firm has good investment opportunity available then it will invest the retained earnings and reduce the dividends or give no dividends at all. If no such opportunity exists, the firm will pay out dividends.

If a firm has to issue securities to finance an investment, the existence of flotation costs needs a larger amount of securities to be issued. Therefore, the pay out of dividends depend on whether any profits are left after the financing of proposed investments as flotation costs increases the amount of profits used. Deciding how much dividends to be paid is not the concern here, in fact the firm has to decide how much profits to be retained and the rest can then be distributed as dividends. This is the theory of residuals, where dividends are residuals from the profits after serving proposed investments.

This residual decision is distributed in three steps:
1. Evaluating the available investment opportunities to determine capital expenditures.
2. Evaluating the amount of equity finance that would be needed for the investment, basically having an optimum finance mix.
3. Cost of retained earnings is less than cost of new equity capital, thus the retained profits are used to finance investments. If there is a surplus after the financing then there is distribution of dividends.

The dividend policy strongly depends on two things:
1. Investment opportunities available to the company.
2. Amount of internally retained and generated funds which lead to dividend distribution if all possible investments have been financed.

The dividend policy of such a kind is a passive one, and does not influence market price. The dividends also fluctuate every year because of different investment opportunities every year. However, it does not really affect the shareholders as they get compensated in the form of future capital gains.

21.3.2 Modigliani-Miller School of Thought: Modigliani and Miller school of thought believes that investors do not state any preference between current dividends and capital gains. They say that dividend policy is irrelevant and is not deterministic of the market value. Therefore, the shareholders are indifferent between the two types of dividends. All they want are high returns either in the form of dividends or in the form of re-investment of retained earnings by the firm.

There are two conditions discussed in relation to this approach: (a) decisions regarding financing and investments are made and do not change with respect to the amounts of dividends received and (b) when an investor buys and sells shares without facing any transaction costs and firms issue shares without facing any floatation cost, it is termed as a perfect capital market.

Modigliani-Miller theorem states that the division of retained earnings between new investment and dividends do not influence the value of the firm. It is the investment pattern and consequently the earnings of the firm which affect the share price or the value of the firm.

21.3.3 Assumptions of the MM theorem

MM approach has taken into consideration the following assumptions:

1. There is a rational behaviour by the investors and there exists perfect capital markets.
2. Investors have free information available for them.
3. No time lag and transaction costs exist.
4. Securities can be split into any parts i.e. they are divisible
5. No taxes and flotation costs.
6. Capital markets are perfectly efficient.
7. The investment decisions are taken firmly and the profits are therefore known with certainty. The dividend policy does not affect these decisions.
8. There is perfect certainty of future profits of firms.

The dividend irrelevancy in this model exists because shareholders are indifferent between paying out dividends and investing retained earnings in new opportunities. The firm finances opportunities either through retained earnings or by issuing new shares to raise capital. The amount used up in paying out dividends is replaced by the new capital raised through issuing shares. This will affect the value of the firm in an opposite way. The increase in the value because of the dividends will be offset by the decrease in the value for new capital raising.

21.4 Dividend Relevance Theories

Despite the suggestion that the dividend policy is irrelevant, it is income for shareholders. Company leaders are often the largest shareholders and have the most to gain from a generous dividend policy.

Various models have been developed to help firms analyse and evaluate the perfect dividend policy. There is no agreement among these schools of thought over the relationship between dividends and the value of the share or the wealth of the shareholders in other words.

Dividends paid by the firms are viewed positively both by the investors and the firms. The firms which do not pay dividends are rated in oppositely by investors thus affecting the share price. The people who support relevance of dividends clearly state that regular dividends reduce uncertainty of the shareholders.

Some important models supporting dividend relevance are given below:

21.4.1 Walter's Model: Propounded by James E. Walter, the model shows the relevance of dividend policy and its bearing on the value of the share.

Assumptions of the Walter model

1. Retained earnings are the only source of financing investments in the firm, there is no external finance involved.
2. The cost of capital, k_e and the rate of return on investment, r are constant i.e. even if new investments decisions are taken, the risks of the business remains same.
3. The firm's life is endless i.e. there is no closing down.

Basically, the firm's decision to give or not give out dividends depends on whether it has enough opportunities to invest the retained earnings i.e. a strong relationship between investment and dividend decisions is considered.

Dividends paid to the shareholders are reinvested by the shareholder further, to get higher returns. This is referred to as the opportunity cost of the firm or the cost of capital, k_e for the firm. Another situation where the firms do not pay out dividends, is when they invest the profits or retained earnings in profitable opportunities to earn returns on such investments. This rate of return r, for the firm must at least be equal to k_e. If this happens then the returns of the firm is equal to the earnings of the shareholders if the dividends were paid. Thus, it is clear that if r, is more than the cost of capital k_e, then the returns from investments is more than returns shareholders receive from further investments.

Walter's model says that if $r<k_e$ then the firm should distribute the profits in the form of dividends to give the shareholders higher returns. However, if $r>k_e$ then the investment opportunities reap better returns for the firm and thus, the firm should invest the retained earnings. The relationship between r and k are extremely important to determine the dividend policy. It decides whether the firm should have zero payout or 100 percent payout.

In a nutshell:

If $r>k_e$, the firm should have zero payout and make investments.

If $r<k_e$, the firm should have 100% payouts and no investment of retained earnings.

If $r=k_e$, the firm is indifferent between dividends and investments.

Although the model provides a simple framework to explain the relationship between the market value of the share and the dividend policy, it has some unrealistic assumptions.

The assumption of no external financing apart from retained earnings, for the firm make further investments is not really followed in the real world. Similarly, the constant r and k_e are seldom found in real life, because as and when a firm invests more the business risks change.

21.4.2 Gordon's Model: Myron J. Gordon has also supported dividend relevance and believes in regular dividends affecting the share price of the firm.

Assumptions of the Gordon model

Gordon''s assumptions are similar to the ones given by Walter. However, there are two additional assumptions proposed by him:

1. The product of retention ratio b and the rate of return r gives us the growth rate of the firm g.
2. The cost of capital k_e, is not only constant but greater than the growth rate i.e. $k_e>g$.

Investors are risk-averse and believe that incomes from dividends are certain rather than incomes from future capital gains, therefore they predict future capital gains to be risky propositions. They discount the future capital gains at a higher rate than the firm's earnings, thereby evaluating a higher value of the share. In short, when retention rate increases, they require a higher discounting rate.

Gordon's ideas are similar to Walter's and therefore the criticisms are also similar. Both of them clearly state the relationship between dividend policies and market value of the firm.

21.4.3 Lintner's Model: John Lintner's dividend policy model is a model theorizing how a publicly-traded company sets its dividend policy. The logic is that every company wants to maintain a constant rate of dividend even if the results in a particular period are not up to the mark. The assumption is that investors will prefer to receive a certain dividend payout.

The model states that dividends are paid according to two factors. The first is the net present value of earnings, with higher values indicating higher dividends. The second is the sustainability of earnings, i.e. a company may increase its earnings without increasing its dividend payouts until managers are convinced that it will continue to maintain such earnings. The theory was adopted based on observations that many companies will set their long-run target dividends-to-earnings ratios based upon the amount of positive net present value projects that they have available.

21.4.4 Capital Structure Substitution (CSS) Theory and Dividends: CSS theory describes the relationship between earnings, stock price and capital structure of public companies. The theory is based on one simple hypothesis: company managements manipulate capital structure such that earnings per share (EPS) are maximized. The resulting dynamic debt-equity target explains why some companies use dividends and others do not. When redistributing cash to shareholders, company managements can typically choose between dividends and share repurchases. But as dividends are in most cases taxed higher than capital gains, investors are expected to prefer capital gains. However, the CSS theory shows that for some companies share repurchases lead to a reduction in EPS. These companies typically prefer dividends over share repurchases.

CSS theory provides more guidance on dividend policy to company managements than the Walter model and the Gordon model. It also reverses the traditional order of cause and effect by implying that company valuation ratios drive dividend policy, and not vice versa. CSS theory does not have *invisible* or *hidden* parameters such as the equity risk premium, the discount rate, the expected growth rate or expected inflation. As a consequence the theory can be tested in an unambiguous way.

To sum up, dividend policy is concerned with financial policies regarding the payment of a cash dividend in the present or paying an increased dividend at a later stage. Whether to issue dividends, and what amount, is determined mainly on the basis of the company's unappropriated profit (excess cash) and influenced by the company's long-term earning power. When cash surplus exists and is not needed by the firm, then management is expected to pay out some or all of those surplus earnings in the form of cash dividends or to repurchase the company's stock through a share buyback programme.

As a general rule, shareholders of growth companies would prefer managers to retain earnings and pay no dividends (use excess cash to reinvest into the company's operations), whereas shareholders of value or secondary stocks would prefer the management of these companies to payout surplus earnings in the form of cash dividends when a positive return cannot be earned through the reinvestment of undistributed earnings. A share buyback programme may be accepted when the value of the stock is greater than the returns to be realized from the reinvestment of undistributed profits. In all instances, the appropriate dividend policy is usually directed by that which maximizes long-term shareholder value.

22

Modigliani-Miller Theorem (M&M Theorem)

Modigliani-Miller Theorem (M&M Theorem) states that the market value of a company is correctly calculated as the present value of its future earnings and its underlying assets, and is independent of its capital structure. At its most basic level, the theorem argues that, with certain assumptions in place, it is irrelevant whether a company finances its growth by borrowing, by issuing stock shares, or by reinvesting its profits.

Companies have only the following three ways to raise money to finance their operations and fuel their growth and expansion.
1. They can borrow money by issuing bonds or obtaining loans.
2. They can re-invest their profits in their operations.
3. They can issue new stock shares to investors.

M&M Theorem argues that the option or combination of options that a company chooses has no effect on its real market value.

According to M&M Theorem a company's capital structure is not a factor in its value. Market value is determined by the present value of future earnings.

M&M Theorem has been highly influential in the area of corporate finance since it was introduced in the 1950s.

22.1 Historical Background

Franco Modigliani and Merton Miller conceptualized and developed this theorem, and published it in an article, "The Cost of Capital, Corporation Finance and the Theory of Investment", which appeared in the *American Economic Review* in the late 1950s.

At the time, both Modigliani and Miller were professors at the Graduate School of Industrial Administration at Carnegie Mellon University. Both were required to teach corporate finance to business students. However, neither had any experience in corporate finance. After reading the course materials that they were to use, the two professors found the information inconsistent and the concepts flawed. So, they worked together to correct them.

Modigliani was awarded the 1985 Nobel Prize in Economics for this and other contributions. Miller was a professor at the University of Chicago when he was awarded the 1990 Nobel Prize in Economics, along with Harry Markowitz and William F. Sharpe, for their "work in the theory of financial economics", with Miller specifically cited for "fundamental contributions to the theory of corporate finance".

Early on, the two economists realized that their initial theorem left out a number of relevant factors. It left out such matters as taxes and financing costs, effectively arguing its point in the vacuum of a *perfectly efficient market*.

Later versions of their theorem addressed these issues, including corporate income taxes and the cost of capital.

22.2 M&M Theorem in Brief

M&M Theorem is an influential element of economic theory. It forms the basis for modern thinking on capital structure. The basic theorem states that in the absence of taxes, bankruptcy costs, agency costs, and asymmetric information, and in an efficient market, the value of a firm is unaffected by how that firm is financed. Since the value of the firm depends neither on its dividend policy nor its decision to raise capital by issuing stock or selling debt, M&M Theorem is often called the *capital structure irrelevance principle*.

The key M&M Theorem was developed in a world without taxes. However, if we move to a world where there are taxes, when the interest on debt is tax deductible, and ignoring other frictions, the value of the company increases in proportion to the amount of debt used. The additional value equals the total discounted value of future taxes saved by issuing debt instead of equity.

Merton Miller, one of the two originators of the theorem, explains the concept behind the theory with an analogy in his book titled *Financial Innovations and Market Volatility*. Consider a firm as a gigantic tub of whole milk. The farmer can sell the whole milk as it is. Or he can separate out the cream and sell it at a considerably higher price than the whole milk would bring. However, the skimmed milk left with the farmer would sell for much less than whole milk. M&M Theorem says that if there were no costs of separation (and no government dairy-support programmes), the cream plus the skim milk would bring the same price as the whole milk.

Consider two firms which are identical except for their financial structures. The first (Firm U) is *unlevered*, i.e. it is financed by *equity* only. The other (Firm L) is *levered*, i.e. it is financed partly by equity, and partly by debt. M&M Theorem states that the value of the two firms is the same.

To see why this should be true, let us suppose an investor is considering buying one of the two firms, U or L. Instead of purchasing the shares of the levered firm L, he could purchase the shares of firm U and borrow the same amount of money B that firm L does. The eventual returns to either of these investments would be the same. Therefore the price of L must be the same as the price of U minus the money borrowed B, which is the value of L's debt.

This discussion also clarifies the role of some of the theorem's assumptions. We have implicitly assumed that the investor's cost of borrowing money is the same as that of the firm, which need not be true in the presence of asymmetric information, in the absence of efficient markets, or if the investor has a different risk profile than the firm.

A higher debt-to-equity ratio leads to a higher required return on equity, because of the higher risk involved for equity-holders in a company with debt. The formula is derived from the theory of weighted average cost of capital (WACC).

These propositions are true under the following assumptions:

1. No transaction costs exist, and
2. Individuals and corporations borrow at the same rates.

These results might seem irrelevant (after all, none of the conditions are met in the real world), but the theorem is still taught and studied because it tells something very important. That is, capital structure matters precisely because one or more of these assumptions is violated. It tells where to look for determinants of optimal capital structure and how those factors might affect optimal capital structure.

22.3 M&M Theorem in Perfectly Efficient Markets

This is the first version of the M&M Theorem with the assumption of perfectly efficient markets. The assumption implies that companies operating in the world of perfectly efficient markets do not pay any taxes, the trading of securities is executed without any transaction costs, bankruptcy is possible but there are no bankruptcy costs, and information is perfectly symmetrical.

Proposition 1:

$V_L = V_U$

Where,

V_U = Value of the unlevered firm (financing only through equity).

V_L = Value of the levered firm (financing through a mix of debt and equity).

The first proposition essentially claims that the company's capital structure does not impact its value. Since the value of a company is calculated as the present value of future cash flows, the capital structure cannot affect it. Also, in perfectly efficient markets, companies do not pay any taxes. Therefore, the company with a 100 percent leveraged capital structure does not obtain any benefits from tax-deductible interest payments.

Proposition 2:

$$r_E = r_a + \frac{D}{E}(r_a - r_D)$$

Where

r_E = Cost of levered equity.

r_a = Cost of unlevered equity.

r_D = Cost of debt.

D/E = Debt-to-equity ratio.

The second proposition of the M&M Theorem states that the company's cost of equity is directly proportional to the company's leverage level. An increase in leverage level induces higher default probability to a company. Therefore, investors tend to demand a higher cost of equity (return) to be compensated for the additional risk.

22.4 M&M Theorem in the Real World

The second version of the M&M Theorem was developed to better suit real-world conditions. The assumptions of the newer version imply that companies pay taxes; there are transaction, bankruptcy, and agency costs; and information is not symmetrical.

Proposition 1:
$V_L = V_U + t_c \times D$
Where
t_c = Tax rate
D = Debt

The first proposition states that tax shields that result from the tax-deductible interest payments make the value of a levered company higher than the value of an unlevered company. The main rationale behind the theorem is that tax-deductible interest payments positively affect a company's cash flows. Since a company's value is determined as the present value of the future cash flows, the value of a levered company increases.

Proposition 2:

$$r_E = r_a + \frac{D}{E} \times (1 - t_c) \times (r_a - r_D)$$

The second proposition for the real-world condition states that the cost of equity has a directly proportional relationship with the leverage level.

Nonetheless, the presence of tax shields affects the relationship by making the cost of equity less sensitive to the leverage level. Although the extra debt still increases the chance of a company's default, investors are less prone to negatively reacting to the company taking additional leverage, as it creates the tax shields that boost its value.

To sum up, M&M Theorem is one of the most important theorems in corporate finance. The theorem was developed by economists Franco Modigliani and Merton Miller in 1958. The main idea of the M&M theory is that the capital structure of a company does not affect its overall value.

The first version of the M&M theory was full of limitations as it was developed under the assumption of perfectly efficient markets, in which the companies do not pay taxes, while there are no bankruptcy costs or asymmetric information. Subsequently, Miller and Modigliani developed the second version of their theory by including taxes, bankruptcy costs, and asymmetric information.

Part V
Indian Financial System

23

Financial Institutions

Financial institutions in India have transited since the mid-1990s from an environment of an administered regime to a system dominated by market-determined interest and exchange rates, and migration of the central bank from direct and quantitative to price-based instruments of monetary policy and operations. However, increased globalisation has resulted in further expansion and sophistication of the financial sector, which has posed new challenges to regulation and supervision, particularly of the banking system. In this context, the capabilities of the existing regulatory and supervisory structures also need to be assessed by benchmarking them against the best international practices.

Emphasizing the need for an efficient financial intermediation, the Twelfth Five Year Plan (2012-17) observed, "While availability of savings in the aggregate is an important part of macroeconomic balance, it is also important to have an efficient financial system that can channel savings to the most productive uses, and also ensure inclusiveness. The past two decades have seen far-reaching change in the character and structure of the country's banking system and the capital markets. These changes have addressed the management of credit risk, provisioning against delinquent loans and a greater focus on fee-based income. The interest rate regime that used to be highly regulated was systematically replaced by a commercially determined framework that helped price-in credit quality, duration and diversification of risk. The kind of loan products available and the servicing of these for the commercial sector have also become more efficient. Retail banking, that is, personal loans for buying homes and other durable assets, and payment and settlement facilities, have become an important and rapidly growing component of banking. Lending to small borrowers typified by the self-help group (SHG) and micro finance has come some distance towards making financial inclusion meaningful.

These changes have also changed the behaviour of corporate borrowers. In many ways, financial risk was not meaningful in the years before 1991. It changed subsequently, and with it the incentives to maintain a clean credit record and a lower leverage. Dismantling of the production licensing system, lower import tariffs and the end of quantitative restrictions on imports made competition a reality in India, that is, both domestic competition and competition vis-à-vis the global producers. Finally, the decline in the ownership functions of government and quasi-governmental agencies, and the enhanced role of capital markets in raising finance has given new importance to the interests of shareholders, especially minority shareholders. Associated with this is the challenge of corporate control, which now has to face up to proactive mergers, acquisition and sale". [1]

23.1 Classification of Financial Institutions in India

Financial institutions in India can be classified as given in Table 23.1.

Table 23.1: Classification of Financial Institutions in India

1. Reserve Bank of India (RBI)
2. Commercial Banks
2.1 Scheduled Commercial Banks
2.1.1 Public Sector Banks: (a) State Bank group, (b) nationalised banks and (c) other public sector banks
2.1.2 Private Sector Banks: (a) old private banks and (b) new private banks
2.1.3 Foreign banks
2.1.4 Regional rural banks
2.2 Non-scheduled commercial banks (local area banks)
2.3 Payment banks
3. Co-operative Banks
3.1 Urban co-operative banks
3.1.1 Scheduled
3.1.2 Non-scheduled
3.2 Rural co-operative banks
3.2.1 Short-term structure: (a) State co-operative banks (SCBs) and (b) District central co-operative banks (DCCBs)
3.2.2 Primary agricultural credit societies (PACS)
3.2.3 Long-term structure: (a) State co-operative agriculture and rural development banks (SCARDBs) and (b) Primary co-operative agriculture and rural development banks (PCARDBs)
4. State Financial Corporations (SFCs)
5. Development Finance Institutions (DFIs)
6. Non-banking Financial Companies (NBFCs)
6.1 NBFCs (Deposit-taking)
6.2 NBFCs (Non-deposit-taking)
6.3 Residuary non-banking companies (RNBCs)
6.4 Primary dealers
6.5 Housing finance companies
7. Mutual Funds
7.1 Bank-sponsored
7.2 Institution-sponsored
7.2.1 Indian
7.2.2 Foreign
7.3 Joint ventures (predominantly Indian)

contd...

7.4 Joint ventures (predominantly foreign)
8. Pension Funds
9. Insurance Institutions
9.1 Life insurance
9.1.1 Public
9.1.2 Private
9.2 Non-life insurance
9.2.1 Public
9.2.2 Private
9.2.3 Others [Deposit Insurance and Credit Guarantee Corporation (DICGC) and Reinsurance Corporation of India Ltd.]
10. Other Institutions
Other institutions established to meet specific financing needs include Power Finance Corporation (PFC) and Rural Electrification Corporation (REC) (financial assistance to the power sector) and Indian Railway Finance Corporation (IRFC), which is the capital market financing arm of Indian Railways. These institutions have been notified as public financial institutions (PFIs) under the Companies Act, 1956 and enjoy less stringent compliance and regulatory norms. In addition, at the state-level, there exists the North Eastern Development Finance Corporation (NEDFC) extending credit to industry and agricultural concerns in the North Eastern region, and Technical Consultancy Organisations, providing technical inputs for feasibility studies on viability of projects. Besides, the State Industrial Development Corporations (SIDCs), registered under the Companies Act, 1956 also provide credit to industries at the state level.
11. Financial Institutions (1 to 10)
12. Banking Sector (1+2+3)

23.2 Financial Institutions in India at a Glance

Financial institutions (intermediaries) in India consist of commercial banks, regional rural banks (RRBs), urban co-operative banks (UCBs), rural co-operative credit institutions, development finance institutions (DFIs), non-banking financial companies (NBFCs), mutual funds, pension funds, and insurance organisations. These institutions, which provide a meeting ground for the savers and the investors, form the core of India's financial sector. Through mobilisation of resources and their better allocation, financial intermediaries play an important role in the development process of underdeveloped countries.

Financial institutions in India have transited since the mid-1990s from an environment of an administered regime to a system dominated by market-determined interest and exchange rates, and migration of the central bank from direct and quantitative to price-based instruments of monetary policy and operations. However, increased globalisation has resulted in further expansion and sophistication of the financial sector, which has posed new challenges to regulation and supervision, particularly of the banking system. In this context, the capabilities of the existing regulatory and supervisory structures also need to be assessed by benchmarking them against the best international practices.

23.2.1 Commercial Banks: Commercial banks are the dominant institutions in the Indian financial landscape. According to Committee on Financial Sector Assessment, "Though public sector banks (PSBs) account for around 70 percent of commercial banking assets, competition in the banking sector has increased in recent years with the emergence of private players as also with greater private shareholding of PSBs. Listing of PSBs on stock exchanges and increased private shareholding have also added to competition. The new private banks which accounted for 2.6 percent of the commercial banking sector in March 1997 have developed rapidly and accounted for nearly 17 percent of the commercial banking assets by end-March 2008. Together with cooperative banks, the banking sector accounts for nearly 70 per cent of the total assets of Indian financial institutions". [2]

Commercial banks in India can be classified in the following ways:

1. Scheduled and non-scheduled banks.
2. Indian and foreign banks.
3. Public sector and private sector banks.

Until the early 1990s, the banking sector suffered from lack of competition, low capital base, low productivity and high intermediation cost. Commenting on the performance of the nationalised banks, the Reserve Bank of India observed, "After the nationalisation of large banks in 1969 and 1980, the Government-owned banks have dominated the banking sector. The role of technology was minimal and the quality of service was not given adequate importance. Banks also did not follow proper risk management systems and the prudential standards were weak. All these resulted in poor asset quality and low profitability". [3]

Prior to reforms, the Indian Government determined the quantum, allocation and the price of credit, a situation referred to as *financial repression* by some experts. It was in this backdrop, that wide-ranging banking sector reforms in India were introduced as an integral part of the economic reforms initiated in the early 1990s. Reforms in the commercial banking sector had two distinct phases.

23.2.2 Regional Rural Banks (RRBs): Regional rural banks (RRBs) form an important segment of the rural financial sector. They were conceived as institutions that combine the local feel and familiarity of the co-operatives with the business capabilities of commercial banks. This sector has an exclusive role in improving financial inclusion and catering to vital sectors like agriculture and allied economic activities. Public policy, therefore, aims at keeping this sector viable and strong through various forms of active intervention.

The renewed emphasis on agricultural and rural development by the Government of India would lead to a growing demand for different types of financial services in the rural areas, as financial needs of the rural economy becomes diversified. The present structure of rural credit may not be able to cater to the same. RRBs would be called upon to play a greater role in providing such services due to their rural character and feel. RRBs have to take over a larger share of credit disbursements calling for much larger resource mobilization, as also greater efforts for their institutional strengthening.

23.2.3 Urban Co-operative Banks (UCBs): The co-operative banking system forms an integral part of the Indian financial system. It comprises urban cooperative banks and rural co-operative credit institutions. Urban co-operative banks have a single-tier structure whereas rural co-operatives have a two- or three-tier structure.

The single tier urban co-operative banks (UCBs)—also referred to as primary cooperative banks—play an important role in meeting the growing credit needs of urban and semi-urban areas of the country. The UCBs, which grew rapidly in the early 1990s, showed certain weaknesses arising out of lack of sound corporate governance, unethical lending, comparatively high levels of non-performing loans and their inability to operate in a liberalised environment. Accordingly, some of the weak UCBs have been either liquidated or merged with other banks.

The financial reforms process initiated in 1991 has tried to achieve regulatory convergence among various financial intermediaries in view of their systemic importance. Therefore, the basic objectives and instruments of reforms for co-operative banks have been the same as for state co-operative banks (SCBs). However, given the special characteristics of co-operative banks, they have been extended certain dispensations in terms of pace and sequencing of reforms.

23.2.4 Rural Co-operative Credit Institutions: Historically, rural co-operative credit institutions (or simply rural co-operatives) have played an important role in providing institutional credit to the agricultural and rural sectors. The structure of rural co-operative banks is not uniform across all the States of the country. Some States have a unitary structure with the State level banks operating through their own branches, while others have a mixed structure incorporating both unitary and federal systems.

The rural credit co-operative system has served as an important instrument of credit delivery in rural and agricultural areas. The separate structure of rural co-operative sector for long-term and short-term loans has enabled these institutions to develop as specialised institutions for rural credit delivery. At the same time, their federal structure has helped in providing support structure for the guidance and critical financing for the lower structure.

23.2.5 Development Finance Institutions (DFIs): Development finance institutions (DFIs) or simply financial institutions were set up in India at various points of time starting from the late 1940s to cater to the medium to long-term financing requirements of industry as the capital market in India had not developed sufficiently. After Independence in 1947, the national government adopted the path of planned economic development and launched the First Five Year Plan in 1951. This strategy of development provided the critical inducement for establishment of DFIs at both all-India and state-levels. In order to perform their role, DFIs were extended funds of the RBI and government guaranteed bonds, which constituted major sources of their funds. Funds from these sources were not only available at concessional rates, but also on a long-term basis with their maturity period ranging from 10-15 years. On the asset side, their operations were marked by near absence of competition.

A large variety of financial institutions have come into existence over the years to perform various types of financial activities. While some of them operate at all-India level, others are state level institutions. Besides providing direct loans (including rupee loans, foreign currency loans), financial institutions also extend financial assistance by way of underwriting and direct subscription and by issuing guarantees. Recently, some DFIs have started extending short-term/working capital finance, although term-lending continues to be their primary activity.

23.2.6 Non-banking Financial Companies (NBFCs): In the multi-tier financial system of India, NBFCs stand apart for more than one reason. Though these companies essentially do the job of financial intermediation, they are still not fully comparable with the other segments of the financial system. This is so in view of the wide variations in the profile of the players in this sector in terms of their nature of activity—lending, investment, lease, hire purchase, chit fund, pure deposit mobilisation, fee based activity etc.—the volume of activity, the sources of funding they rely on (public deposits and non-public deposits), method of raising resources, deployment pattern etc. This has naturally resulted in the creation of multifarious categories of NBFCs and therefore, diverse regulatory dispensation by RBI.

Although NBFCs in India have existed for a long time, they shot into prominence in the second half of the 1980s and in the first-half of the 1990s, as deposits raised by them grew rapidly. NBFCs were historically subjected to a relatively lower degree of regulation *vis-à-vis* banks. Prior to reforms in this sector, operations of NBFCs were characterized by several distinctive features *viz.*, no entry barriers, limited fixed assets and no holding of inventories-all of which led to a proliferation of NBFCs. Primarily engaged in the area of retail banking, they face competition from banks and financial institutions. With the increasing services sector activity in India, the NBFCs have been playing a critical role in providing credit. NBFCs have extensive networks with some of them accepting public deposits.

23.2.7 Mutual Funds: Mutual funds are very popular all over the world and they play an important role in the financial system of many countries. Mutual funds are an ideal medium for investment by small investors in the stock market. Mutual funds pool together the investments of small investors for participation in the stock market. Being institutional investors, mutual funds can afford market analysis generally not available to individual investors. Furthermore, mutual funds can diversify the portfolio in a better way as compared with individual investors due to the expertise and availability of funds.

23.2.8 Pension Funds: Pension sector reforms were initiated in India to establish a robust and sustainable social security arrangement in the country seeing that only about 12-13 percent of the total workforce was covered by any formal social security system. The New Pension System (NPS) was introduced by the Government from January 1, 2004 for new entrants to the Central Government service, except the Armed Forces, and was extended to the general public from May 1, 2009 on a voluntary basis. The features of the NPS design are self-sustainability, portability and scalability. Based on individual choice, it is envisaged as a low-cost and efficient pension system backed by sound regulation. As a pure "defined contribution" product with no defined benefit element, returns are totally market-related. The NPS provides various investment options and choices to individuals to switch over from one option to another or from one fund manager to another, subject to certain regulatory restrictions.

Pension Fund Regulatory and Development Authority (PFRDA), set up as a regulatory body for the pension sector, is engaged in consolidating the initiatives taken so far regarding the full NPS architecture and expanding the reach of the NPS distribution network. The full NPS architecture comprising a central recordkeeping agency (CRA), pension fund managers (PFMs), trustee bank, custodian and NPS Trust has been put in place and is fully operational. The National Securities Depository Limited (NSDL) has been selected as the CRA. The PFRDA has also appointed 7 pension fund managers (PFM) for the unorganized sector, namely UTI Retirement Solutions Limited, SBI Pension Funds Pvt. Ltd., ICICI Prudential Pension Fund Management Co. Ltd., LIC Pension Fund Ltd., Reliance Capital Pension Fund Ltd., Kotak Mahindra Pension Fund Ltd. and HDFC Pension Management Co. Ltd. as pension fund sponsors under the NPS.

23.2.9 Insurance Organisations: Insurance has been an important part of the Indian financial system. Until recently, insurance services were provided by the public sector i.e. life insurance by the Life Insurance Corporation of India (LIC) since the mid-1950s, and general insurance by the General Insurance Corporation (GIC) and its four subsidiaries since the 1970s. The insurance industry was opened up to the private sector in August 2000. The primary objective of liberalisation in the insurance sector was to deepen insurance penetration by enlarging consumer choices through product innovation. The increased competition has led to rapid product innovations for catering to the diverse requirements of the various segments of the population. Besides statutory commitments in respect of weaker sections of society, competitive pressures are pushing life insurers to adopt innovative marketing strategies to extend insurance penetration, especially targeting lower income groups. Insurance industry in India is broadly classified into: (a) life insurance, and (b) non-life insurance business.

The Indian insurance industry has witnessed a sea-change since opening up to private players in 1999. The liberalisation has transformed the industry's outlook towards the vast Indian market. The spurt in the number of players has led to innovation in product development and distribution channels, thus treating the Indian customer to a whole new range of insurance products, each suited to match unique requirements of different societal segments.

The ultimate objective of reforms is to increase insurance-density and insurance penetration levels by designing more tailor-made products for customers, both individuals and institutions. Overall, the reach of the sector has increased since opening up with a wider choice available to the policy holder. Simultaneously, the increase in resource mobilisation has resulted in the investment in the infrastructure and social sectors.

23.3 Regulation and Supervision of Financial Institutions in India

Financial institutions in India are regulated and supervised by various authorities and legislations (Table 23.2).

Table 23.2: Regulation and Supervision of Financial Institutions in India

Institutions	Regulator(s)	Act(s)
Commercial banks	- Reserve Bank of India (RBI)	- Banking Regulation Act, 1949 - Reserve Bank of India Act, 1934 - State Bank of India Act, 1955 - State Bank of India (Subsidiary) Banks Act, 1959 - Banking Companies (Acquisition and Transfer of Undertaking) Acts, 1970 and 1980 - Deposit Insurance and Credit Guarantee Co-operation (DICGC) Act, 1961
Urban co-operative banks	- RBI - Registrar of Co-operative Societies	- Banking Regulation Act, 1949 - Co-operative Societies Act of various State Governments - Multi-State Co-operative Societies Act, 2002 - DICGC Act, 1961
Regional rural banks (RRBs)	- RBI - National Bank for Agriculture and Rural Development (NABARD)	- Banking Regulation Act, 1949 - DICGC Act, 1961 - Regional Rural Banks Act, 1976 - Reserve Bank of India, Act, 1934
State co-operative banks/district central co-operative banks	- RBI - Registrar of Co-operative Societies - NABARD	- Banking Regulation Act, 1949 - Co-operative Societies Act of various State Governments - DICGC Act, 1961
Development finance institutions (DFIs)/Non-banking financial companies (NBFCs)	- RBI - Ministry of Corporate Affairs	- Reserve Bank of India, Act, 1934 - Companies Act, 1956
Housing finance companies	- National Housing Bank (NHB) - Ministry of Corporate Affairs	- Reserve Bank of India, Act, 1934 - National Housing Bank Act, 1987 Companies Act, 1956
Mutual funds	- Securities and Exchange Board of India (SEBI)	- Securities and Exchange Board of India (SEBI) Act, 1992

contd...

Insurance companies	- Insurance Regulatory and Development Authority (IRDA)	- Insurance Regulatory and Development Authority (IRDA) Act, 1999

Endnotes

1. Government of India, Planning Commission, *Twelfth Five Year Plan* (2012-17), Volume I, Chapter 2, paras 2.78 and 2.79.
2. Reserve Bank of India, *Committee on Financial Sector Assessment* (Chairman: Rakesh Mohan), March 2009, Volume II, p. 64.
3. Reserve Bank of India, Report on Currency and Finance, 2001-02, p. VI-1.

24

Financial Markets

Financial market is a mechanism which allows people to buy and sell financial securities and other fungible items of value. Fungible means interchangeable or exchangeable items (like goods, services, currencies) as contrasted with non-fungible items such as human beings. Thus, financial market can mean capital market (trading in shares and bonds etc.), commodity market (trading in gold and silver etc.), foreign exchange market (trading in different currencies) and other such markets.

24.1 Importance of Financial Markets

A well-functioning financial market enables efficient use of market-based instruments of monetary policy by improving interest rate signals in the economy. Apart from enhancing the efficiency of monetary policy, deep and well-functioning financial markets promote mobilisation of domestic savings and improve the allocative efficiency of financial intermediation, and foster the necessary conditions to emerge as an international or a regional financial centre. Strong domestic financial markets also act as a buffer against external disturbances and help in absorbing shocks to the domestic banking system during crises. Further, they provide incentives for development of hedging instruments, and lower macroeconomic volatility and financial instability. Efficient financial markets also have several indirect benefits such as rapid accumulation of physical and human capital, more stable investment financing, and faster technological progress.

Developed and well-integrated financial markets are critical for sustaining high growth, for the effective conduct of monetary policy, for developing a diversified financial system, financial integration and ensuring financial stability. The question therefore is not whether developed financial markets are needed, but how to go about in developing them fully. Financial markets presently deal with complex and sophisticated products. Introduction of such products would require clear regulatory frameworks, appropriate institutions and development of human resource skills. The speed for further changes in the financial markets would thus depend on how quickly are we able to meet these requirements.

The need for developed financial markets also arises in the context of increasing integration of domestic financial markets with international financial markets. The concept of globalisation is no longer restricted to its traditional sense—variety of cross-border transactions in goods and services—but also extends to international capital flows, driven by rapid and widespread diffusion of technology. In fact, most of the literature in recent years on globalisation has centred around financial integration due to the emergence of worldwide financial markets and the possibility of better access to external financing for a variety of domestic entities.

Financial market development is a complex and time-consuming process. There are no short cuts for developing well-functioning markets with depth and liquidity. Some of the preconditions for financial market reform are the following.
1. Macroeconomic stability.
2. Sound and efficient financial institutions and structure.
3. Prudential regulation and supervision.
4. Strong creditor rights.
5. Contract enforcement.

24.2 Regulation and Supervision of Financial Markets in India

Financial markets in India have evidenced significant development since the financial sector reforms initiated in the 1990s. The development of these markets has been done in a calibrated, sequenced manner and in step with those in other markets in the real economy. The emphasis has been on strengthening price discovery, easing restrictions on flows or transactions, lowering transaction costs, and enhancing liquidity. Benefiting from a series of policy initiatives over time, greater domestic market integration has also been witnessed.

The equity, government securities, foreign exchange and money markets along with their corresponding derivatives segments have developed into reasonably deep and liquid markets and there has been significant increase in domestic market integration over the years. However, the credit derivative market is yet to take off in any significant manner. As regards corporate bonds, though the primary market has seen an increase in issuance, the secondary market has not developed commensurately.

Financial markets in India are regulated and supervised by the Reserve Bank of India (RBI) and the Securities and Exchange Board of India (SEBI). Financial markets under the purview of the RBI include the following:
1. Money market and derivatives.
2. Foreign exchange market and derivatives.
3. Government securities market and interest rate derivatives.
4. Credit markets and derivatives.
Financial markets under the control and supervision of SEBI are as under:
1. Equity market and derivatives.
2. Corporate bond market.

24.3 Money Market

Money market is the most important segment of the financial system as it provides the fulcrum for equilibrating short-term demand for and supply of funds, thereby facilitating the conduct of monetary policy. It is a market for short-term funds with a maturity of up to one year and includes financial instruments that are close substitutes for money. [1]

The main instruments comprising the money market are as under:

1. Call money/notice money.
2. Certificates of deposit (CD).
3. Treasury bills.
4. Repurchase agreements (repos).
5. Commercial bills.
6. Commercial papers (CPs).
7. Inter-corporate funds.
   The money market is generally expected to perform three broad functions.
1. It provides an equilibrating mechanism to even out demand for and supply of short-term funds.
2. It also presents a focal point for central bank intervention for influencing liquidity and general level of interest rates in the economy.
3. It provides reasonable access to providers and users of short-term funds to fulfil their borrowing and investment requirements at an efficient market clearing price.

24.3.1 Reserve Bank of India (RBI) and the Money Market: The RBI is the most important constituent of the money market. Owing to its implications for conducting monetary policy, the money market falls under the direct purview of regulation of the RBI. The primary objective of the RBI's operations in the money market has been to ensure that short-term interest rates and liquidity are maintained at levels which are consistent with the overall monetary policy objectives, viz. maintaining price stability, ensuring adequate flow of credit to the productive sectors of the economy and maintaining orderly conditions in the financial markets. Liquidity and interest rates in the system are influenced by the RBI through the use of various instruments at its disposal which, *inter alia*, include the following.

1. Variations in cash reserve ratio.
2. Standing facilities/refinance schemes.
3. Repo and reverse repo transactions.
4. Changes in the Bank Rate.
5. Open market operations.
6. Foreign exchange swaps operations.

Recognising the important role of the market in the monetary policy process, the RBI has taken active interest in continuously refining the money market instruments in order to have greater control over the liquidity in the system and for creating an efficient mechanism to impart interest rate signals.

24.4 Government Securities Market

Under Section 2 of the Securities Contracts (Regulation) Act, 1956, securities include the following:
1. Shares, scrips, stocks, bonds, debentures, debenture stocks, or other marketable securities of a like nature in or of any incorporated company or other body corporate.
2. Government securities.
3. Such other instruments as may be declared by the Central government to be securities.

4. Rights or interests in securities.

Government Securities mean securities created and issued—whether before or after the commencement of the Securities Contracts (Regulations) Act, 1956—by the Central Government or a State Government for the purpose of raising a public loan and having one of the forms specified in Section 2(2) of the Public Debt Act, 1944 (since replaced by the Government Securities Act, 2006).

The government securities market deals with tradable debt instruments issued by the Government for meeting its financing requirements. It is an important segment of the financial market in most countries. The development of the primary segment of this market enables the managers of public debt to raise resources from the market in a cost effective manner with due recognition to associated risks. A vibrant secondary segment of the government securities market helps in the effective operation of monetary policy through application of indirect instruments such as open market operations, for which government securities act as collateral.

Existence of a well-developed government securities market is essential for the pursuit of a market-based monetary policy. The Government securities market in India forms an overwhelming part of the overall debt market. Interest rates in this market provide benchmarks for other segments of the financial market. Historically, the impetus for development of the Government securities market in India has come from the large Government borrowing requirements while an additional reason during the 1990s was the increased capital flows and the need for sterilisation.

As a debt manager to the Government, the development of a deep and liquid market for government securities is of critical importance to the RBI as it results in better price discovery and cost effective Government borrowing. The government securities market also provides an effective transmission mechanism for monetary policy, facilitates the introduction and pricing of hedging products and serves as a benchmark for pricing other debt instruments. Although the government securities market has developed considerably over the years, more needs to be done for it to become fully developed.

The government securities market is also regarded as the backbone of fixed income securities markets as it provides the benchmark yield and imparts liquidity to other financial markets. The existence of an efficient government securities market is seen as an essential precursor, in particular, for development of the corporate debt market. Furthermore, the government securities market acts as a channel for integration of various segments of the domestic financial market and helps in establishing inter-linkages between the domestic and external financial markets.

From the perspective of the issuer, i.e. the Government, a deep and liquid government securities market facilitates its borrowings from the market at reasonable cost. A greater ability of the Government to raise resources from the market at market determined rates of interest allows it to refrain from monetisation of the deficit through central bank funding. It also obviates the need for a captive market for its borrowings. Instead, investor participation is voluntary and based on risk and return perception.

24.5 Capital Market

Capital market is a market for long-term funds. The distinction between capital market and money market is not watertight. Broadly speaking, capital market focuses on financing of fixed investment (machinery and equipment) while money market provides working capital finance (raw material etc.).

Capital market channelises household savings to the corporate sector and allocates funds to firms. In this process, it allows both firms and households to share risks associated with business. Moreover, capital market enables the valuation of firms on an almost continuous basis and plays an important role in the governance of the corporate sector.

An efficient capital market is an important constituent of a sound financial system. In India, efforts have been made in recent years to set up an effective regulatory framework covering major participants in the capital market. Similarly, the technology of trading and settlements in the stock exchanges has been upgraded. Internet-based trading in securities has been permitted. Foreign institutional investors (FIIs) and pension funds were allowed to enter the Indian stock market from 1993 onwards. The market has undergone a major transformation in terms of its structure, products, practices, spread, institutional framework and other important aspects like transparency, integrity and efficiency since then. The size of the market has also grown manifold.

The capital market fosters economic growth in following ways:
1. It augments the quantum of savings and capital formation in the economy.
2. It allocates capital efficiently thereby raising the productivity of investment.
3. It enhances the efficiency of a financial system as diverse competitors vie with each other for financial resources.
4. It adds to the financial deepening of the economy by enlarging the financial sector and promoting the use of innovative, sophisticated and cost-effective financial instruments, which ultimately reduce the cost of capital.
5. Well-functioning capital markets also impose discipline on firms to perform.
6. Equity and debt markets stress on the banking sector by diversifying credit risk across the economy.

24.5.1 Securities and Exchange Board of India: The Securities and Exchange Board of India (SEBI) was constituted on April 12, 1988 as a non-statutory body through an Administrative Resolution of the Government for dealing with all matters relating to development and regulation of the securities market and investor protection and to advise the government on all these matters. SEBI was given statutory status and powers through an Ordinance promulgated on January 30, 1992. SEBI was established as a statutory body on February 21, 1992. The Ordinance was replaced by Securities and Exchange Board of India Act, 1992 on April 4, 1992.

In 1992, the Capital Issues (Control) Act, 1947 was repealed and the office of the Controller of Capital Issues (CCIs) was abolished. With this ended all controls related to raising of funds from the market. The move was aimed at enhancing the efficiency, safety, integrity and transparency of the market. Presently, issuers of capital are required to meet the guidelines of SEBI on disclosures and protection of investors.

In short, though SEBI was originally set up in 1988, it did not have any legal status to control securities market transactions. Legal status was granted to SEBI in 1992 to help it curb malpractices in securities market like rigging of stock prices, insider trading, pricing of new issues without any basis etc.

A. Objectives of SEBI: SEBI has emerged as an autonomous and independent statutory body. Its legally mandated objectives are the following:
1. Development of the securities market.
2. Regulation of the securities market activities.
3. Protection of the interests of investors in securities.
4. Prevention of malpractices.
5. Code of conduct for intermediaries.
6. Matters connected therewith and incidental thereto.

SEBI prohibits fraudulent and unfair trade practices, including insider trading. It also regulates substantial acquisition of shares and takeovers. In order to ensure protection of investors and to safeguard the integrity of the markets, there is a comprehensive surveillance system. Stock exchanges are the primary targets for detection of market manipulation, price rigging and other regulatory breaches regarding capital market functioning.

B. Functions of SEBI: SEBI performs the following functions:
(a) Protective Functions:
1. Preventing price rigging.
2. Curbing insider trading.
3. Checking fraudulent and unfair trade practices.
4. Developing and monitoring investor grievance redressal mechanism.
5. Initiating punitive action against erring entities.
(b) Developmental Functions:
1. Certification for intermediaries.
2. Technology adoption for faster business.
3. Investment products.
(c) Regulatory Functions:
1. Registration of intermediaries.
2. Framing rules for intermediary operations.
3. Regulation of mutual funds.

24.5.2 Stock Exchanges: A stock (or share) market deals mainly in corporate securities. The securities are chiefly in the form of equity shares and debentures. The purpose of these securities is to raise long-term funds for companies engaged in production. The function of the stock market is two-fold: (a) to arrange for the raising of new capital (primary market function), and (b) to provide liquidity to existing securities (secondary market function). The new capital is raised by the issue of shares and debentures. The corporate enterprises raising new capital may be new companies or existing companies planning expansion of their operations. Sometimes, existing private firms go public, i.e. become public limited companies.

The stock market helps the floatation of new issues by providing a variety of services like underwriting, distribution, and listing of the issue. Underwriting means guaranteeing the purchase of a fixed amount of new issues by the underwriter. The new issues of capital may be a public issue or a rights issue or both in certain proportions. It may be in the form of equity shares or debentures. Debentures, in turn, may be fully convertible, partly convertible, or non-convertible into shares. A public issue implies that the general public is invited to subscribe to the new issue. A rights issue is restricted for subscription by existing shareholders.

Stock market provides facilities for secondary market, i.e. transaction in existing securities. People desirous of converting their cash into securities can go to the stock exchange and buy securities with the help of brokers there. Similarly, securities can be converted into cash by selling them in the market. Transactions in the secondary market reflect the investment climate in the economy. A well-developed stock market helps to access external capital which allows financially constrained domestic firms to expand. It is argued that countries with developed stock markets tend to grow faster.

A. Bombay Stock Exchange (BSE): BSE is a stock exchange located on Dalal Street, Mumbai. It was the 11th largest stock exchange in the world by market capitalisation as of March 2017.

Established in 1875, BSE Ltd. (formerly known as Bombay Stock Exchange Ltd.), is India's second oldest stock exchange (Oldest being the Calcutta Stock Exchange located at Lyons Range, Kolkata) and one of India's leading exchange groups.

In August 31, 1957, the BSE became the first stock exchange to be recognized by the Indian Government under the Securities Contracts Regulation Act. In 1980 the exchange moved to the Phiroze Jeejeebhoy Towers at Dalal Street, Fort area. In 1986 it developed the BSE SENSEX index, giving the BSE a means to measure overall performance of the exchange. In 2000, the BSE used this index to open its derivatives market, trading SENSEX futures contracts. The development of SENSEX options along with equity derivatives followed in 2001 and 2002, expanding the BSE's trading platform.

BSE has facilitated the growth of the Indian corporate sector by providing it an efficient capital-raising platform. BSE is a corporatized and demutualised entity, with a broad chorholder-base which includes two leading global exchanges, Deutsche Bourse, Fuse and Singapore Exchange as strategic partners. BSE provides an efficient and transparent market for trading in equity, debt instruments, derivatives, mutual funds. It also has a platform for trading in equities of small-and-medium enterprises (SME). More than 5,500 companies are listed on BSE making it world's top most exchange in terms of listed members.

B. National Stock Exchange of India Limited (NSE): It is located in Mumbai, India. NSE was established in the mid-1990s as a demutualised electronic exchange. NSE provides a modern, fully automated screen-based trading system, with over 2 lakh trading terminals, through which investors in every nook and corner of India can trade. NSE has played a critical role in reforming the Indian securities market and in bringing unparalleled transparency, efficiency and market integrity.

Though a number of other exchanges exist, NSE and the Bombay Stock Exchange (BSE) are the two most significant stock exchanges in India, and between them are responsible for the vast majority of share transactions. NSE's flagship index, the CNX NIFTY 50, is used extensively by investors in India and around the world to take exposure to the Indian equities market.

24.5.3 Demutualisation and Corporatisation of Stock Exchanges: Stock exchanges all over the world were traditionally formed as *mutual* organisations. The trading members not only provided broking services, but also owned, controlled and managed such exchanges for their mutual benefit. Demutualisation refers to the transition process of an exchange from a *mutually-owned* association to a company *owned by shareholders*. In other words, transforming the legal structure of an exchange from a mutual form to a business corporation form is referred to as demutualisation. The above, in effect means that after demutualisation, the ownership, the management and the trading rights at the exchange are segregated from one another.

In a mutual exchange, the three functions of ownership, management and trading are intervened into a single group. Here, the broker members of the exchange are both the owners and the traders on the exchange and they further manage the exchange as well. A demutualised exchange, on the other hand, has all these three functions clearly segregated, i.e. the ownership, management and trading are in separate hands.

In India, NSE was set up as a demutualised corporate body, where ownership, management and trading rights are in the hands of three different sets of groups from its inception. The Stock Exchange, Mumbai—one of the two premier exchanges in the country—has since been corporatised and demutualised and renamed as the Bombay Stock Exchange Ltd. (BSE).

Corporate governance has emerged as an important tool for protection of shareholders. The corporate governance framework in India has evolved over a period of time since the setting up of the Kumar Mangalam Birla Committee by SEBI. India has a reasonably well-designed regulatory framework for the issuance and trading of securities, and disclosures by the issuers with strong focus on corporate governance standards.

To enhance the level of continuous disclosure by the listed companies, SEBI amended the listing agreement to incorporate segment reporting, related party disclosures, consolidated financial results and consolidated financial statements. The listing agreement between the stock exchanges and the companies has been strengthened from time to time to enhance corporate governance standards.

24.6 Foreign Exchange Market

The Indian foreign exchange market is a decentralised multiple dealership market comprising two segments—the spot and the derivatives market. In the spot market, currencies are traded at the prevailing rates and the settlement or value date is two business days ahead. The two-day period gives adequate time for the parties to send instructions to debit and credit the appropriate bank accounts at home and abroad.

The derivatives market encompasses forwards, swaps and options. Though forward contracts exist for maturities up to 1 year, majority of forward contracts are for 1 month, 3 months, or 6 months. Forward contracts for longer periods are not common because of the uncertainties involved and related pricing issues.

A swap transaction in the foreign exchange market is a combination of a spot and a forward in the opposite direction.

The spot market is the dominant segment of the Indian foreign exchange market. The derivative segment of the foreign exchange market is assuming significance and the activity in this segment is gradually rising.

24.6.1 Market Players: Players in the Indian foreign exchange market include: (a) authorised dealers (ADs), mostly banks who are authorised to deal in foreign exchange, (b) foreign exchange brokers who act as intermediaries, and (c) customers—individuals and corporates who need foreign exchange for their transactions. Though customers are major players in the foreign exchange market, for all practical purposes they depend upon ADs and brokers. In the spot foreign exchange market, foreign exchange transactions were earlier dominated by brokers. However, the situation has changed with the evolving market conditions and as of now the transactions are dominated by ADs. Brokers continue to dominate the derivatives market.

The RBI intervenes in the market essentially to ensure orderly market conditions. The RBI undertakes sales/purchases of foreign currency in periods of excess demand/supply in the market.

Foreign Exchange Dealers' Association of India (FEDAI) plays a special role in the foreign exchange market for ensuring smooth and speedy growth of the foreign exchange market in all its aspects. All ADs are required to become members of the FEDAI and execute an undertaking to the effect that they would abide by the terms and conditions stipulated by the FEDAI for transacting foreign exchange business. The FEDAI is also the accrediting authority for the foreign exchange brokers in the inter-bank foreign exchange market.

The licences for ADs are issued to banks and other institutions, on their request, under Section 10(1) of the Foreign Exchange Management Act, 1999. ADs are divided into different categories.

All scheduled commercial banks—which include public sector banks, private sector banks and foreign banks operating in India—belong to category I of ADs.

All upgraded full-fledged money changers (FFMCs) and select regional rural banks (RRBs) and co-operative banks belong to category II of ADs.

Select financial institutions such as EXIM Bank belong to category III of ADs.

All merchant transactions in the foreign exchange market have to be necessarily undertaken directly through ADs. However, to provide depth and liquidity to the inter-bank segment, ADs have been permitted to utilise the services of brokers for better price discovery in their inter-bank transactions.

The customer segment of the foreign exchange market comprises major public sector units, corporates and business entities with foreign exchange exposure. It is generally dominated by select large public sector units such as Indian Oil Corporation (IOC), Oil and Natural Gas Commission (ONGC), Bharat Heavy Electrical Limited (BHEL), Steel Authority of India Limited (SAIL), Maruti Udyog and also the Government of India (for defence and civil debt service) as also big private sector corporates like Reliance Group, Tata Group and Larsen and Toubro, among others.

In recent years, foreign institutional investors (FIIs) have emerged as major players in the foreign exchange market.

Endnote

1. There is no demarcated distinction between the short-term money market and the long-term capital market, and in fact there are integral links between the two markets as the array of instruments in the two markets invariably forms a continuum.

25

Financial Instruments

The maturity and sophistication of financial system depends upon the prevalence of a variety of financial instruments to suit the varied investment requirements of heterogeneous investors so as to enable it to mobilize savings from as wide section of the investing public as possible. Since early 1990s, the Indian financial system has witnessed tremendous growth in financial product innovation by corporates as well as financial institutions.

Capital market instruments fall into two broad groups:
1. Direct Financial Instruments.
2. Derivates Financial Instruments.

25.1 Direct Financial Instruments

Direct instruments include the following:
1. Ordinary (or equity) shares.
2. Preference shares.
3. Debentures.
4. Bonds

While the ordinary and preference shares represent ownership instruments, debentures and innovating debt instruments are creditorship securities.

For details, see chapter 18 of this book.

25.2 Derivative Financial Instruments

India has introduced different equity derivatives in a phased manner. This phased approach was adopted in India with index futures being introduced in June 2000, index options in June 2001 and individual stock options in July 2001.

25.2.1 L.C. Gupta Committee on Derivatives Trading in India: Securities and Exchange Board of India (SEBI) set up a 24-member committee under the Chairmanship of L.C. Gupta on November 18, 1996 to develop appropriate regulatory framework for derivatives trading in India. The Committee submitted its report on March 17, 1998 prescribing necessary preconditions for introduction of derivatives trading in India. The committee recommended that derivatives should be declared as *securities* so that regulatory framework applicable to trading of *securities* could also govern trading of derivatives. [1]

25.2.2 Amendment of Securities Contract Regulation Act (SCRA): In pursuance of the recommendations of the L.C. Gupta Committee, SCRA was amended in December 1999 to include derivatives within the ambit of *securities* and the regulatory framework was developed for governing derivatives trading. The Act also made it clear that derivatives shall be legal and valid only if such contracts are traded on a recognised stock exchange, thus precluding OTC derivatives. The government also rescinded in March 2000, the three-decade old notification, which prohibited forward trading in securities.

Derivatives trading commenced in India in June 2000 after SEBI granted the final approval to this effect in May 2000. SEBI permitted the derivatives segments of two stock exchanges NSE and BSE, and their clearing house/corporation to commence trading and settlement in approved derivative contracts. To begin with, SEBI approved trading in index future contracts based on S&P CNX Nifty and BSE-30 (Sensex) index. This was followed by approval for trading in options which commenced in June 2001 and the trading in options on individual securities commenced in July 2001. Future contracts on individual stocks were launched in November 2001. Trading and settlement in derivative contracts is done in accordance with the rules, by-laws, and regulations of the respective exchanges and their clearing house/corporation duly approved by SEBI and notified in the official gazette.

25.2.3 Measures to Protect the Rights of Investors in the Derivatives Market: Investors' money has to be kept separate at all levels and is permitted to be used only against the liability of the investor and is not available to the trading member or clearing member or even any other investor.

A trading member is required to provide every investor with a risk disclosure document which will disclose the risks associated with the derivatives trading so that investors can take a conscious decision to trade in derivatives.

Investors get the contract note duly time stamped for receipt of the order and execution of the order. The order is executed with the identity of the client and without client ID order is not accepted by the system. The investors can demand the trade confirmation slip with their respective ID in support of the contract note. This protects them from the risk of price favours, if any, extended by the Member.

In the derivatives market all money paid by the investors towards margins on all open positions is kept in trust with the clearing house/clearing corporation and in the event of default of the trading or clearing member the amounts paid by the client towards margins are segregated and not utilized towards the default of the member. However, in the event of default of a member, losses suffered by the investors, if any, on settled/closed out position are compensated from the investors' protection fund, as per the rules, by-laws and regulations of the derivative segment of the exchanges.

25.2.4 Credit Derivatives in India: The credit market refers to the market where financial instruments that embrace credit risk are traded. In addition to traditional instruments, such as loans and advances, corporate bonds, and commercial papers the credit market now includes securitised products in which various credit risks have been pooled as well as credit derivatives whose underlying assets encompass credit risks.

As a financial system which is dominated by bank intermediation, credit has traditionally been the main source of funds to various sectors in the Indian economy, and loans and advances continue to be the preferred part of asset books of banks. However, the implementation of risk management guidelines and the requirement for providing a capital charge for credit risk in the balance sheet has given banks an incentive to look for innovative methods of transferring credit risk from their books.

While simple techniques for transferring credit risk, such as financial guarantees, collateral and credit insurance have long been prevalent in the Indian banking industry, the recent innovative instruments in credit risk transfer are yet to make an impact. However, in recent years the risk management architecture of banks in India has strengthened and they are on the way to becoming Basel II compliant, providing adequate comfort level for the introduction of credit derivatives.

The Reserve Bank in its Annual Policy announced in April 2007 mentioned that as part of the gradual process of financial sector liberalization in India, it was considered appropriate to introduce credit derivatives in a calibrated manner. Furthermore, the amendment to the Reserve Bank of India Act, 1934 had provided legality to OTC (over the counter) derivative instruments, including credit derivatives.

Although derivative instruments were introduced in July 1999 in the money/foreign exchange market in the form of forward rate agreements (FRAs) [2] and interest rate swaps (IRS), [3] credit derivatives are yet to be introduced. The RBI's Annual Policy Statement 2007-08 announced the introduction of credit derivatives in India in a calibrated manner. In view of certain adverse developments in the international financial markets, especially credit markets, resulting from recent financial turmoil, it was widely felt that time is not opportune to introduce the credit derivatives in India for the present. As such, the RBI announced on June 19, 2008 its decision to keep in abeyance the issuance of the final guidelines on introduction of credit derivatives in India.

25.2.5 Traders and Trading System of Derivatives:

A. Traders in Derivatives Market:

(a) Hedgers: Hedgers are the traders who wish to eliminate the risk (of price change) to which they are already exposed. They may take a long position on, or short sell, a commodity and would, therefore, stand to lose should the prices move in the adverse direction. The trader can sell future (or forward) contracts with a matching price, to hedge.

Stocks carry two types of risk: company specific and market risk. While company risk can be minimized by diversifying your portfolio, market risk cannot be diversified but has to be hedged.

Hedging involves protecting an existing asset position from future adverse price movements. In order to hedge a position, a market player needs to take an equal and opposite position in the futures market to the one held in the cash market.

How does one measure the market risk? Market risk can be known from Beta which measures the relationship between movement of the index to the movement of the stock. The beta measures the percentage impact on the stock prices for 1 percent change in the index. Therefore, for a portfolio whose value goes down by 11 percent when the index goes down by 10 percent, the beta would be 1.1. When the index increases by 10 percent, the value of the portfolio increases 11 percent. The idea is to make beta of your portfolio zero to nullify your losses.

(b) Speculators: If hedgers are the people who wish to avoid the price risk, speculators are those who are willing to take such risk. These are the people who take position in the market and assume risks to profit from fluctuations in prices. In fact, the speculators consume information, make forecasts about the prices and put their money in these forecasts. Depending on their perceptions, they may take long or short positions on futures and/or options, or may hold spread positions (simultaneous long and short positions on the same derivatives).

Speculators are those who do not have any position on which they enter in futures and options market. They only have a particular view on the market, stock, commodity etc. In short, speculators put their money at risk in the hope of earning profit from an anticipated price change. They consider various factors such as demand, supply, market position, open interests, economic fundamentals and other data to take their positions.

(c) Arbitrageurs: Arbitrageurs thrive on market imperfections. An arbitrageur profits by trading a given commodity, or other item, that sells for different prices in different markets. This becomes possible by simultaneous purchase of securities in one market where the price is low and sale in another market, where the price is comparatively higher.

This is done when the same securities are being quoted at different prices in the two markets. Arbitrageurs derive advantage from difference in prices of securities prevailing in the two markets.

An arbitrageur is basically risk averse. He enters into those contracts were he can earn riskless profits. When markets are imperfect, buying in one market and simultaneously selling in other market gives riskless profit. Arbitrageurs are always in the look out for such imperfections.

In the futures market one can take advantages of arbitrage opportunities by buying from lower priced market and selling at the higher priced market. In index futures arbitrage is possible between the spot market and the futures market.

B. Trading System:

(a) National Exchange for Automated Trading (NEAT-F&O): Futures and options trading system of NSE—called NEAT-F&O trading system—provides a fully automated screen-based trading for index futures and options, stock futures and options and futures on interest rate on a nationwide basis as well as an online monitoring and surveillance mechanism. It supports an order driven market and provides complete transparency of trading operations. It is similar to that of trading of equities in the cash market segment.

The software for the F&O market has been developed to facilitate efficient and transparent trading in futures and options instruments. Keeping in view the familiarity of trading members with the current capital market trading system, modifications have been introduced in the existing capital market trading system so as to make it suitable for trading futures and options.

(b) Trading Mechanism: The NEAT-F&O system supports an order driven market, wherein orders match automatically. Order matching is essentially on the basis of security, its price, time and quantity. All quantity fields are in units and price in rupees.

The lot size on the futures and options market is 50 for Nifty. The exchange notifies the regular lot size and tick size for each security traded on this segment from time to time. Orders, as and when they are received, are first time stamped and then immediately processed for potential match. When any order enters the trading system, it is an active order. If it finds a match, a trade is generated. If a match is not found, then the orders are stored in different books. Orders are stored in price-time priority in various books in the following sequence: (a) best price, and (b) within price, by time priority.

(c) **Entities in the Trading System:** There are four entities in the trading system:

1. **Trading Members:** Trading members are members of NSE. They can trade either on their own account or on behalf of their clients including participants. The exchange assigns ID to each trading member. Each trading member can have more than one user.

2. **Clearing Members:** Clearing members are members of NSCCL. They carry out risk management activities and confirmation/inquiry of trades through the trading system.

3. **Professional Clearing Members:** Professional clearing members are clearing members who are not trading member. Typically, banks and custodians become professional clearing members and clear and settle for their trading members.

4. **Participants:** A participant is a client of trading members like financial institutions. These clients may trade through multiple trading members but settle through a single clearing member.

(d) **Corporate Hierarchy:** In the F&O trading software, a trading member has the facility of defining a hierarchy amongst users of the system. This hierarchy comprises corporate manager, branch manager and dealer.

1. **Corporate Manager:** The term *corporate manager* is assigned to a user placed at the highest level in a trading firm. Such a user can perform all the functions such as order and trade-related activities, receiving reports for all branches of the trading member firm and also all dealers of the firm. Additionally, a corporate manager can define exposure limits for the branches of the firm. This facility is available only to the corporate manager.

2. **Branch Manager:** The branch manager is a term assigned to a user who is placed under the corporate manager. Such a user can perform and view order and trade-related activities for all dealers under that branch.

3. **Dealer:** Dealer is a user at the lower level of the hierarchy. A dealer can perform trade-related activities only for himself and does not have access to information on other dealers under either the same branch or other branches.

C. Order Types and Conditions: The system allows the trading members to enter orders with various conditions attached to them as per their requirements. These conditions are broadly divided into the following three categories:

(a) **Time Conditions:**

1. **Day Order:** A day order, as the name suggests, is an order which is valid for the day on which it is entered. If the order is not executed during the day, the system cancels the order automatically at the end of the day.

2. **Immediate or Cancel (IOC):** An IOC order allows the user to buy or sell a contract as soon as the order is released into the system, failing which the order is cancelled from the system. Partial match is possible for the order, and the unmatched portion of the order is cancelled immediately.

(b) Price Conditions:

1. **Stop-loss:** This facility allows the user to release an order into the system, after the market price (last traded price) of the security reaches or crosses a threshold price, e.g. if for stop-loss buy order, the trigger is 1027, the limit price is 1030 and the market (last traded) price is 1023, then this order is released into the system once the market price reaches or exceeds 1027. This order is added to the regular lot book with time of triggering as the time stamp, as a limit order of 1030. For the stop-loss sell order, the trigger price has to be greater than the limit price.

(c) Other Conditions:

1. **Market Price:** Market orders are orders for which no price is specified at the time the order is entered (i.e. price is market price). For such orders, the system determines the price.
2. **Limit Price:** Price of the order after triggering from stop loss book.
3. **Pro:** Pro means that the orders are entered on the trading member's own account.
4. **Cli:** Cli means that the trading member enters the orders on behalf of a client.
5. **Trigger Price:** It is the price at which an order gets triggered from stop-loss book. Several combinations of the above are allowed thereby providing enormous flexibility to the users.

D. Market Watch: The purpose of market watch is to allow continuous monitoring of contracts or securities that are of specific interest to the user. It displays trading information for contracts selected by the user. The user also gets a broadcast of all the cash market securities on the screen. This function is also available if the user selects the relevant securities for display on the market watch screen. Display of trading information related to cash market securities is in *read only* format, i.e. the dealer can only view the information on cash market but cannot trade in them through the system. This is the main window from the dealer's perspective.

The following windows are displayed on a trader's workstation screen.

1. Title bar.
2. Ticker window of futures and options market.
3. Ticker window of underlying (capital) market.
4. Tool bar.
5. Market watch window.
6. Inquiry window.
7. Snap quote.
8. Order/trade window.
9. System message window.

E. Placing Orders on the Trading System: While entering orders on the trading system—for both futures and the options market—members are required to identify orders as being proprietary or client orders. Proprietary orders should be identified as *Pro* and those of clients should be identified as *Cli*. Apart from this, in the case of *Cli* trades, the client account number should also be provided. The futures and options market is a zero sum game, i.e. the total number of long in contracts always equals the total number of short in contracts. The total number of outstanding contracts (long/short) at any point in time is called the *open interest*. This open interest figure is a good indicator of the liquidity in the contract. Based on studies carried out in international exchanges, it is found that open interest is maximum in near month expiry contracts.

F. Eligibility Criteria for Securities/Indices Traded in F&O:

(a) Eligibility Criteria for Stocks:

1. The stock is chosen from amongst the top 500 stocks in terms of average daily market capitalisation and average daily traded value in the previous 6 months on a rolling basis.

2. A stock's median quarter-sigma order size over the last 6 months should not be less than ₹ 1 lakh. For this purpose, a stock's quarter-sigma order size should mean the order size (in value terms) required to cause a change in the stock price equal to one-quarter of a standard deviation.

3. The market wide position limit in the stock should not be less than ₹ 50 crore. The market wide position limit (number of shares) is valued taking into account the closing prices of stocks in the underlying cash market on the date of expiry of contract in the month. The market wide position limit of open position (in terms of the number of underlying stock) on futures and option contracts on a particular underlying stock should be lower of 20 percent of the number of shares held by non-promoters in the relevant underlying security i.e. free-float holding.

If an existing security fails to meet the eligibility criteria for 3 months consecutively, then no fresh month contract will be issued on that security.

However, the existing unexpired contracts can be permitted to trade till expiry and new strikes can also be introduced in the existing contract months.

For unlisted companies coming out with initial public offering, if the net public offer is ₹ 500 crore or more, then the exchange may consider introducing stock options and stock futures on such stocks at the time of its listing than in cash market.

(b) Eligibility Criteria for Indices: The exchange may consider introducing derivative contracts on an index if the stocks contributing to 80 percent weightage of the index are individually eligible for derivative trading. However, no single eligible stock in the index should have a weightage of more than 5 percent in the index. The above criteria is applied every month, if the index fails to meet the eligibility criteria for 3 months consecutively, then no fresh month contract would be issued on that index.

(c) Eligibility Criteria for Stocks for Derivatives Trading on Account of Corporate Restructuring: The criteria in this case are as under:

1. All the following conditions shall be met in the case of shares of a company undergoing restructuring through any means for eligibility to reintroduce derivative contracts on that company from the first day of listing of the post- restructured company's stock in the underlying market:

- Futures and options contracts on the stock of the original (pre-restructure) company were traded on any exchange prior to its restructuring.
- Pre-restructured company had a market capitalisation of at least ₹ 1,000 crore prior to its restructuring.
- Post-restructured company would be treated like a new stock and if it is, in the opinion of the exchange, likely to be at least one-third the size of the pre-restructured company in terms of revenues, or assets, or (where appropriate) analyst valuations.
- In the opinion of the exchange, the scheme of restructuring does not suggest that the post-restructured company would have any characteristic (for example extremely low free float) that would render the company ineligible for derivatives trading.

2. If the above conditions are satisfied, then the exchange takes the following course of action in dealing with the existing derivative contracts on the pre-restructured company and introduction of fresh contracts on the post- restructured company:

- In the contract month in which the post-restructured company begins to trade, the exchange introduces near month, middle month and far month derivative contracts on the stock of the restructured company.
- In subsequent contract months, the normal rules for entry and exit of stocks in terms of eligibility requirements would apply. If these tests are not met, the exchange shall not permit further derivative contracts on this stock and future month series shall not be introduced.

To sum up, financial derivatives are of recent origin in India, barring trade-related forward contracts in the forex market. Over-the-counter (OTC) as well as exchange-traded derivatives have been introduced, marking an important development in the structure of financial markets in India. Forward contracts in the forex market have also been liberalised. OTC derivatives, viz. interest rate swaps (IRS) and forward rate agreements (FRAs) were introduced in July 1999. The IRS and FRA were introduced with a view to deepening the money market as also to enable banks, primary dealers and financial institutions to hedge interest rate risks.

Endnotes

1. SEBI also set up a group in June 1998 (Chairman: J.R. Varma) to recommend measures for risk containment in derivatives market in India. The report, which was submitted in October 1998, worked out the operational details of margining system, methodology for charging initial margins, net worth of brokers, deposit requirements and real-time monitoring requirements.
2. The FRA is an off-balance sheet contract between two parties under which one party agrees on the start date for trade and the party that agrees, would lodge a notional deposit with the other for a specified sum of money for a specified period of time (the FRA period) at a specified rate of interest (the contract rate). The party that has agreed to make the notional deposit has, thus, sold the FRA to the other party who has bought it.
3. The IRS is a contract between two counter-parties for exchange interest payment for a specified period based on a notional principal amount. The notional principal is used to calculate interest payments, but is not exchanged. Only interest payments are exchanged.

26

Financial Inclusion

26.1 Origins of the Current Approach to Financial Inclusion

The present concern for financial inclusion can be traced to the United Nations Capital Development Fund (UNCDF) initiatives [1], which broadly underlined the main goals as also the broad frameworks and parameters of inclusive finance, as access to a range of financial services, including savings, credit, insurance, remittance and other banking/payment services to all 'bankable' households and enterprises at a reasonable cost.

According to UNCDF the main goals of inclusive finance are as under:

1. Access at a reasonable cost of all households and enterprises to the range of financial services for which they are 'bankable', including savings, short and long-term credit, leasing and factoring, mortgages, insurance, pensions, payments, local money transfers and international remittances.
2. Sound institutions, guided by appropriate internal management systems, industry performance standards, and performance monitoring by the market, as well as by sound prudential regulation where required.
3. Financial and institutional sustainability as a means of providing access to financial services over time.
4. Multiple providers of financial services, wherever feasible, so as to bring cost-effective and a wide variety of alternatives to customers (which could include any number of combinations of sound private, non-profit and public providers).

The Report of the Centre for Global Development (CGD) Task-Force on Access to Financial Services further laid down the broad policy principles for expanding financial access, including the implicit institutional mechanisms, with particular emphasis on the need for ensuring data collection, monitoring and evaluation. [2]

G-20 Toronto Summit [3] had also outlined the "Principles for Innovative Financial Inclusion", which serves as a guide for policy and regulatory approaches aimed at fostering safe and sound adoption of innovative, adequate, low-cost financial delivery models, helping provide conditions for fair competition and a framework of incentives for the various bank, insurance, and non-bank actors involved in the delivery of a full-range of affordable and quality financial services. The G-20's highest priority, as declaration goes, is to safeguard and strengthen the recovery and lay the foundation for strong, sustainable and balanced growth, and strengthen our financial systems against risks.

26.2 Financial Exclusion and Financial Inclusion Defined

In most developing countries, a large segment of society, particularly low-income people, has very little access to financial services, both formal and semi-formal. As a consequence, many of them have to necessarily depend either on their own or high cost informal sources of finance such as moneylenders. This is particularly true for the sporadic financing requirements of low income households for non-productive consumption purposes and other emergency requirements such as medical expenditure. Benefits of growth, therefore, tend to concentrate in the hands of those already served by the formal financial system.

Despite the rapid spread of banking over the years, a significant segment of the population, predominantly in the rural areas, is excluded from the formal financial system. It is well-known that poor people, potential entrepreneurs, small enterprises and others are excluded from the financial sector, which leads to their marginalisation and denial of opportunity for them to grow and prosper. Therefore, access to a greater proportion of the population to the organised financial system should be high on the agenda of the Government of India. The key issue, however, is how to mainstream the institutional sources so as to achieve wider coverage in terms of extending credit. There are also a large number of households with low income and small savings, which need to be mobilised.

Apart from the rural areas, there is significant degree of financial exclusion in urban areas as well. The cost of financial exclusion is recognised to be enormous for the society as well as for individuals, particularly in terms of inability to realise full potential due to financial constraints.

The recent developments in banking technology have transformed banking from the traditional brick-and-mortar infrastructure like staffed branches to a system supplemented by other channels like automated teller machines (ATMs), credit/debit cards, internet banking, online money transfers etc. However, the access to such technology is restricted only to certain segments of the society. Indeed, some trends, such as increasingly sophisticated customer segmentation technology—allowing, for example, more accurate targeting of sections of the market—have led to restricted access to financial services for some groups. There is a growing divide, with an increased range of personal finance options for a segment of high and upper middle income population and a significantly large section of the population who lack access to even the most basic banking services. This is termed *financial exclusion*. These people, particularly, those living on low incomes, cannot access mainstream financial products such as bank accounts, credit, remittances and payment services, financial advisory services, insurance facilities etc.

Merely having a bank account may not be a good indicator of financial inclusion. The ideal definition should look at people who want to access financial services but are denied the same. If genuine claimants for credit and financial services are denied the same, then that is a case of exclusion. As this aspect would raise the issue of credit worthiness or bankability, it is also necessary to dwell upon what could be done to make the claimants of institutional credit bankable or creditworthy. This would require re-engineering of existing financial products or delivery systems and making them more in tune with the expectations and absorptive capacity of the intended clientele.

According to the Committee on Financial Inclusion (Chairman: C. Rangarajan), 2008, "Financial inclusion may be defined as the process of ensuring access to financial services and timely and adequate credit where needed by vulnerable groups such as weaker sections and low income groups at an affordable cost".

The essence of financial inclusion is in trying to ensure that a range of appropriate financial services is available to every individual and enabling them to understand and access those services. Apart from the regular form of financial intermediation, it may include a basic no-frills banking account for making and receiving payments, a savings product suited to the pattern of cash flows of a poor household, money transfer facilities, small loans and overdrafts for productive, personal and other purposes, insurance (life and non-life) etc. While financial inclusion, in the narrow sense, may be achieved to some extent by offering any one of these services, the objective of *comprehensive financial inclusion* would be to provide a holistic set of services encompassing all of the above.

26.3 Advantages of Financial Inclusion

The objective of financial inclusion is to extend financial services to the large hitherto unserved population of the country to unlock its growth potential. In addition, it strives towards a more inclusive growth by making financing available to the poor in particular. Government of India has been actively pursuing the agenda of financial inclusion, with key interventions in four groups, viz. expanding banking infrastructure, offering appropriate financial products, making extensive and intensive use of technology and through advocacy and stakeholder participation.

Access to safe, easy and affordable credit and other financial services by the poor and vulnerable groups, disadvantaged areas and lagging sectors is recognised as a pre-condition for accelerating growth and reducing income disparities and poverty. A developing country can benefit from financial inclusion in the following ways:

1. Access to a well-functioning financial system—by creating equal opportunities—enables economically and socially excluded people to integrate effectively into the economy and contribute to development and protect themselves against economic shocks.

2. Availability of external finance to potential entrepreneurs and small firms enables new entrants, leading to increased competition to incumbents. This, in turn, encourages entrepreneurship and productivity.

3. Inclusive finance—including safe savings, appropriately designed loans for poor and low-income households and for micro, small and medium-sized enterprises, and appropriate insurance and payments services—can help people to enhance incomes, acquire capital, manage risk, and come out of poverty.

4. Access to financial services contributes to higher production and social protection, as the financial sector—through stored savings, credit and insurance—serves as a measure of crisis mitigation.

5. Financial inclusion can improve the efficiency of the process of intermediation between savings and investments while facilitating change in the composition of the financial system with regard to the transactions that take place, the clients that use the various services, the new risks created, and possibly the institutions that operate in newly created or expanded markets. As the balance sheet of the financial sector grows more diversified and encompasses a broader spectrum of economic agents, its contribution to a more

resilient economy is commensurately higher.

6. For financial institutions, especially banks, financial inclusion helps provide a more stable retail base of deposits. As the recent global crisis also demonstrated, stable retail sources of funding, as against reliance on borrowed funds, can greatly enhance the soundness and resilience of financial institutions and can reduce volatility in earnings. It has been well-recognised that access to financial services facilitates making and receiving financial payments and reduces transaction costs. Financial inclusion enables to finance activities or firms or individuals that are at the margin, thereby promoting their growth-inducing productive activities.

7. Financial inclusion facilitates greater participation by different segments of the economy in the formal financial system. The presence of a large informal sector can impair the transmission of monetary policy as a significant segment of financially excluded households and small businesses make financial decisions independent of and un-influenced by, the monetary policy actions of the central bank. As the share of the formal financial sector increases through greater financial inclusion, it yields an important positive externality by making monetary policy transmission more effective.

8. To the extent that financial inclusion helps people move from the cash economy to bank accounts which can be monitored, it helps facilitate implementation of anti-money laundering and combating the financing of terrorism.

9. Financial inclusion can contribute to enhanced financial stability through contributing to the improved health of the household sector, of small businesses and, to some extent, that of the corporate sector. The health of the household sector is improved through improved economic linkages, reducing reliance on the costly informal sector and through improved ability to make and receive payments.

10. Financial inclusion can improve the access to finance and the social quality (including gender equality) and cost of the service that small businesses receive from banks. These factors are a key to the profitability and prosperity of these businesses and that are the backbones of the growing economy. Therefore, achieving greater financial inclusion and maintaining financial stability are now complementary policy compulsions in so far as India is concerned.

26.4 Measures Taken by Reserve Bank of India (RBI) for Financial Inclusion

Given the socio-demographic complexities in India, the policy endeavour of the RBI has been to adopt a multi-institutional and multi-instrument approach to comprehensively address the issue of financial inclusion in all its dimensions, going beyond mere availability of credit to the masses. The term *financial inclusion* needs to be understood in a broader perspective to mean the provision of the full range of affordable financial services, viz. access to payments and remittance facilities, savings, loans and insurance services by the formal financial system to those who tend to be excluded from these services. The RBI, while recognising the concerns in regard to the banking practices that tend to exclude rather than attract vast sections of population, has been urging the banks to review their existing practices to align them with the objective of achieving greater financial inclusion. The RBI too has taken a number of measures with the objective of attracting the financially excluded population into the formalised financial system. Some of the measures taken in this direction are as follows.

26.4.1 No Frills Account: RBI vide Mid-term Review of Annual Policy Statement for the year 2005-2006, advised banks to align their policies with the objective of financial inclusion. Banks were advised to make available a basic banking *No frills* account either with *nil* or very minimum balances as well as charges that would make such accounts accessible to vast sections of population. Besides, it was emphasized upon by the RBI for deepening and widening the reach of financial services so as to cover a large segment of the rural and poor sections of population.

All the public and the private sector banks as well as the foreign banks, except those not having significant retail presence, are reported to have introduced the basic banking 'no-frills' account.

26.4.2 General Credit Card (GCC): With the objective of providing hassle-free credit to the banks' constituents in rural and semi urban areas, the banks were advised in December 2005, to consider introduction of a *General Credit Card* (GCC) to such constituents. The card was to have a credit limit of up to ₹ 25,000, based on the assessment of income and cash flows of the household without insistence on security or purpose or end-use of credit. The credit facility was to be in the nature of revolving credit entitling the holder to withdraw up to the limit sanctioned. The banks are required to charge appropriate and reasonable Interest rate on the facility.

26.4.3 Business Facilitator and Business Correspondent (BC) Models: In January 2006, banks were permitted to utilise the services of non-governmental organisations (NGOs/SHGs), micro finance institutions and other civil society organisations as intermediaries in providing financial and banking services through the use of *business facilitator* and *business correspondent (BC) models*. The BC model allows banks to do *cash in-cash out* transactions at the location of the BC and allows branchless banking.

26.4.4 Passbook Facility: The matter of issuing passbooks to the small depositors has been a nagging issue for sometime past. Pass books provide the account holders a ready reckoner of the transactions in their accounts and is a convenient reference document—which can not be substituted by periodical bank account statements, particularly by the small account holders. Since non-issuance of the passbooks to the small customers could indirectly lead to their financial exclusion, the RBI had advised the banks in October 2006 to invariably offer the passbook facility to all its savings bank account holders (individuals) and not to levy any charge on the customers thereof.

26.4.5 Simplified KYC Procedure: With a view to facilitating the opening of bank accounts by the common man through a simplified KYC procedure, in the Mid-Term Review of the Annual Policy of the RBI for the year 2006-07, it was announced that the "banks could open accounts of low balance/turnover (where the balance does not exceed ₹ 50,000 in all the accounts taken together and the total credit in all the accounts taken together is not expected to exceed rupees two lakh in a year) only with self certification of address by the customers and his photograph". However, this policy announcement is yet to be operationalised as the matter is under consideration of the Government in the light of the provisions of the Rules framed under Prevention of Money Laundering Act.

26.4.6 Credit Counselling and Financial Education: Promoting *credit counselling and financial education* of the clientele of the banks is also an area that deserves due attention of the banking community. Towards this objective, the banks were also advised by the RBI to make available all printed material used by retail customers in the concerned regional language. As far as RBI itself is concerned, it has launched on June 18, 2007, a multilingual website in 13 Indian languages on all matters concerning banking and the common person so that the language does not become a barrier to acquiring financial education by the public at large.

26.4.7 Use of Technology: Recognizing that technology has the potential to address the issues of outreach and credit delivery in rural and remote areas in a viable manner, banks have been advised to make effective use of information and communications technology (ICT), to provide doorstep banking services through the business communication (BC) model where the accounts can be operated by even illiterate customers by using biometrics, thus ensuring the security of transactions and enhancing confidence in the banking system.

26.4.8 Simplified Branch Authorization: To address the issue of uneven spread of bank branches, in December 2009, domestic scheduled commercial banks were permitted to freely open branches in tier III to tier VI centres with a population of less than 50,000 under general permission, subject to reporting.

26.4.9 Banking Services in Unbanked Villages: Banks were advised to draw up a road map to provide banking services in every unbanked village having a population of over 2,000 by March 2012. RBI advised banks that such banking services need not necessarily be extended through a bricks and mortar branch, but could also be provided through any of the various forms of ICT-based models. About 73,000 such unbanked villages were identified and allotted to various banks through state-level bankers' committees.

26.4.10 Financial Inclusion Plans of Banks for Three Years: RBI advised all public and private sector banks to submit a board-approved, three-year financial inclusion plan (FIP) starting April, 2010. These plans broadly include self-set targets in respect of rural bricks and mortar branches opened, BCs employed, coverage of unbanked villages with a population above 2,000 as also other unbanked villages with population below 2,000 through branches.

Government of India had set up the Financial Stability and Development Council (FSDC), which is mandated, *inter alia,* to focus on financial inclusion and financial literacy issues. In order to further strengthen the ongoing financial inclusion agenda in India, a high level Financial Inclusion Advisory Committee has been constituted by RBI. The Committee would pave the way for developing a viable and sustainable banking services delivery model focusing on accessible and affordable financial services, developing products and processes for rural and urban consumers presently outside the banking network and for suggesting appropriate regulatory framework to ensure that financial inclusion and financial stability move in tandem. India has, for a long time, recognized the social and economic imperatives for broader financial inclusion and has made an enormous contribution to economic development by finding innovative ways to empower the poor.

26.5 Financial Inclusion Measures by NABARD

Set up in 1982, National Bank for Agriculture and Rural Development (NABARD) is the apex institution accredited with all matters concerning policy, planning and operations in the field of credit for agriculture and other economic activities in rural areas in India.

NABARD serves as an apex refinancing agency for the institutions providing investment and production credit in rural areas.

NABARD has been instrumental in facilitating various activities under micro finance sector, involving all possible partners at the ground level in the field. NABARD has been encouraging voluntary agencies, bankers, socially spirited individuals, other formal and informal entities and also government functionaries to promote and nurture self-help groups (SHGs).

The focus in this direction has been on training and capacity building of partners, promotional grant assistance to self-help promoting institutions (SHPIs), revolving fund assistance (RFA) to MFIs, equity/capital support to MFIs to supplement their financial resources and provision of 100 percent refinance against bank loans provided by various banks for microfinance activities.

In view of the large outreach and pre-dominant position of the micro finance programme, it is important to keep a continuous track of the status, progress, trends, qualitative and quantitative performance comprehensively. To achieve this objective, Reserve Bank of India and NABARD issued guidelines in the year 2006-07 to commercial banks, regional rural banks and co-operative banks to furnish data on progress under micro finance.

The data so collected covers various parameters like savings of SHGs with banks, bank loan disbursed to SHGs, bank loan outstanding against SHGs, gross non-performing assets of bank loans to SHGs, recovery performance of loans to SHGs. Further, the banks also furnish the data regarding bank loans provided to micro finance institutions (MFIs). NABARD has been bringing out the consolidated document annually.

The data furnished by the banks have been analysed on a region-wise, state-wise, agency-wise, bank-wise and also for SHGs exclusively under Swarnajayanti Gram Swarojgar Yojana and exclusive women SHGs.

The major support provided by NABARD under Micro Finance Development and Equity Fund relates to promotion and nurturing of SHGs by self-help promoting institutions and training and capacity building of the stakeholders in the sector. NABARD is also experimenting innovative projects for further developing the micro finance through Joint Liability Groups.

Since 2006-07, NABARD has been compiling and analysing the data on progress made in micro finance sector, based on the returns furnished by commercial banks (CBs), regional rural banks (RRBs) and co-operative banks operating in the country.

Most of the banks participating in the process of microfinance have reported the progress made under the programme.

26.6 Committee on Financial Inclusion

Committee on Financial Inclusion (Chairman: C. Rangarajan) [4] was constituted by the Government of India on June 26, 2006 to prepare a strategy of financial inclusion. The Committee submitted its Final Report on January 4, 2008.

As is evident from the preamble of the report, the Committee interpreted financial inclusion as an instrumentality for social transformation: "Access to finance by the poor and vulnerable groups is a prerequisite for inclusive growth. In fact, providing access to finance is a form of empowerment of the vulnerable groups. Financial inclusion denotes delivery of financial services at an affordable cost to the vast sections of the disadvantaged and low-income groups.

The various financial services included credit, savings, insurance and payments and remittance facilities. The objective of financial inclusion is to extend the scope of activities of the organized financial system to include within its ambit people with low incomes. Through graduated credit, the attempt must be to lift the poor from one level to another so that they come out of poverty".

The Report viewed financial inclusion as a comprehensive and holistic process of ensuring access to financial services and timely and adequate credit, particularly to vulnerable groups such as weaker sections and low income groups at an affordable cost.

Financial inclusion, therefore, according to the Committee, should include access to mainstream financial products such as bank accounts, credit, remittances and payment services, financial advisory services and insurance facilities.

The Report observed that in India, 51.4 percent of farmer households are financially excluded from both formal/informal sources and 73 percent of farmer households do not access formal sources of credit.

Exclusion is most acute in Central, Eastern and North Eastern regions with 64 percent of financially excluded farmer households. According to the Report, the overall strategy for building an inclusive financial sector should be based on the following policy measures:
1. Effecting improvements within the existing formal credit delivery mechanism.
2. Suggesting measures for improving credit absorption capacity especially amongst marginal and sub-marginal farmers and poor non-cultivator households.
3. Evolving new models for effective outreach.
4. Leveraging on technology based solutions.

Keeping in view the enormity of the task involved, the Committee recommended the setting up of a mission mode National Rural Financial Inclusion Plan (NRFIP) with a target of providing access to comprehensive financial services to at least 50 percent (55.77 million) of the excluded rural households by 2012 and the remaining by 2015. This would require semi-urban and rural branches of commercial banks and RRBs to cover a minimum of 250 new cultivator and non-cultivator households per branch per annum. The Committee also recommended that the Government should constitute a National Mission on Financial

Inclusion (NaMFI) comprising representatives of all stakeholders for suggesting the overall policy changes required, and supporting stakeholders in the domain of public, private and NGO sectors in undertaking promotional initiatives.

The major recommendations relating to commercial banks included: (a) target for providing access to credit to at least 250 excluded rural households per annum in each rural/semi-urban branches, (b) targeted branch expansion in identified districts in the next three years, (c) provision of customised savings, credit and insurance products, (d) incentivising human resources for providing inclusive financial services, and (e) simplification of procedures for agricultural loans.

The major recommendations relating to regional rural banks (RRBs) included: (a) extending their services to unbanked areas and increasing their credit-deposit ratios, (b) no further merger of RRBs, (c) widening of network and expanding coverage in a time-bound manner, and (d) separate credit plans for excluded regions and strengthening of their boards.

In the case of co-operative banks, the major recommendations were: (a) early implementation of Vaidyanathan Committee Revival Package, (b) use of primary agricultural credit societies (PACS) and other primary co-operatives as business correspondents, and (c) co-operatives to adopt group approach for financing excluded groups.

Other important recommendations of the Committee included: (a) encouraging self-help groups (SHGs) in excluded regions, (b) legal status for SHGs, and (c) measures for urban micro-finance and separate category of micro finance institutions (MFIs).

The Committee recommended setting up of two funds: Financial Inclusion Fund (FIF) and Financial Inclusion Technology Fund (FITF). Each of the Funds shall consist of an overall corpus of ₹ 500 crore, with initial funding to be contributed by the Government of India, Reserve Bank of India (RBI) and NABARD in the ratio of 40:40:20.

The two funds have been established with NABARD which is the coordinating agency for financial inclusion initiatives with its Financial Inclusion Department (FID) as the nodal department. The core activities of the FID are to carry forward the agenda of financial inclusion of the excluded population at the national level as per the framework described by the Committee on Financial Inclusion in general and operationalising the Financial Inclusion Fund (FIF) and Financial Inclusion Technology Fund (FITF), in particular. The implementation is under the guidance of the two Advisory Boards set up for FIF and FITF respectively.

26.7 Committee on Comprehensive Financial Services for Small Businesses and Low-income Households (CCFS), 2014

On September 23, 2013, the Reserve Bank of India (RBI) constituted a Committee on Comprehensive Financial Services for Small Businesses and Low Income Households (Chairman: Nachiket Mor). On January 7, 2014, the Committee submitted its final report.

CCFS emphasized that in order to achieve the task of financial inclusion in a manner that enhances both financial inclusion and stability, there was need to move away from an exclusive focus on any one model to an approach where multiple models and partnerships were allowed to thrive, particularly between national full-service banks, regional banks of various types, non-banking financial companies (NBFCs), and financial markets. The common theme of all the recommendations made by the CCFS was that instead of focusing only on large generalist institutions, specialization and partnerships between specialists must be encouraged. Such an approach, in its view, would be far more effective at delivering high quality financial inclusion, without compromising financial stability or responsibility towards customers.

Some of the key recommendations of the CCFS included the following:

1. Universal Electronic Bank Account for every resident to be made available at the time of issuing the Aadhaar number.

2. Licensing, with lowered entry barriers but otherwise equivalent treatment, more functionally focused banks, including payment banks, wholesale consumer banks, and wholesale investment banks.

3. Developing risk-based supervision processes for regional banks and strengthening existing ones before creating new regional banks.

4. Reorienting the focus of NABARD, SIDBI, and NHB to be market-makers and providers of risk-based credit enhancements.

5. Consolidating NBFC definitions into two categories: core investment companies and other NBFCs.

6. On priority sector lending, while the CCFS acknowledged that the current focus of the policy, on small farmers, small businesses, and weaker sections, was well placed, it recommended an approach that incentivizes each provider to specialise in one or more sectors of the economy and regions of the country. Government subsidies should be channelled as direct benefit transfers (DBTs) rather than as subventions or waivers.

7. All financial firms regulated by the RBI should be required to have an internal process to assess suitability of products prior to advising clients with regard to them.

26.8 Pradhan Mantri Jan-Dhan Yojana (PMJDY), 2014

Exclusion from the banking system excludes people from all benefits that come from a modern financial system. Thus, financial inclusion is a national priority of the Government of India as it is an enabler for inclusive growth. Financial inclusion is important as it provides an avenue to the poor for bringing their savings into the formal financial system, a means to remit money to their families in villages besides taking them out of the clutches of the usurious money lenders.

26.8.1 Background: The efforts to include the financially excluded segments of the society in India are not new. The concept was first mooted by the Reserve Bank of India in 2005 and branchless banking through banking agents called *Bank Mitras* [Business Correspondents (BCs)] was started in the year 2006. In the year 2011, banks covered 74,351 villages, with population of more than 2,000 (as per 2011 Census), with banking facilities under the *Swabhimaan* campaign. However, the programme had a very limited reach and impact.

This campaign was limited in its approach in terms of reach and coverage. Convergence of various aspects of comprehensive financial inclusion like opening of bank accounts, access to digital money, availing of micro credit, insurance and pension was lacking.

The campaign focused only on the supply side by providing banking facility in villages of population greater than 2,000 but the entire geography was not targeted. There was no focus on the households. Also, some technology issues hampered further scalability of the campaign. Consequently, the desired benefits could not be achieved and a large number of bank accounts remained dormant. A comprehensive plan was felt necessary to keep the accounts active and use them as an instrument of some economic activity leading to livelihoods.

In order to provide the much needed thrust, a flagship programme called the Pradhan Mantri Jan-Dhan Yojana (PMJDY) was announced by the Prime Minister Narendra Modi in his Independence Day address to the nation on August 15, 2014. PMJDY was launched on August 28, 2014, across the country simultaneously. PMJDY lies at the core of development philosophy of *Sab Ka Sath Sab Ka Vikas* (inclusive growth).

26.8.2 PMJDY: Brief Introduction: PMJDY is a National Mission on financial inclusion. This Mission would enable all households—urban and rural—to gain easy and universal access to financial services. In this Mission, households will not only have bank accounts with indigenous RuPay debit cards but will also gain access to credit for economic activity and to insurance and pension services for their social security. The Mission has a strong focus on the use of technology and incorporates lessons learnt from earlier efforts.

PMJDY encompasses an integrated approach to bring about comprehensive financial inclusion of all the households in the country. The Plan envisages universal access to banking facilities with at least one basic banking account for every household, financial literacy, access to credit, insurance and pension facility. In addition, the beneficiaries would get RuPay Debit card having in-built accident insurance cover of ₹ 1 lakh. The plan also envisages channelling all Government benefits (from Centre/State/Local Body) to the beneficiaries' accounts and pushing the direct benefits transfer (DBT) scheme of the Union Government. The technological issues like poor connectivity, online transactions would also be addressed. Mobile transactions through telecom operators and their established centres as Cash Out Points are also planned to be used for financial inclusion under the Scheme. Also, an effort is being made to reach out to the youth of the country to participate in this Mission Mode Programme.

PMJDY aims to provide bank account to every household in the country and make available the following basic banking services facilities:

1. Opening of bank account with RuPay debit card and mobile banking facility.
2. Cash withdrawal and deposits.
3. Transfer.
4. Balance enquiry.
5. Mini statement.

Other services are also to be provided in due course in a time-bound manner apart from financial literacy which is to be disseminated side by side to make citizens capable to use optimum utilization of available financial services. To provide these banking services, banking outlets are to be provided within 5 kilometres distance of every village. Necessary infrastructure also needs to be placed to enable e-KYC for account opening and AEPS for withdrawal of cash-based biometric authentication from UIDAI database.

26.8.3 Six Pillars of PMJDY: PMJDY, to be executed in the Mission Mode, envisages provision of affordable financial services to all citizens within a reasonable distance. It comprises of the following six pillars:

1. **Universal Access to Banking Facilities:** Mapping of each district into sub service area (SSA) catering between 1,000-1,500 households in a manner that every habitation has access to banking services within a reasonable distance, say 5 km. by August 14, 2015. Coverage of parts of J&K, Himachal Pradesh, Uttarakhand, North East and the Left Wing Extremism affected districts which have telecom connectivity and infrastructure constraints would spill over to the Phase II of the programme (August 15, 2015 to August 15, 2018).

2. **Providing Basic Banking Accounts with Overdraft Facility and RuPay Debit Card to all Households:** The effort would be to first cover all uncovered households with banking facilities by August 2015, by opening basic bank accounts. Account holder would be provided a RuPay debit card. Facility of an overdraft to every basic banking account holder would be considered after satisfactory operation/credit history of six months.

3. **Financial Literacy Programme:** Financial literacy would be an integral part of the Mission in order to let the beneficiaries make best use of the financial services being made available to them.

4. **Creation of Credit Guarantee Fund:** Creation of a Credit Guarantee Fund would be to cover the defaults in overdraft accounts.

5. **Micro Insurance:** To provide micro insurance to all willing and eligible persons by August 14, 2018, and then on an ongoing basis.

6. **Unorganized Sector Pension Schemes like Swavalamban:** By August 14, 2018 and then on an ongoing basis.

Under the Mission, the first three pillars would be given thrust in the first year.

To sum up, the banking industry in India has grown both horizontally and vertically but the branch penetration in rural areas has not kept pace with the rising demand and the need for accessible financial services. Even after decades of bank nationalization—whose rationale was to shift the focus from class banking to mass banking—usurious money lenders in rural areas and urban slums continue to exploit the poor. After economic reforms initiated in 1991, the country can ill-afford not to include the poor in the growth paradigm. Financial inclusion of the poor will help in bringing them to the mainstream of growth and would also provide the financial institutions an opportunity to be partners in inclusive growth.

The Indian experience has proved that financial inclusion can work within the framework of financial stability given an enabling regulatory environment. A combination of viable business strategies targeted towards the population at the bottom of the pyramid, lower transactions costs with technological innovations and appropriate regulatory environment have helped foster greater financial inclusion with stability. The twin objectives of financial stability and financial inclusion are arguably two sides of a coin but it is imperative that a robust risk-mitigating framework which exploits their complementarities while minimizing the conflicts is adopted to ensure that they do not work at cross purposes. Looking to the immense potential lying ahead, rapid progress of financial inclusion efforts in India is the need of the hour. The stakeholders have come to realize the need for viable and sustainable business models which can sharply focus on accessible and affordable financial services, products and processes, synergistic partnerships with non-bank entities including the technology service providers.

There is substantial progress towards opening of accounts, providing basic banking services during the recent years. However, it is essential that all the sections be financially included in order to have financial stability and sustainability of the economic and social order. There is urgent need to push forward the financial inclusion agenda to ensure that people at the bottom of the pyramid join the mainstream of the formal financial system.

Endnotes

1. United Nations Capital Development Fund (UNCDF), *Building Inclusive Financial Sectors for Development*, UNCDF, May 2006. UNCDF is the UN's capital investment agency for the world's 48 least developed countries. It creates new opportunities for poor people and their communities by increasing access to micro finance and investment capital.

   UNCDF focuses on Africa and the poorest countries of Asia, with a special commitment to countries emerging from conflict or crisis. It provides seed capital—grants and loans—and technical support to help micro finance institutions reach more poor households and small businesses, and local governments finance the capital investments—water systems, feeder roads, schools, irrigation schemes—that will improve poor peoples' lives.

   UNCDF works to enlarge peoples' choices. It believes that poor people and communities should take decisions about their own development. Its programmes help to empower women—over 50 percent of the clients of UNCDF-supported micro finance institutions are women—and its expertise in micro finance and local development is shaping new responses to food insecurity, climate change and other challenges. All UNCDF support is provided via national systems, in accordance with the Paris Principles. UNCDF works in challenging environments—remote rural areas, countries emerging from conflict—and paves the way for others to follow. Established by the General Assembly in 1966 and with headquarters in New York, UNCDF is an autonomous UN organization affiliated with UNDP.

2. Report of the Taskforce set up by the Centre for Global Development, October 2009.

3. G-20 Toronto Summit Declaration, June 26-27, 2010.

4. Government of India, Planning Commission, *Report of the Committee on Financial Inclusion* (Chairman: C. Rangarajan), 2008.

27

Financial Regulators

Financial regulators in India are multiple. There is a plethora of legislations, rules and regulations to regulate and supervise the financial sector. In this context, the Report of the Financial Sector Legislative Reforms Commission (Chairman: B.N. Srikrishna), 2013 remarked, "The institutional framework governing the financial sector has been built up over a century. There are over 60 Acts and multiple rules and regulations that govern the financial sector. Many of the financial sector laws date back several decades, when the financial landscape was very different from that seen today. For example, the Reserve Bank of India (RBI) Act and the Insurance Act are of 1934 and 1938 vintage respectively. Financial economic governance has been modified in a piecemeal fashion from time to time, without substantial changes to the underlying foundations. Over the years, as the economy and the financial system have grown in size and sophistication, an increasing gap has come about between the requirements of the country and the present legal and regulatory arrangements". [1]

The Commission further observed, "The existing regulatory environment in India is fragmented and complex. There are multiple regulators, each one tasked with a silo within the financial sector. Given the fluidity and the fungibility of financial markets, such a fragmented approach cannot possibly achieve the results desired in terms of providing an organicunity to the sector in addressing domestic and global co-ordination, addressing financial development and inclusion, and dealing with systemic stability and other concerns. In fact, the experience of regulatory co-operation in India has not been very encouraging and has witnessed escalation of conflicts in the recent past. The Commission, therefore, feels that the fragmented approach to financial sector regulation in India has failed on many grounds, which need to be corrected. But at the same time, learning from the global crisis and the consequential regulatory rethinking in multiple jurisdictions, and the need for aligning the regulatory requirements to our own milieu, the Commission deliberated the issue of appropriate regulatory structure in detail". [2]

The chief regulators and supervisors of the Indian financial system are described below.

27.1 Ministry of Finance, Government of India
The work of the Ministry is divided into 5 departments.

27.1.1 Department of Economic Affairs (DEA): DEA is the nodal agency of the Union Government to formulate and monitor country's economic policies and programmes having a bearing on domestic and international aspects of economic management. A principal responsibility of this Department is the preparation of the Union Budget annually (excluding the Railway Budget). Other main functions include the following:

1. Formulation and monitoring of macroeconomic policies, including issues relating to fiscal policy and public finance, inflation, public debt management and the functioning of capital market including stock exchanges. In this context, it looks at ways and means to raise internal resources through taxation, market borrowings and mobilization of small savings.
2. Monitoring and raising of external resources through multilateral and bilateral official development assistance (ODA), sovereign borrowings abroad, foreign investments and monitoring foreign exchange resources including balance of payments.
3. Production of bank notes and coins of various denominations, postal stationery, postal stamps; and cadre management, career planning and training of the Indian Economic Service (IES).

27.1.2 Department of Expenditure: It is the nodal Department for overseeing the public financial management system in the Central Government and matters connected with State finances. The principal activities of the Department include the following:
1. Pre-sanction appraisal of major schemes/projects (both Plan and non-Plan expenditure).
2. Handling the bulk of the Central budgetary resources transferred to States.
3. Implementation of the recommendations of the Finance Commission and Central Pay Commission.
4. Overseeing the expenditure management in the Central Ministries/Departments through the interface with the financial advisors and the administration of the financial rules, regulations and orders through monitoring of audit comments and observations.
5. Preparation of Central Government Accounts.
6. Managing the financial aspects of personnel management in the Central Government.
7. Assisting Central Ministries/Departments in controlling the costs and prices of public services.
8. Assisting organizational re-engineering through review of staffing patterns and reviewing systems and procedures to optimize outputs and outcomes of public expenditure.

The Department also coordinates matters concerning the Ministry of Finance including Parliament-related work of the Ministry. The Department has under its administrative control the National Institute of Financial Management (NIFM), Faridabad.

27.1.3 Department of Revenue: It exercises control in respect of matters relating to all the Direct and Indirect Union Taxes through two statutory Boards namely, the Central Board of Direct Taxes (CBDT) and the Central Board of Excise and Customs (CBEC). Each Board is headed by a Chairman who is also ex-officio Special Secretary to the Government of India. Matters relating to the levy and collection of all Direct taxes are looked after by the CBDT whereas those relating to levy and collection of Customs and Central Excise duties and other Indirect taxes fall within the purview of the CBEC. The two Boards were constituted under the Central Board of Revenue Act, 1963.

27.1.4 Department of Financial Services: It looks after the following matters:
1. Citizen's Charter.

2. Industrial finance and micro, small and medium enterprise sector.
3. Banking, insurance and pension reforms.
4. Work allocation and advertisements.

27.1.5 Department of Disinvestment: It promotes people's ownership of Central Public Sector Enterprises to share in their prosperity through disinvestment. The Mission of the Department is as follows:

1. List all profitable Central Public Sector Enterprises (CPSEs) on stock exchanges.
2. Listing to result in: (a) improvement in corporate governance, (b) higher disclosure levels due to listing to bring about greater transparency and accountability in the functioning of the CPSEs, and (c) adding market discipline to the functioning of CPSEs
3. Disinvestment process to facilitate unlocking the true value of the CPSEs for all stakeholders—investors, employees, company and the Government.

27.2 Reserve Bank of India (RBI)

There is only one central bank in a country whose main function is to control the operations of the rest of the banking system. Reserve Bank of India (RBI), the central bank of India, is the apex institution responsible for managing and supervising the monetary and financial system of the economy.

27.2.1 Changing Role of RBI in the Financial Sector: Since the setting up of the Reserve Bank of India in 1935, its role in the financial sector and financial market development has undergone significant changes. Emerging primarily as a bank-based financial system, the development of financial structure in India has been to finance the planned development efforts. To this end, institutional development received considerable attention of the RBI. The broad-based development of the banking sector to meet short-term financing needs was supplemented by the setting up of specialised development finance institutions by the RBI to cater to long-term financing needs. Since the early 1990s, the introduction of financial sector reforms has provided a strong impetus to the development of financial markets. The introduction of market-based monetary policy instruments, the liberalisation of capital controls and integration of the Indian economy with global markets have exposed the country to potentially volatile capital inflows, posing new challenges and dilemmas for the RBI in monetary and exchange rate management.

The RBI has been suitably reorienting the regulatory and supervisory framework so as to meet the challenges of a new environment. It has been the endeavour of the RBI to develop a competitive, strong and dynamic banking system so that it plays an effective role in supporting the growth process of the economy. The emphasis has been on safeguarding the financial stability of the overall system through increased emphasis on prudential guidelines and effective monitoring, improving institutional soundness, strengthening the regulatory and supervisory processes by aligning with international best practices and by developing the necessary technological and legal infrastructure. While the approach towards the reforms has essentially been gradual and relevant to the context, consultative processes and appropriate timing and sequencing of measures have succeeded in aiding growth, enhancing efficiency, avoiding crises and imparting resilience to the financial system.

27.2.2 Global Financial Crisis and the RBI: Though adversely affected by global meltdown, Indian economy has shown considerable absorption capacity and resilience. Soon after the start of the crisis, net portfolio flows to India turned negative as foreign institutional investors (FIIs) rushed to sell equity stakes in a bid to replenish overseas cash balances. This had a knock-on effect on the stock market which nosedived to record levels. Supply and demand imbalance in the foreign exchange market led to depreciation of rupee vis-à-vis other currencies. The current account was affected mainly after September 2008 through slowdown in exports. Despite setbacks, however, the balance of payments situation of the country has remained comfortable.

India has remained relatively immune from the fallout of the crisis due to several reasons including prudential, supervisory and regulatory framework of the Reserve Bank of India (RBI). Moral suasions on the part of Government of India, RBI and Securities and Exchange Board of India (SEBI) have also worked. More importantly, the Indian banking system has shown remarkable market discipline, docility, and sincerity of purpose as against the financial gimmicks and dubious practices of the financial institutions in the US. It is heartening to note that in India, complex structures like synthetic securitisations have not been permitted so far.

RBI has the necessary framework for provision of liquidity to the banking system, in terms of Sections 17 and 18 of the Reserve Bank of India Act, 1934. RBI can undertake purchase/sale of securities of the Central or State Governments and can purchase, sell and rediscount bills of exchange and promissory notes drawn on and payable in India and arising out of bonafide commercial or trade transactions for provision/absorption of liquidity for normal day-to-day liquidity management operations as also for provision of emergency liquidity assistance to the banks under the lender-of-last-resort function.

RBI is empowered under the existing legal framework to deal with the resolution of weak and failing banks. The Banking Regulation Act provides the legal framework for voluntary amalgamation and compulsory merger of banks under Sections 44 (A) and 45, respectively. The Deposit Insurance and Credit Guarantee Corporation (DICGC) offers deposit insurance cover in India. The mergers of many weak private sector banks with healthy banks have improved overall stability of the system. Not a single scheduled commercial bank in the country has capital adequacy ratio which is less than the minimum regulatory requirement of 9 percent.

RBI took a number of monetary easing and liquidity enhancing measures including reduction in cash reserve ratio (CRR), statutory liquidity ratio (SLR) and key policy rates. The objective has been to facilitate flow of funds from the financial system to meet the needs of productive sectors. RBI's monetary policy stance has consistently been to balance growth, inflation and financial stability concerns. It has taken a slew of measures aimed at infusing rupee as well as foreign exchange liquidity into the system and to maintain credit flow to productive sectors of the economy.

In tune with the national economic objectives, RBI has followed a monetary policy usually called the policy of *controlled expansion*. The money supply has expanded sufficiently to meet the growing needs of industry and trade. However, it has been ensured that the expansion is not reckless. Broadly speaking, the expansion of money supply has been somewhat more than the increase in output thereby allowing a reasonable increase in the price level.

27.3 Ministry of Corporate Affairs

The Ministry is primarily concerned with administration of the Companies Act, 2013 for regulating the functioning of the corporate sector in accordance with law. The Ministry is also responsible for administering the Competition Act, 2002. Besides, it exercises supervision over the three professional bodies—Institute of Chartered Accountants of India (ICAI), Institute of Company Secretaries of India (ICSI) and the Institute of Cost and Works Accountants of India (ICWAI)—which are constituted under three separate Acts of the Parliament for proper and orderly growth of the professions concerned. The Ministry also has the responsibility of carrying out the functions of the Central Government relating to administration of Partnership Act, 1932, the Companies (Donations to National Funds) Act, 1951 and Societies Registration Act, 1980.

27.3.1 Companies Act, 2013

A. Background: The Companies Act, 1956 Act was in need of a substantial revamp for quite some time, to make it more contemporary and relevant to corporates, regulators and other stakeholders in India. While several unsuccessful attempts were made in the past to revise the 1956 Act, the most recent attempt was the Companies Bill, 2009 which was introduced in the Lok Sabha on August 3, 2009. This Companies Bill, 2009 was referred to the Parliamentary Standing Committee on Finance, which submitted its report on August 31, 2010 and was withdrawn after the introduction of the Companies Bill, 2011. The Companies Bill, 2011 was also considered by the Parliamentary Standing Committee on Finance which submitted its report on June 26, 2012. Subsequently, the Bill was considered and approved by the Lok Sabha on December 18, 2012 as the Companies Bill, 2012. The Bill was then considered and approved by the Rajya Sabha too on August 8, 2013. After having obtained the assent of the President of India on August 29, 2013, it came into effect.

B. Significance: The 2013 Act introduces significant changes in the provisions related to governance, e-management, compliance and enforcement, disclosure norms, auditors and mergers and acquisitions. Also, new concepts such as one-person company, small companies, dormant company, class action suits, registered valuers and corporate social responsibility have been included.

An attempt has been made to reduce the content of the substantive portion of the related law in the Companies Act, 2013 as compared to the Companies Act, 1956. In the process, much of the aforesaid content has been left, *to be prescribed*, in the Rules which are yet to be finalised and notified.

The changes in the 2013 Act have far-reaching implications that are set to significantly change the manner in which corporates operate in India. The 2013 Act has introduced several new concepts and has also tried to streamline many of the requirements by introducing new definitions.

C. Main Provisions:

(a) Types of Companies:

1. **One-person Company:** The 2013 Act introduces a new type of entity to the existing list i.e. apart from forming a public or private limited company, the 2013 Act enables the formation of a new entity a 'one-person company' (OPC). An OPC means a company with only one person as its member [Section 3(1) of 2013 Act].

2. **Private Company:** The 2013 Act introduces a change in the definition for a private company, *inter alia*, the new requirement increases the limit of the number of members from 50 to 200 [Section 2(68) of 2013 Act].

3. **Small Company:** A small company has been defined as a company, other than a public company.

- Paid-up share capital of which does not exceed ₹ 50 lakh or such higher amount as may be prescribed which shall not be more than ₹ 5 crore.

- Turnover of which as per its last profit-and-loss account does not exceed ₹ 2 crore INR or such higher amount as may be prescribed which shall not be more than ₹ 20 crore:

  As set out in the 2013 Act, this section will not be applicable to the following: (a) a holding company or a subsidiary company, (b) a company registered under Section 8, and (c) a company or body corporate governed by any special Act [Section 2(85) of 2013 Act].

4. **Dormant Company:** The 2013 Act states that a company can be classified as dormant when it is formed and registered under this 2013 Act for a future project or to hold an asset or intellectual property and has no significant accounting transaction. Such a company or an inactive one may apply to the ROC in such manner as may be prescribed for obtaining the status of a dormant company [Section 455 of 2013 Act].

(b) Mergers and Acquisitions: The 2013 Act features some new provisions in the area of mergers and acquisitions, apart from making certain changes from the existing provisions. While the changes are aimed at simplifying and rationalising the procedures involved, the new provisions are also aimed at ensuring higher accountability for the company and majority shareholders and increasing flexibility for corporates. The 2013 Act has streamlined as well as introduced concepts such as reverse mergers (merger of foreign companies with Indian companies) and squeeze-out provisions, which are significant. The 2013 Act has also introduced the requirement for valuations in several cases, including mergers and acquisitions, by registered valuers.

(c) Prohibition of Association or Partnership of Persons Exceeding Certain Number: The 2013 Act puts a restriction on the number of partners that can be admitted to a partnership at 100. To be specific, the 2013 Act states that no association or partnership consisting of more than the given number of persons as may be prescribed shall be formed for the purpose of carrying on any business that has for its object the acquisition of gain by the association or partnership or by the individual members thereof, unless it is registered as a company under this 1956 Act or is formed under any other law for the time being in force.

As an exception, the aforesaid restriction would not apply to the following: (a) A Hindu undivided family carrying on any business, and (b) an association or partnership, if it is formed by professionals who are governed by special acts like the Chartered Accountants Act etc. [Section 464 of 2013 Act].

(d) Insider Trading and Prohibition on Forward Dealings: The 2013 Act for the first time defines insider trading and price-sensitive information and prohibits any person including the director or key managerial person from entering into insider trading [Section 195 of 2013 Act]. Further, the Act also prohibits directors and key managerial personnel from forward dealings in the company or its holding, subsidiary or associate company [Section 194 of 2013 Act].

(e) Corporate Governance: The 2013 Act intends to improve corporate governance by requiring disclosure of nature of concern or interest of every director, manager, any other key managerial personnel and relatives of such a director, manager or any other key managerial personnel and reduction in threshold of disclosure from 20 percent to 2 percent. The term 'key managerial personnel' has now been defined in the 2013 Act and means the chief executive officer, managing director, manager, company secretary, whole-time director, chief financial officer and any such other officer as may be prescribed.

(f) Accounts and Audit: The 2013 Act has introduced certain significant amendments in this chapter. It has also introduced several additional requirements such as preparation of consolidated financial statements, additional reporting requirements for the directors in their report such as the development and implementation of the risk management policy, disclosures in respect of voting rights not exercised directly by the employees in respect of shares to which the scheme relates, etc., in comparison with the requirements of the 1956 Act.

The 2013 Act features extensive changes within the area of audit and auditors with a view to enhance audit effectiveness and accountability of the auditors. These changes undoubtedly, have a considerable impact on the audit profession. However, it needs to be noted that these changes will also have a considerable impact on the company in terms of time, efforts and expectations involved. Apart from introducing new concepts such as rotation of audit firms and class action suits, the 2013 Act also increases the auditor's liability substantially in comparison with the 1956 Act.

Unlike the appointment process at each annual general meeting under the 1956 Act, the auditor will now be appointed for a period of 5 years, with a requirement to ratify such an appointment at each annual general meeting [Section 139(1) of 2013 Act].

(g) Dividend: The 2013 Act proposes to introduce significant changes to the existing provisions of the 1956 Act in respect of declaration of dividend. The changes are likely to affect the existing practices followed by companies with regard to the declaration of dividend.

The existing provisions of the 1956 Act in relation to the transfer of a specified percentage of profit to reserve is no longer applicable and thus, companies will be free to transfer any or no amount to its reserves.

(h) Revival and Rehabilitation of Sick Companies: Chapter XIX of the 2013 Act lays down the provisions for the revival and rehabilitation of sick companies. The chapter describes the circumstances which determine the declaration of a company as a sick company, and also includes the rehabilitation process of the same. Although it aims to provide comprehensive provisions for the revival and rehabilitation of sick companies, the fact that several provisions such as particulars, documents as well as content of the draft scheme in respect of application for revival and rehabilitation, etc. have been left to substantive enactment, leaves scope for interpretation.

The coverage of this chapter is no longer restricted to industrial companies, and the determination of the net worth would not be relevant for assessing whether a company is a sick company.

(i) Corporate Social Responsibility: The 2013 Act makes an effort to introduce the culture of corporate social responsibility (CSR) in Indian corporates by requiring companies to formulate a corporate social responsibility policy and at least incur a given minimum expenditure on social activities.

27.4 Securities and Exchange Board of India (SEBI)

SEBI is an autonomous and independent statutory body. Its legally mandated objectives are the following: (a) protection of the interests of investors in securities, (b) development of the securities market, (c) regulation of the securities market, and (d) matters connected therewith and incidental thereto.

For details, see section 24.5.1 of chapter 24 of this book.

27.5 Insurance Regulatory and Development Authority (IRDA)

The supervisory control of insurance companies is exercised by Insurance Regulatory and Development Authority (IRDA) and these powers flow from Insurance Act, 1938 as well as from IRDA Act, 1999. IRDA Act 1999 states: "Subject to the provisions of this Act and any other law for the time being in force, the Authority shall have the duty to regulate, promote and ensure orderly growth of insurance business and reinsurance business".

27.5.1 Mission Statement of IRDA:

1. To protect the interest of and secure fair treatment to policyholders.
2. To bring about speedy and orderly growth of the insurance industry (including annuity and superannuation payments), for the benefit of the common man, and to provide long term funds for accelerating growth of the economy.
3. To set, promote, monitor and enforce high standards of integrity, financial soundness, fair dealing and competence of those it regulates.
4. To ensure speedy settlement of genuine claims, to prevent insurance frauds and other malpractices and put in place effective grievance redressal machinery.
5. To promote fairness, transparency and orderly conduct in financial markets dealing with insurance and build a reliable management information system to enforce high

standards of financial soundness amongst market players.

6. To take action where such standards are inadequate or ineffectively enforced.

7. To bring about optimum amount of self-regulation in day-to-day working of the industry consistent with the requirements of prudential regulation.

27.5.2 Regulatory and Supervisory Powers of IRDA: These are wide and pervasive. These can be summarised as under.

1. **Registration/Licensing:** Any company proposing to enter in the insurance business has to apply to the authority for registration certificate. The authority has the powers to issue the licence subject to its satisfaction that the proposed company is financially sound and has the managerial expertise to run the business. The authority has also got the powers to renew it, modify it or even suspend and cancel such registration.

2. **Product and its Pricing:** The authority shall be satisfied about the nature of the product and its pricing before it is placed for marketing amongst the consumers. The powers to control the price of the product is in addition to the premium rates which are fixed by the Tariff Advisory Committee (TAC) constituted under Section 64U of Insurance Act, 1938. Chairman of the authority is also ex-officio Chairman of TAC. The authority should also be satisfied with the terms and conditions mentioned in the policy documents.

3. **Investment of Funds:** The investment policy of the insurance companies is governed by the broad guidelines framed by the authority. It may direct the insurer to invest certain proportion of their funds in specified securities. For instance, the present directives are that general insurance companies have to invest minimum of 30 percent of their funds in government securities and 15 percent in housing projects including purchase of fire fighting equipments by state governments. Only 55 percent of the funds may be invested in market securities and amongst market securities only in approved securities.

4. **Solvency Margin:** The authority has to ensure that insurers maintain the solvency margin as laid down in the Act. In case companies fail to comply to solvency margin requirements, the authority can initiate disciplinary action against the defaulting companies.

5. **Appointment of Actuary:** As per the directives of the authority, it is mandatory for insurer to appoint an actuary. The qualifications of actuary have been laid down. The functions and duties of actuary have been prescribed by the authority.

6. **Appointment to Chief Executive/Managing Director:** It is obligatory on the part of insurance companies to take prior approval of the authority before appointing chief executive, managing director or whole time director in the company. The authority has also been vested with the power to remove any managerial person and also appoint any additional director in the company.

7. **Power of Investigation and Inspection:** The authority can institute any inquiry against the insurer to investigate the affairs of the company and for this purpose can appoint any person as investigator. Based on the report, authority can take

disciplinary action against the insurer including suspension of its registration.

8. **Accounts and Balance Sheets:** The insurers are required to prepare a balance sheet, a profit and loss account, a separate account of receipts and payments and a revenue account in respect of each class of business. These are to be audited by a qualified auditor.

9. **Intermediaries:** The authority shall also monitor the activities of intermediaries who are being engaged by the insurers to market their products. The licence to the agents will be issued by the authority. As and when brokers are allowed to operate, they will also have to obtain the licence from the authority.

10. **Surveyors and Loss Assessors:** The qualifications for surveyors to be eligible to obtain a licence are prescribed by the authority. Their licences are also being issued by the authority.

11. **Reinsurance:** Reinsurance programmes of insurance companies are being monitored by the authority on a continuous basis. As per the directives of the authority, insurance companies are required to cede a part of their premium income to designated Indian reinsurer. Insurers are supposed to keep the authorities apprised of their insurance programme, both outward and inward, and seek authority's approval.

27.6 Pension Fund Regulatory and Development Authority (PFRDA)

PFRDA was established by Government of India on August 23, 2003. The Government has, through an executive order dated October 10, 2003, mandated PFRDA to act as a regulator for the pension sector. The mandate of PFRDA is development and regulation of pension sector in India.

PFRDA, set up as a regulatory body for the pension sector, is engaged in consolidating the initiatives taken so far regarding the full NPS architecture and expanding the reach of the NPS distribution network.

Presently, PFRDA has appointed the following 7 pension fund managers (PFMs) for government and private sector NPS:

1. Aditya Birla Sun Life Pension Management Ltd.
2. HDFC Pension Management Company Ltd.
3. ICICI Prudential Pension Funds Management Company Ltd.
4. Kotak Mahindra Pension Fund Ltd.
5. LIC Pension Fund Ltd.
6. SBI Pension Funds Pvt. Ltd.
7. UTI Retirement Solutions Ltd.

PFMs manage three separate schemes consisting of three asset classes, namely: (i) equity, (ii) Government securities, and (iii) credit risk-bearing fixed income instruments, with the investment in equity subject to a cap of 50 percent. The fund managers will invest only in index funds that replicate either the BSE sensitive index or NSE Nifty 50 index. The subscriber will have the option to decide the investment mix of his pension wealth. In case the subscriber is unable/unwilling to exercise any choice regarding asset allocation, his contribution will be invested in accordance with the *auto choice* option with a predefined portfolio.

PFRDA has set up a Trust under the Indian Trusts Act, 1882 to oversee the functions of the PFMs. The NPS Trust is composed of members representing diverse fields and brings wide range of talent to the regulatory framework. PFRDA also intends to intensify its effort towards financial education and awareness as a part of its strategy to protect the interest of the subscribers. PFRDA's efforts are an important milestone in the development of a sustainable and efficient voluntary defined contribution based pension system in India.

PFRDA has also enhanced the maximum entry age into NPS from 55 years to 60 years. These initiatives are expected to help realize the full potential of the NPS in terms of economies of scale and benefit the subscribers in terms of lower fees and charges and higher returns.

For all citizens including workers in the unorganized sector, NPS is currently available through over 1,000 service provider (SP) branches of 57 Points of Presence (PoP). PFRDA has also recently appointed the Department of Posts as PoP in addition to other financial institutions which will expand the PoP-SP network by more than five times.

While Tier I, the non-withdrawable pension account under the NPS has been in operation since May 1, 2009, Tier II, the withdrawable account was made operational from December 1, 2009.

NPS implementation in the Central Government has stabilized with more than 5.64 lakh employees already covered. NPS has also been well received by the State Governments and 23 State Governments/Union Territories have notified similar schemes for their new recruits under the ambit of the NPS. PFRDA has been working with all the States to enable them to log on to the NPS architecture with ease.

NPS represents a major reform of Indian pension arrangements, and lays the foundation for a sustainable solution to ageing in India by shifting to an individual account, defined-contribution system.

27.7 Monitoring Framework for Financial Conglomerates (FCs)

The quickening pace of technological innovations coupled with blurring of sectoral distinctions has enabled financial intermediaries to effectively compete in sectors beyond their domain by deconstructing and recombining risks. Financial liberalisation has led to the emergence of financial conglomerates, cutting across not only various financial sectors such as banking, insurance and securities but across geographical boundaries as well.

These developments have also ushered in the attendant risks like that of contagion whereby the problems of different sectors and different geographies could have an adverse impact upon the balance sheets of parent regulated entity viz. the bank, insurance company or the securities company. Supervisors have realised the inadequacy of the sectoral regulations to deal with the complexities interwoven into operations of financial conglomerates.

In order to address the limitations of the segmental approach to supervision, the Reserve Bank, in consultation with SEBI and IRDA, decided upon putting in place a special monitoring system for systemically important financial intermediaries (SIFIs) or Financial Conglomerates. Accordingly, a financial conglomerates (FCs) monitoring mechanism was put in place in June 2004.

For the purpose of monitoring of FCs, the above three regulators are designated as the principal regulators to whom the identified FCs submit the FC Returns through their designated entities. The mechanism involves a quarterly reporting of relevant data by the identified FCs to their respective principal regulators with a focus on the extent of intra-group transactions and exposures of the identified groups. Primarily, the review of the intra-group transactions is conducted with a view to track build-up of large exposures to entities within the Group, to outside counterparties and to various financial market segments (equity, debt, money market, and derivatives markets), identify cases of migration/transfer of 'losses' and detecting situations of regulatory/supervisory arbitrage. The monitoring mechanism, thus, seeks to capture the 'contagion risk' within the group as also its cumulative exposure to specific outside entities, sectors and market segments.

The identification of financial groups for specialized monitoring under the FC framework is incumbent upon the scale of their operations in respective financial market segments (banking, insurance, securities, and non-banking finance). The size of the off-balance sheet position of the entities is also being additionally included as a parameter for determining the size of operations of the entities in respective market segments. While a group having a significant presence in two or more of these financial market segments qualifies to be an *identified FC*, few other financial groups which are otherwise important from a *systemic* standpoint (mainly on account of their size, involvement in specialised transactions like derivatives and securitisation and on account of market feedback), also get identified as FCs and are subjected to focused monitoring.

Since the monitoring framework also covers the housing finance segment which falls under the jurisdiction of the National Housing Bank (NHB), it has been named as a specified regulator.

The High Level Co-ordination Committee on Financial Markets (HLCCFM) Technical Committee on RBI Regulated Entities has been designated as the inter-regulatory forum for having an overarching view of the FC monitoring mechanism and for providing guidance/directions on concerns arising out of analysis of FC data and for sharing of other significant information in the possession of the Principal Regulators, which might have a bearing on the Group as a whole. Thus, the FC monitoring framework endeavours to identify contagion like situations at the incipient stage, which could snowball into a systemic concern unless addressed promptly. The framework also aims at addressing market disruptions issues by undertaking assessments of sources of liquidity for the group which is quite critical from a financial stability angle.

Endnotes

1. Government of India, Ministry of Finance, *Report of the Financial Sector Legislative Reforms Commission* (Chairman: B.N. Srikrishna), Volume I, March 2013, p. xiii.
2. Ibid., p. 9.

28

Legislative and Institutional Measures to Strengthen Financial Sector

An efficient financial system requires a regulatory framework with well-defined objectives, adequate and clear legal framework and transparent supervisory procedure. This, in turn, requires comprehensive legislations to enable the regulatory authorities to discharge their responsibilities effectively. The RBI has, therefore, been making constant efforts to upgrade and strengthen the legal framework in tune with the changing environment.

Some recent Acts enacted by the Parliament are as under.

28.1 Prevention of Money Laundering Act (PMLA), 2002

Money laundering is the process of transforming the proceeds of crime and corruption into ostensibly legitimate assets. In a number of legal and regulatory systems, however, the term money laundering has become conflated with other forms of financial and business crime, and is sometimes used more generally to include misuse of the financial system, including terrorism financing and evasion of international sanctions. Most anti-money laundering laws openly conflate money laundering with terrorism financing when regulating the financial system.

Some countries define money laundering as obfuscating sources of money, either intentionally or by merely using financial systems or services that do not identify or track sources or destinations. Other countries define money laundering to include money from activity that *would have been* a crime in that country, even if it was legal where the actual conduct occurred. This broad brush of applying money laundering to incidental, extraterritorial or simply privacy-seeking behaviours has led some to label it *financial thought crime.*

PMLA, 2002 was enacted in January 2003. The Act along with the Rules framed thereunder came into force with effect from July 1, 2005. Section 3 of PMLA defines offence of money laundering as whosoever directly or indirectly attempts to indulge or knowingly assists or knowingly is a party or is actually involved in any process or activity connected with the proceeds of crime and projecting it as untainted property shall be guilty of offence of money-laundering. It prescribes obligation of banking companies, financial institutions and intermediaries for verification and maintenance of records of the identity of all its clients and also of all transactions and for furnishing information of such transactions in prescribed form to the Financial Intelligence Unit-India (FIU-IND). It empowers the Director of FIU-IND to impose fine on banking company, financial institution or intermediary if they or any of their officers fails to comply with the provisions of the Act.

PMLA empowers certain officers of the Directorate of Enforcement to carry out investigations in cases involving offence of money laundering and also to attach the property involved in money laundering. PMLA envisages setting up of an Adjudicating Authority to exercise jurisdiction, power and authority to confirm attachment or order confiscation of attached properties. It also envisages setting up of an Appellate Tribunal to hear appeals against the order of the Adjudicating Authority and the authorities like Director FIU-IND.

PMLA envisages designation of one or more courts of sessions as Special Court or Special Courts to try offences punishable under PMLA and offences with which the accused may, under the Code of Criminal Procedure, 1973, be charged at the same trial. PMLA allows Central Government to enter into an agreement with Government of any country outside India for enforcing the provisions of the PMLA, exchange of information for the prevention of any offence under PMLA or under the corresponding law in force in that country or investigation of cases relating to any offence under PMLA.

PMLA seeks to combat money laundering in India and has three main objectives:
1. To prevent and control money laundering.
2. To confiscate and seize the property obtained from the laundered money.
3. To deal with any other issue connected with money laundering in India.

Special Courts have been set-up in a number of States/UTs by the Central Government to conduct the trial of the offences of money laundering. The authorities under the Act, like the director, adjudicating authority and the appellate tribunal, have been constituted to carry out the proceedings related to attachment and confiscation of any property derived from money laundering.

In order to enlarge the scope of this Act and to achieve the desired objectives, the Act provides for bilateral agreements between countries to cooperate with each other and curb the menace of money laundering. These agreements shall be for the purpose of either enforcing the provisions of this Act or for the exchange of information which shall help in the prevention in the commission of an offence under this Act or the corresponding laws in that foreign State.

In certain cases the Central Government may seek/provide assistance from/to a contracting State for any investigation or forwarding of evidence collected during the course of such investigation. The Act provides for reciprocal arrangements for processes/assistance with regard to accused persons.

The Government constituted the Financial Intelligence Unit-India, in November, 2004. The organization has started receiving Cash Transaction Reports and Suspicious Transaction Reports from the banking companies etc. in terms of Section 12 of the PMLA.

28.2 Credit Information Companies (Regulation) Act, 2005

It is aimed at providing for regulation of credit information companies and to facilitate efficient distribution of credit. No company can commence or carry on the business of credit information without obtaining a certificate of registration from the RBI. The Act sets out procedures for obtaining certificate of registration, the requirements of minimum capital and management of credit information companies. The Act also empowers the RBI to determine policy in relation to functioning of credit information companies and to give directions to such companies, credit institutions and specified users.

The Act also lays down the functions of credit information companies, powers and duties of auditors, obtaining of membership by credit institutions in credit information companies, information privacy principles, alterations of credit information files and credit reports, regulation of unauthorised access to credit information, offences and penalties, obligations as to fidelity and secrecy.

Other salient features of the Act include settlement of disputes between credit institutions and credit information companies or between credit institutions and their borrowers. The Act also provides for amendment of certain enactments so as to permit disclosure of credit information.

28.3 Government Securities Act, 2006

This Act was enacted by the Parliament with a view to consolidating and amending the law relating to Government securities and its management by the Reserve Bank of India. The Act applies to Government securities created and issued, whether before or after the commencement of the Act, by the Central or a State Government. Accordingly, the Public Debt Act, 1944 ceased to apply to the Government securities. The Indian Securities Act, 1920 was repealed.

The new Act would facilitate widening and deepening of the Government securities market and its more effective regulation by the Reserve Bank in various ways, such as:

1. Stripping or reconstitution of Government securities.
2. Legal recognition of beneficial ownership of the investors in Government securities through the constituents' subsidiary general ledger (CSGL).
3. Statutory backing for the Reserve Bank's power to debar subsidiary general ledger (SGL) account holders from trading, either temporarily or permanently, for misuse of SGL account facility.
4. Facility of pledge or hypothecation or lien of Government securities for availing of loan.
5. Extension of nomination facility to hold the securities or receive the amount thereof in the event of death of the holder.
6. Recognition of title to Government security of the deceased holder on the basis of documents other than succession certificate such as will executed by the deceased holder, registered deed of family settlement, gift deed, deed of partition, etc., as prescribed by the Reserve Bank of India.
7. Recognition of mother as the guardian of the minor for the purpose of holding Government Securities.
8. Statutory powers to the Reserve Bank to call for information, cause inspection and issue directions in relation to Government securities.

28.4 Payment and Settlement Systems Act, 2007

This Act, along with Payment and Settlement Systems Regulations, 2008, stipulates that no person other than the Reserve Bank of India (RBI), shall commence or operate a payment system except under and in accordance with an authorisation issued by the RBI under the provisions of the Act.

All persons currently operating a payment system or desirous of setting up a payment system, as defined in Section 2(1)(i) of the Act should apply for authorisation to the Reserve Bank, unless specifically exempted in terms of the Act. Existing payment systems will cease to have the right to carry on their operations, unless they obtain an authorisation within six months from the commencement of the Act (i.e. August 12, 2008).

The Payment and Settlement Systems Regulations, 2008 detail the form and manner in which the application is to be made to the Reserve Bank for grant of authorisation.

28.5 Black Money (Undisclosed Foreign Income and Assets) and Imposition of Tax Act, 2015

Individuals and institutions globally are engaged in evading taxes and generating surplus which do not get accounted for in the formal economy. These funds are generated from activities which may be legal or illegal by nature. However, the mere fact that taxes have not been paid on such incomes, as per the rules of the land, converts such funds to form a part of the parallel economy or black money generation. The Government has been focused on the black money peril both within the confines of India and the sums of money parked abroad. To tackle the complex issue of black money abroad which has been in the headlines, a separate regime for taxation of The Black Money (Undisclosed Foreign Income and Assets) and Imposition of Tax Act, 2015 has been introduced.

The Act was passed by Lok Sabha on May 11, 2015 and by the Rajya Sabha on May 13, 2015. It received President's assent on May 26, 2015 and came into force on July 1, 2015. The Act extends to the whole of India.

The Act makes provisions to deal with the problem of the black money (i.e. undisclosed foreign income and assets), to frame procedures for dealing with such income and assets and to provide for imposition of tax on any undisclosed foreign income and asset held outside India and for matters connected therewith or incidental thereto.

28.6 Benami Transactions (Prohibition) Amendment Act, 2016

It came into force from November 1, 2016. The new law seeks to give more teeth to the authorities to curb benami transactions and hence black money. The Act was an amendment of the existing Benami Transactions (Prohibition) Act, 1988. After coming into force, it was renamed as Prohibition of Benami Property Transactions Act, 1988 (PBPT Act). The Act defines *benami* transactions and also provides imprisonment up to 7 years and fine for violation of the Act. The earlier law provided for up to 3 years of imprisonment or fine or both.

The PBPT Act prohibits recovery of the property held benami from benamidar by the real owner. Properties held benami are liable for confiscation by the government without payment of compensation. The new law also provides for an appellate mechanism in the form of an adjudicating authority and appellate tribunal.

The amendments aim to strengthen the Act in terms of legal and administrative procedure. The *benami* (without a name) property refers to property purchased by a person in the name of some other person. The person on whose name the property is purchased is called the *benamdar* and the property so purchased is called the *benami* property. The person who finances the deal is the real owner.

The PBPT Act prohibits recovery of the property held benami from benamdar by the real owner. As per the Act, properties held benami are liable for confiscation by the government, without payment of compensation. An appellate mechanism has been provided under the act, in the form of an adjudicating authority and appellate tribunal.

The four authorities who will conduct inquiries or investigations are the initiating officer, approving authority, administrator and adjudicating authority. In the case of charitable or religious organisation properties, the government has the power to grant exemption.

28.7 High Level Committee on Financial Sector Reforms, 2008

With a view to outlining a comprehensive agenda for the evolution of the financial sector—indicating especially the priorities and sequencing decisions which the Government of India must keep in minds—a High Level Committee on Financial Sector Reforms was set up by the Planning Commission of India in August 2007. The Committee (Chairman: Raghuram G. Rajan) submitted its report in September 2008, and made the following main recommendations:

1. Allow more entry to private well-governed, deposit-taking small finance banks.
2. Liberalise the banking correspondent regulation so that a wide range of local agents can serve to extend financial services. Use technology both to reduce costs and to limit fraud and misrepresentation.
3. Offer priority sector loan certificates (PSLC) to all entities that lend to eligible categories in the priority sector. Allow banks that undershoot their priority sector obligations to buy the PSLC and submit it towards fulfilment of their target.
4. Sell small under-performing public sector banks, possibly to another bank or to a strategic investor, to gain experience with the process and gauge outcomes.
5. Create stronger boards for large public sector banks, with more power to outside shareholders (including possibly a private sector strategic investor), devolving the power to appoint and compensate top executives to the board.
6. After starting the process of strengthening boards, delink the banks from additional government oversight, including by the Central Vigilance Commission and Parliament, with the justification that with government-controlled boards governing the banks, a second layer of oversight is not needed.
7. Be more liberal in allowing takeovers and mergers, including by domestically incorporated subsidiaries of foreign banks.
8. Free banks to set up branches and ATMs anywhere.

28.8 Committee on Financial Sector Assessment (CFSA), 2009

In March 2009, the Government and RBI jointly released the report of the Committee on Financial Sector Assessment (CFSA) that was co-chaired by Deputy Governor Rakesh Mohan and Finance Secretary Ashok Chawla. The report is the culmination of work started in September 2006 to undertake a comprehensive self-assessment of India's financial sector, particularly focusing on stability assessment and stress testing and compliance with all financial standards and codes.

CFSA owed its origins to the Financial Sector Assessment Programme (FSAP) that was initiated in 1999 and carried out jointly by the IMF and the World Bank after the Asian crisis. Several countries, including India, participated in this long- drawn and resource-intensive exercise. This programme so far has been conducted by the IMF and the World Bank using experts from around the world to carry out the assessment with participation from the host country.

The CFSA followed a forward-looking and holistic approach to self-assessment, based on three mutually reinforcing pillars:
1. Financial stability assessment and stress testing.
2. Legal, infrastructural and market development issues.
3. Assessment of the status of implementation of international financial standards and codes.

The first pillar is essentially concerned with stability assessment. Taking into account the legal, regulatory and supervisory architecture in India, the CFSA felt the need for involving, and associating closely, all the major regulatory institutions in the financial sector—RBI, SEBI and IRDA [1], besides the relevant government departments. Direct official involvement at different levels brought about enormous responsibility, ownership, and commitment to the process, ensuring constructive pragmatism when faced with contentious issues.

Since the assessment required comprehensive domain knowledge in the various technical areas examined, the CFSA initially constituted Technical Groups comprising officials with first-hand experience in handling the respective areas from the regulatory agencies concerned as well as the government to undertake the preliminary assessment and to prepare technical notes and background material in the concerned areas. This ensured that officials who are well-conversant with their own systems and are aware of the existing strengths and weaknesses could identify the best alternative solutions.

To ensure an impartial assessment, the CFSA constituted four external independent advisory panels, comprising non-official experts drawn from within the country. These Panels made their assessments after thorough debate and rigorous scrutiny of inputs provided by the technical groups. To further strengthen the credibility of this assessment, the advisory panels' assessments were reviewed by eminent international experts.

The CFSA then drew up its own overview report at the final stage, drawing upon the assessments, findings and recommendations of the advisory panels and the comments of the peer reviewers. The assessments and recommendations comprise six volumes.

Overall, the CFSA found that India's financial system is essentially sound and resilient, and that systemic stability is by and large robust. India is broadly compliant with most of the standards and codes though gaps were noted in the timely implementation of bankruptcy proceedings.

Of immediate interest, and related closely to the current macroeconomic conditions, the CFSA also carried out single-factor stress-tests for credit and market risks and liquidity ratio and scenario analyses. These tests show that there are no significant vulnerabilities in the banking system. This does not mean that NPAs will not rise in this economic slowdown. NPAs may indeed rise. However, given the strength of the banks' balance sheets, that rise is not likely to pose any systemic risks, as it might in many advanced countries. Risk assessment, however, is a continuous process and the stress tests need to be conducted taking into account the macroeconomic linkages as also the second round and contagion risks.

28.9 Financial Sector Legislative Reforms Commission (FSLRC), 2013

The Indian financial system is increasingly out of touch with the requirements of the economy today and the even greater requirements of the economy in the future. Most changes in the framework of financial regulation in India have been made in response to the need of the hour. This has meant piecemeal changes to the various laws that give powers to regulators to regulate finance.

In recent years, a consensus has emerged about the direction of reforms through a series of expert committees, which have drawn on hundreds of independent experts and a body of research on the failings of Indian finance. However, many of the changes proposed are incompatible with the basic structure of existing laws.

With a view to revamping financial sector laws to bring them in tune with current requirements, the Government set up the FSLRC (Chairman: B.N. Srikrishna) on March, 24, 2011. [2] FSLRC in its Report, submitted in March 2013, gave wide-ranging recommendations, both legislative and non-legislative, on the institutional, legal, and regulatory framework and operational changes in the Indian financial sector. The draft Indian Financial Code (IFC) was proposed by FSLRC has provisions that aim at replacing a large numbers of existing financial laws. FSLRC has designed a modified financial regulatory architecture which would increase accountability by achieving clarity of purpose for each organization and avoid conflicts of interest. The modified arrangements also facilitate achieving economies of scope and scale of related activities, for the private sector and for the government.

The FSLRC was set up to review and redraft the laws so that Indian finance can be reformed to prepare India for growing into a modern economy, without having to constantly amend existing laws to incorporate each new step for the financial system.

The task for FSLRC was to question the fundamental arrangements between regulators, the Government, the regulated, and the consumer for whose protection regulation is ultimately being done. FSLRC proposed a new draft law, viz. the Indian Financial Code. This law puts consumer protection at the heart of all financial regulations. In order to protect the consumer without putting a burden on the taxpayer, regulators do micro-prudential regulation and reduce the risk of failure of financial firms. They protect policy holders and prevent unsuitable products from being sold through regulations about consumer protection and through redressal forums. When financial firms fail, shareholders should bear the full brunt of the failure, but consequences for consumers and the economy should be blocked using a resolution corporation. Through systemic risk regulation, the regulators and the government prevent a large-scale disruption of financial services. This adds up to a rational approach to interventions by financial agencies in the financial system, as opposed to the existing approach of command and control.

A major theme of many of the recommendations of previous committee reports in India has been the impediments placed by financial agencies against progress. This issue has been addressed by FSLRC by giving regulators clear objectives and enumerated powers. The regulator in this scenario needs to demonstrate that the regulation is required to meet the objectives assigned to him, and it lies within his powers, and that a cost-benefit analysis of the regulation shows that the additional cost, monetary or otherwise, of complying with this regulation is going to bring clear benefits to the economy.

28.10 Indian Financial Code (IFC)

The Report of FSLRC contained the Draft Indian Financial Code. IFC replaces most existing Indian financial laws. It seeks to address present weaknesses of the Indian financial system, and meet the requirements of the Indian economy over the coming 30 years.

IFC articulates clear objectives for financial regulation where Government intervention is required. These include: (a) consumer protection, (b) micro-prudential regulation, (c) systemic risk reduction, (d) market abuse in organized financial trading, (e) consumer redress, (f) debt management, (g) capital controls, and (h) monetary policy. In each area, precise objectives are stated and precise powers given to financial agencies.

IFC lays great emphasis on the formal process through which the legislative, executive, and judicial functions take place in financial regulation. The principles of rule of law and accountability are emphasized to create a better environment of checks and balances around regulators.

The present financial regulatory architecture has come about through numerous episodes in the past decades, without a coherent design. FSLRC has designed a modified financial regulatory architecture, which would increase accountability by achieving clarity of purpose for each organization and avoid conflicts of interest. The modified arrangements also facilitate achieving economies of scope and scale.

Financial Stability and Development Council (FSDC) decided that while the draft IFC is a bill that requires Parliamentary action, a number of changes proposed by the FSLRC can be implemented voluntarily, without any legislative changes. To provide examples of best practices, and to guide regulators on compliance with the measures recommended by the FSLRC, the Ministry of Finance has published a handbook on adoption of governance enhancing and non-legislative elements of the draft Indian Financial Code.

IFC is on the legislative agenda. This legislative and non-legislative work is now the centrepiece of financial reforms in India.

28.11 Financial Stability and Development Council (FSDC)

Following the recent global financial crisis, several nations have been revisiting their regulatory architecture. India has also been prompt to act on this front. In pursuance of the announcement made in the Budget 2010-11, an apex-level Financial Stability and Development Council was set up under the Chairmanship of the Finance Minister for strengthening and institutionalizing the mechanism for maintaining financial stability and enhancing inter-regulatory coordination. FSDC is a non-statutory apex council for coordination among various regulatory bodies, since in India's increasingly complex economy, issues arise that straddle multiple financial jurisdictions.

FSDC monitors macro-prudential supervision of the economy, including functioning of large financial conglomerates, and addresses inter-regulatory coordination and financial-sector development issues. It also focuses on financial literacy and financial inclusion.

A sub-committee of the FSDC has also been set up under the chairmanship of the Governor of Reserve Bank of India (RBI). Under the aegis of the FSDC, two empowered technical groups (i.e. Technical Group on Financial Literacy and Financial Inclusion and Inter-Regulatory Technical Group) have been formed.

28.12 Financial Action Task Force (FATF)

FATF is an inter-governmental policy-making body established in 1989 by the Ministers of its Member jurisdictions. The objectives of the FATF are to set standards and promote effective implementation of legal, regulatory and operational measures for combating money laundering, terrorist financing and other related threats to the integrity of the international financial system. The FATF is therefore a *policy-making body* which works to generate the necessary political will to bring about national legislative and regulatory reforms in these areas.

The FATF has a ministerial mandate to establish international standards for combating money laundering and terrorist financing. India joined the FATF as its 34th member in June 2010. At present the FATF has 37 members comprising 35 countries and two organizations, namely the European Commission and Gulf Cooperation Council. India participated in the FATF plenary and Working Group Meetings held in Mexico from June 20-24, 2011.

FATF has developed a series of Recommendations that are recognised as the international standard for combating of money laundering and the financing of terrorism and proliferation of weapons of mass destruction. They form the basis for a co-ordinated response to these threats to the integrity of the financial system and help ensure a level playing field. First issued in 1990, the FATF Recommendations were revised in 1996, 2001, 2003 and 2012 to ensure that they remain up to date and relevant, and they are intended to be of universal application.

FATF monitors the progress of its members in implementing necessary measures, reviews money laundering and terrorist financing techniques and counter-measures, and promotes the adoption and implementation of appropriate measures globally. In collaboration with other international stakeholders, the FATF works to identify national-level vulnerabilities with the aim of protecting the international financial system from misuse.

FATF's decision-making body, the FATF Plenary, meets three times per year.

28.13 Financial Stability Board (FSB)

FSB was established in 2009 under the aegis of the G20 bringing together the national authorities, standard-setting bodies, and international financial institutions to address vulnerabilities and to develop and implement strong regulatory, supervisory, and other policies in the interest of financial stability. India is an active Member of the FSB. Financial Stability and Development Council (FSDC) Secretariat in the Department of Economic Affairs, Ministry of Finance coordinates with the various financial sector regulators and other relevant agencies to represent India's views with the FSB. As a member of the FSB, Basel Committee on Banking Supervision (BCBS), and International Monetary Fund (IMF), India actively participates in post-crisis reforms of the international regulatory and supervisory framework under the aegis of the G20. India remains committed to adoption of international standards and best practices, in a phased manner and calibrated to local conditions, wherever necessary.

Endnotes

1. The supervisory control of insurance companies is exercised by Insurance Regulatory and Development Authority (IRDA) and these powers flow from Insurance Act, 1938 as well as from IRDA Act, 1999. IRDA Act 1999 states: "Subject to the provisions of this Act and any other law for the time being in force, the Authority shall have the duty to regulate, promote and ensure orderly growth of insurance business and reinsurance business". Regulatory and supervisory powers of the IRDA are wide and pervasive.
2. Government of India, Ministry of Finance, *Report of the Financial Sector Legislative Reforms Commission* (Chairman: B.N. Srikrishna), March 2013.

Suggested Readings

Suggested Readings

Baker, M., and J. Wurgler (2002), "Market Timing and Capital Structure", *The Journal of Finance,* 57(1), (February).

Berens, J.L. and C.J. Cuny (1995), "The Capital Structure Puzzle Revisited", *The Review of Financial Studies,* 8(4), (Winter).

Bhavani, T.A. and N.R. Bhanumurthy (2012), "Financial Access in Post-Reform India", Oxford University Press, New Delhi.

Bhole, L.M. and J. Mahukud (2011), "Financial Institutions and Markets", Tata McGraw-Hill, New Delhi.

Brealey, Richard A. and Stewart C. Myers (2002), "Principles of Corporate Finance", McGraw-Hill, Seventh Edition.

Brennan, M., and E. Schwartz (1984), "Optimal Financial Policy and Firm Valuation", *The Journal of Finance*, 39.

Castanias, R. (1983), "Bankruptcy Risk and Optimal Capital Structure", *The Journal of Finance*, 38(5), December.

Chandra, Prasanna (2008), "Financial Management: Theory and Practice", Tata McGraw-Hill, New Delhi.

Copeland, Thomas E., J. Fred Weston and Kuldeep Shastri (2003), "Financial Theory and Corporate Policy", Prentice Hall, fourth edition.

Cornell, B., and A.C. Shapiro (1987), "Corporate Stakeholders and Corporate Finance", *Financial Management* (Spring).

David, G. and M. Luenberger (1997), "Investment Science", Oxford University Press, USA.

De Angelo, H. and R. Masulis (1980), "Optimal Capital Structure under Corporate and Personal Taxation", *Journal of Financial Economics.*

Fabozzi, F.B., F. Modigliani, F.J. Jones and M.G. Ferri (2009), "Foundations of Financial Markets and Institutions", Pearson Education, third edition.

Fama, E.F. and K.R. French (2002), "Testing Trade-off and Pecking Order Predictions about Dividends and Debt", *The Review of Financial Studies*, 15(1), (Spring).

Fischer, E.O., R. Heinkel and J. Zechner (1989), "Dynamic Capital Structure Choice: Theory and Tests", The Journal of Finance, 44(1), March.

Harris, M. and A. Raviv (1990), "Capital Structure and the Informational Role of Debt", *The Journal of Finance*, 45(2), (June).

Huang, Chi-fu, and Robert H. Litzenberger (1988), "Foundations for Financial Economics", North-Holland.

Hull, John C. (2005), "Options, Futures and Other Derivatives", Pearson Education, sixth edition.

Ingersoll Jr., Jonathan E. (1987), "Theory of Financial Decision Making", Rowman & Littlefield.

Khan, M.Y. (2011), "Indian Financial System", Tata McGraw-Hill, New Delhi.

Merton, R.C. (2005), "Financial Innovation and Economic Performance", *Journal of Applied Corporate Finance*, Volume 4, Issue 4.

Mishkin, F.S. and S.G. Eakins (2009), "Financial Markets and Institutions", Pearson Education, sixth edition.

Modigliani, F. and M.H. Miller (1958), "The Cost of Capital, Corporation Finance and the Theory of Investment", *The American Economic Review,* 48(3), June.

Modigliani, F. and M.H. Miller (1963), "Corporate Income Taxes and the Cost of Capital: A Correction", *The American Economic Review,* 53(3), June.

Myers, S.C. (1977), "Determinants of Corporate Borrowing", *Journal of Financial Economics,* November.

Myers, S.C., and N.S. Majluf (1984), "Corporate Financing and Investment Decisions When Firms Have Information That Investors Do Not Have", *Journal of Financial Economics.*

Rene, S. (1990), "Managerial Discretion and Optimal Financing Policies", *Journal of Financial Economics.*

Ross, Stephen A., Randolph W. Westerfield and Bradford D. Jordan (2005), "Fundamentals of Corporate Finance", McGraw-Hill, seventh edition.

Sharpe, William, Gordon Alexander and Jeffery Bailey (2002), "Investments", Prentice Hall of India, sixth edition.

Titman, S. and R. Wessels (1988), "The Determinants of Capital Structure Choice", *The Journal of Finance,* 43(1), March.

Van Horne, J.C. (2007), "Financial Management and Policy", Prentice Hall of India, New Delhi.

Index

Index

A

Advantages of Financial Inclusion, 174
Advantages of Fixed Income Securities, 31
Advantages of Forwards, 74
Advantages of Option Trading, 89
Arbitrage Pricing Theory (APT), 106
Arbitrage-Free Market, 103
Arbitrageurs, 67
Aspects of Financial Economics, 8
Assumptions of Black-Scholes Model, 95

B

B.N. Srikrishna, 203
Badla System, 83
Binomial Option Pricing Model (BOPM), 98
Binomial Tree Pricing Model, 91
Black-Scholes Formula, 95
Black-Scholes Model, 91
Bombay Stock Exchange, 83, 104, 160
Bond Rating, 128

C

C. Rangarajan, 179
Calculating Price with the Binomial Model, 99
Call Options, 86
Callable Bond, 127
Capital Asset Pricing Model (CAPM), 48, 107
Capital Budgeting, 117
Capital Investments, 116
Capital Market Line (CML), 54
Capital Market, 12, 158
Capital Structure Substitution (CSS) Theory, 138
Causes of Differences in Interest Rates, 23
Chicago Board of Trade, 68, 72
Chicago Board Options Exchange (CBOE), 71
Chicago Mercantile Exchange (CME), 69, 79
Classification of Financial Institutions in India, 146
Commercial Paper, 130
Companies Act, 2013, 189
Conditions for Arbitrage, 103
Constant Dividend Policy, 134
Consumption Capital Asset Pricing Model (CCAPM), 51
Convertible Bond, 127
Corporate Bonds, 126
Credit Derivatives in India, 165
Credit Information Companies (Regulation) Act, 2005, 198
Currency Futures, 80, 84

D

Debentures, 115
Delhi Stock Exchange, 83
Dennis Robertson, 18
Derivative Financial Instruments, 164
Determinants of Access to Financial Services, 5
Development Finance Institutions (DFIs), 149
Disadvantages of Fixed Income Securities, 31
Distinction between Forwards and Futures, 82
Diversification of Portfolio, 35
Dividend Irrelevance Theories, 134
Dividend Puzzle, 133
Dividend Relevance Theories, 136

E

Economic Role of Derivatives, 67
Equated Monthly Instalment (EMI), 25

Exchange-traded Options, 90
Expectations Theory, 29
Expected Net Present Value (NPV), 40

F
Financial Derivatives, 14
Financial Futures, 77
Financial Institutions in India at a
    Glance, 147
Financial Institutions, 10
Financial Instruments, 13
Financial Markets, 11
Financial Neutrality versus Financial
    Activism, 5
Financial Repression, 5
Financial Stability Board (FSB), 206
Financial Volatility versus Financial
    Stability, 6
First Five Year Plan, 149
Fitch Ratings, 128
Fixed Income Securities, 30
Flat Rate Loans, 25
Floating Rate Loans, 25
Foreign Exchange Market, 161
Forms of Option Trading, 90
Forward Markets Commission
    (FMC) of India, 75
Franco Modigliani, 119, 139
Functions of Financial System, 4

G
General Credit Card (GCC), 176
Gordon's Model, 137
Government Securities Act, 2006, 199
Government Securities Market, 156
Grain Futures Act, 69
Gross and Net Rate of Interest, 17

H
Harry Markowitz, 39, 44
Hedgers, 67
History of Derivatives, 68

History of Futures, 77
Hong Kong Futures Exchange, 71

I
Initial Public Offer (IPO), 13
Insurance Regulatory and Development
    Authority (IRDA), 192
International Monetary Fund (IMF), 64
International Monetary Markets
    (IMM), 78
Inter-temporal Capital Asset Pricing
    Model (ICAMP), 52
Introduction of Futures in India, 83

J
James E. Walter, 136
John Cox, 91
John Lintner, 137

K
Kansas City Board of Trade, 69
Knut Wicksell, 18
Kolkata Stock Exchange, 104

L
L.C. Gupta, 164
Lake Michigan, 68
Lintner's Model, 137
Liquidity Preference Theory of the
    Rate of Interest, 18
Liquidity Premium Theory, 29
Liquidity Trap, 20
Loanable Fund Theory of the Rate of
    Interest, 18
London Inter-bank Offer Rate, 132

M
Margin Requirement, 80
Mark Rubinstein, 91
Markowitz Bullet, 47
Markowitz Efficient Frontier, 46
Markowitz Efficient Set, 44

Meaning and Significance of Financial
    Economics, 7
Meaning of Derivatives, 64
Mean-variance Analysis, 39
Merton Miller, 119, 139
Ministry of Corporate Affairs, 189
Modigliani-Miller School of
    Thought, 135
Modigliani-Miller Theorem (M&M
    Theorem), 119, 139
Money Market, 12, 155
Moody's Investor Services, 128
Motives for Holding Cash, 18
Mutual Funds, 140
Myron J. Gordon, 137

N
National Exchange for Automated
    Trading (NEAT-F&O), 167
National Securities Clearing
    Corporation (NSCC), 71
National Stock Exchange of India
    Limited (NSE), 160
No Frills Account, 176
Non-banking Financial Companies
    (NBFCs), 150

O
Option Valuation, 100
Options in Historical Perspective, 86
Options Risk Metrics, 92
Options, 66
Ordinary Shares, 113
Organisation for Economic Cooperation
    and Development (OECD), 70
Over-the-counter Options, 90

P
Pecking Order Theory, 120
Pension Fund Regulatory and
    Development Authority (PFRDA),
    151, 194

Pension Funds, 150
Political Arbitrage, 106
Portfolio Defined, 33
Portfolio Management, 34
Portfolio Manager, 33
Pradhan Mantri Jan-Dhan Yojana
    (PMJDY), 181
Preference Shares, 115
Primary Market, 13
Private Placement Market, 128
Problems of Forward Contracts, 74
Put Options, 87
Putable Bond, 127

R
Real and Money Rate of Interest, 17
Regional Rural Banks (RRBs), 148
Regulation and Supervision of Financial
    Institutions in India, 151
Regulation and Supervision of Financial
    Markets in India, 155
Regulation and Supervision of Financial
    System, 7
Reserve Bank of India (RBI), 25, 187
Residual Dividend Policy, 134
Residuals Theory of Dividends, 134
Revolving Line of Credit, 25
Risk-Return Trade-off, 49
Risks Involved in Arbitrage, 104
Risks with Forward Contracts, 75
Role of Clearing House, 80
Role of the State in Financial
    Development, 4
Rural Co-operative Credit Institutions, 149

S
Salient Features of Forward Contracts, 73
Secondary Market, 13
Secured versus Unsecured Debt, 126
Securities and Exchange Board of
    India, 158
Security Market Line (SML), 56

Segmented Market Theory, 29
Shapes and Uses of Yield Curve, 27
Significance of Interest Rate, 17
Singapore International Monetary
    Exchange (SIMEX), 71
Sources of Capital, 113
Speculators, 67
Stable Dividend Policy, 134
Standard & Poor's Global Ratings, 128
Stephen Ross, 91
Stock Exchanges, 159
Sydney Futures Exchange, 71
Syndicated Loan, 129
Systematic Risks versus Unsystematic
    Risks, 48

T
Tata Steel, 104
Telecom Arbitrage, 106
Trade-off Theory, 120
Triangular Arbitrage, 106
Twelfth Five Year Plan (2012-17), 145
Types of Arbitrage, 105

U
United Nations Capital Development
    Fund (UNCDF), 172
Urban Co-operative Banks (UCBs), 149

V
Valuation Models, 91

W
Walter's Model, 136
Weighted Average Cost of Capital
    (WACC), 122
William Sharpe, 48, 98